SOE SINGAPORE
1941–42

SOE SINGAPORE

1941–42

Richard Gough

WILLIAM KIMBER · LONDON

First published in 1985 by
WILLIAM KIMBER & CO. LIMITED
100 Jermyn Street, London, SW1Y 6EE

© Richard Gough, 1985
ISBN-0-7183-0584-1

Photoset by Rapidset and Design Ltd
Printed and bound in Great Britain by
Redwood Burn Limited, Trowbridge, Wiltshire

To Rona for her patience

Contents

List of Illustrations

List of Maps

Author's Preface

The Orient Mission was a little known, ill-fated, section of Special Operations Executive (SOE) which was overwhelmed when the Japanese launched their attack on the Malayan Barrier in 1941. Its survivors provided Force 136 and other special units with a nucleus of experienced officers who carried out deep penetration behind enemy lines throughout the Far East.

This story, which is not its history, was put together with the help of Major-General Jim Gavin, one of the survivors. In 1941 he was responsible for creating the first jungle warfare school in Singapore and played a large and important part in the Orient Mission's operations. Further help was received from the late Alan Ferguson Warren, who was, at that time, a lieutenant-colonel in the Royal Marines and liaison officer with GHQ Far East. He was an authority on clandestine activities and although part of the War Office staff initially he was later absorbed into SOE. Like Jim Gavin he gave me every co-operation – pleased that the Mission's work was at last being recognised. In addition I received valuable assistance from Colonel Jack Knott who, as a captain, was responsible for all wireless communications and later became Chief Wireless Officer for Force 136: also from John Davis who became the main link with the Chinese in Malaya and later spent a considerable time there, behind enemy lines. After the war he carried out an important role with security forces during the Emergency. Last but not least, Frank Brewer who was an instructor at 101 Special Training School.

The effective life of the Mission was about twelve months. For clarity the story unfolds month by month rather than pursue the adventures of the various units within the Mission. I also make no apology for introducing the reader to many of the staff and operatives including the Free French. They all played their part and not only do they deserve a mention but their involvement in the story gives some idea of the problems and frantic scramble Gavin and Warren faced to get the show on the road.

Although this is not an official history and most of the opinions expressed are my own, nevertheless it is as accurate as possible. The events took place more than forty years ago and the stories related have been taken from the memories of some of the participants and from research from earlier publications. A full bibliography is included but readers who may wish to obtain a more definitive picture of some of the operations mentioned may wish to read *The Jungle is Neutral* (F. Spencer Chapman), *The Three They Couldn't Kill* (John Cross) and *The Naked Island* (Russell Braddon).

I would like to thank Jim Gavin, John David, Doug Cuthbertson and Peter Nunn for their generous help in providing photographs. My thanks are also due to Messrs A.D. Peters for premission to quote from *Japan's Imperial Conspiracy* by David Bergamini, and to the controller of Her Majesty's Office for permission to use the map of the pacific from *Grand Strategy, Vol 3*.

Finally, the book couldn't have been completed without Moira Feeney's help with the typing, and above all, my wife's encouragement and her sufferance of my ten years of research into the subject.

RICHARD GOUGH

CHAPTER ONE

'You're going to Singapore!'

Singapore, in April 1941, was far away from any war zone. The battles raging in Europe and the Western Desert were ten thousand miles away. The Sino-Japanese conflict in China wasn't really considered, being at least four thousand miles in the opposite direction.

For the 50,000 servicemen on the island it was a tropical peacetime station, where every morning it seemed to rain at 8 am for five minutes, then it became very warm with temperatures of 90°. They played soldiers for half a day then swam or did sports before relaxing with pints of Tiger beer in downtown Singapore, with taxi-dancers or in the Happy World. Local civilians, Indians, Malays and Chinese, kept the barracks clean, did cookhouse fatigues or cleaned the other-ranks' boots and webbing for a small sum.

A recent arrival that month was a tall, smartly dressed colonel in the Royal Marines, sent by the War Office to develop the concept of irregular warfare. He was no stranger to the East having served his first tour in Shanghai during the twenties. Even after fifteen years he considered nothing had changed. The same rickshaws, beggars, smells and the homeless living on the pavements. No wonder the Japanese slogan – Asia for the Asians – attracted revolutionaries.

He had arrived on the island with a plan to raise a native guerrilla force which could operate in the jungle, behind the lines, should Malaya be over-run by the Japanese in the event of war. The military refused to consider the idea and his unofficial discussions with European Colonial government officials and local business people met with a cool reception.

They quickly pointed out that the military's need to recruit workers to build defence works in Johore was creating a labour shortage which could force up wages. Recruiting others into a jungle-based irregular army would only increase the problems. There were already too many problems up-country with tin miners clashing with the police when they protested for better working conditions and pay. Summing-up the attitude of the business community, one senior officer, anxious to get back to Europe for the war, commented to Colonel Warren that the civilians 'didn't give a bloody damn' about the war. All they wanted was to be left alone like they were in the Kaiser's war and earn money for the war effort. He thought they would have a fit if his plans to arm the natives leaked out.

At the War Office in London, Warren was regarded as a high flier. When he returned from his last tour of duty in Shanghai he was sent to Staff College, Camberley. This was followed by a tour as Commandant of the Royal Marine Barracks at Chatham. Then in 1938 he was in 'Special Operations', running secret training courses, in a country house, for businessmen who worked overseas. The object was to encourage and develop unorthodox methods of warfare and, before war broke out, his section had men in Havana, most major ports in Africa, the Balkans and the USA.

As the threat of war began to develop it was soon realised in the War Office that if Britain went to war with Germany the latter would rely heavily on iron ore shipments from Sweden, so Warren and his men put together a project to 'take-out' the mines. Unfortunately this was leaked to the King of Sweden who complained to His Majesty King George and the project was cancelled.

When war eventually broke out he was sent to France to build up an underground organisation in areas likely to be over-run by the Germans. The collapse of the front line came unexpectedly. The last few days before the Dunkirk evacuation were spent rushing lorry loads of arms along roads, choked with refugees and retreating troops, to secret caches often only hours before the area was over-run.

When he returned to England via the beaches, he became involved in a plan to put a sabotage group ashore in Norway to join up with Norwegian troops still active behind German lines. The submarine carrying the group ran into a minefield and was badly damaged. The vessel returned to Rosyth and the operation was cancelled.

Almost immediately he was called to see the Controller. News was continually coming in during May that large groups of leaderless British troops were wandering around France, having missed the Dunkirk evacuation and the later one which brought out the Canadians and the 2nd BEF in June. He was told to go back across the Channel and slip ashore into enemy-occupied France. He was to search for these men, who had been left behind south of Cherbourg, and mould them into commando units, just like the Boer Columns in South Africa forty years earlier. He was given a small hand-held wireless, told to attend Woolwich Military Establishment for a briefing and collect three French-speaking officer cadets who would be waiting for him at Dover, Command HQ. The Dover chaps would fix him up with a launch.

Two days later he drove into Dover and although the evacuation had finished, he found the town still packed with servicemen from France and ambulances full of casualties. Command HQ confirmed that small groups of soldiers were still making their way back to England in stolen boats but none he spoke to could confirm that large bands were roaming free in France.

That evening he collected his officer cadets and went down to the East Dock to look for his launch. This turned out to be a small open fishing boat and he discovered its civilian owner, with his head buried in the engine hatch, trying to repair the motor. By the time they got started and out into the Channel it was daylight and a thick fog descended. Warren had hoped for a night landing. Some miles along the coast the engine stopped and refused to start and the launch just drifted. No one had any idea where they were and they occasionally caught glimpses of the shoreline, but which one was anyone's guess. Apart from the clatter of the owner's tools in the engine hatch, everything was silent until they were horrified to hear the thump, thump, thump of a ship's engine. The owner stopped working and joined them at the boat's side and the fog slowly parted to reveal the Dungeness pilot boat.

The coastguards had seen them earlier and informed the crew who had been searching for them. As the vision of a prison camp began to recede Warren and his cadets clambered over the ship's side and transferred their kit to the other boat. He then persuaded the coxswain to take them across the Channel and put them ashore in France.

By the time they reached the French shore they had been at sea for about 18 hours. Dawn was not far away as the boat crept in, as far as it could without going aground, leaving them to wade, chest deep, through the swell. The fog still hung around and as the boat slipped back into the mist, the party, wet and tired, dragged their weapons and supplies across the beach to the dunes. Warren, with one of the cadets, followed a path to the top of the dunes. These stretched for some miles along the beach but after climbing over the dunes for about a hundred yards inland, the ground dropped away to flat lowland. Above the low mist were tree tops, ridge tents and lorries. Below slept a company of German troops from one of Rommel's armoured columns. Suddenly, they were hailed by a sentry partly shrouded by the mist, Warren waved, turned and hurried along the dune parallel with the beach. Hidden for a moment by some scrub they both ran, scrambling down to the beach where they grabbed their packs and, followed by the others, fled along the beach.

When they turned inland later in the day they found themselves in a water-logged soggy area which, as they walked deeper into it became a marsh, which they struggled through often waist deep in mud and water. That first night they hid naked in a wood, their clothes hung around on branches and bushes to dry. After this demoralising start they moved slowly inland making contacts with local priests who in turn made their own enquiries. But the answers were always the same: all the soldiers had either surrendered or been captured. They found one evader, however, by accident when they stumbled into a barn one night to hide and found him beneath the hay. He thought they were a German patrol. Contacts told them that the Germans knew they were in the area and were carrying out a full scale search for them.

So Warren, after three weeks of fruitless searching and with their money running out, decided to evacuate. This promised to be easier than getting to France. The new hand-held wireless transmitter could bring in a launch to pick them up within twelve hours. They were to be sadly disillusioned, again. Despite the assurances from the boffins at Woolwich, the transmitter remained mute and after 48 hours' pointless calling, Warren gave up in disgust and bribed a local fishermen to sell him a boat (it later transpired that the boat belonged to a neighbour). That night the party moved along the beach in the shadow of the dunes, fully expecting treachery. It was with some misgiving that he had earlier parted with the money before seeing the boat, but their contact was as good as his word and the boat, clothes and food were waiting for them. They found the rowing boat upturned in the sand, well above the high tide mark. It was sun-bleached and dried out and they suspected that it hadn't been used for some time. Their suspicions proved correct: the boat was well embedded in the sand. By now it was early morning and dawn was not far away. Between them they dug it out with their hands, turned it over and half carried and dragged it to the water's edge.

When they tried to launch it in the face of four-foot waves and an incoming tide they repeatedly finished up back upon the beach in a tangle of arms, legs and oars. Eventually the tide changed and they got it through the surf and afloat. As the four struggled with the oars

Warren bailed out and caulked the seams with paper, bits of shirts and socks. Once, when he looked over the side he found they were less than a mile off shore, serenely drifting past enemy soldiers, taking a morning swim.

They spent most of the next twenty-four hours pulling across the English Channel and when dawn came they were again in sight of land. The fickle tide changed and the English coast line began to recede. All four oarsmen gave up and slumped exhausted over the oars. Furious, Warren, sitting in the stern, drew his pistol and fired two shots in the air. The startled rowers, shocked to attention, were verbally abused and to the beat of his pistol against the boat's side the rowers found new strength and pulled against the tide. But it was to no avail and the boat, caught in the tidal race, ignored their efforts and took them back out to sea.

They were eventually rescued and hauled aboard the lightship off Dungeness Point where their morale was revived with large mugs of cocoa. Later, ashore, Warren remembers being fed doorstep slices of bread and butter by the wife of the local policeman while waiting for a staff car from Dover Command.

When Churchill was told about it – he was not amused and called it 'a silly little episode'.

It was late August when Warren arrived back in London and he found everyone in the middle of an invasion scare. Hitler was massing his troops and armour at embarkation ports in France and intelligence reports spoke of landing barges and troop transports being assembled in creeks and rivers along the French coast. In London preparations were well in hand to form a secret army, in Britain, to harass the enemy's lines of communications when – and not if – German troops carried out successful seaborne landings along the south coast. His old 'D' Section fellow officer, General Gubbins, had been put in charge of the 'army' and Warren, who everyone thought had been captured, was welcomed back with enthusiasm and sent to Kent to co-ordinate matters. He was joined by another old 'D' Section hand, Peter Fleming. He had just returned from China where he had been running another covert operation. The third member of the team was Captain Michael Calvert, fresh from a course at the recently opened SOE training school in Scotland. For Warren it was France all over again. Civilians were taught how to make petrol bombs and be tank killers. Secret arms caches were buried, miners dug underground hideaways along the Weald and a local hunt joined en-masse as cavalry. Most of its members were ex-officers, veterans of the Boer War who still retained their swords.

Winter came without the expected invasion and Kent was covered with a particularly heavy fall of snow. Intelligence reports gave details of troop movements to Poland while the troops in France began to construct beach defences. The invasion scare began to recede and the SOE team in Kent was disbanded. Peter Fleming was posted to the Western Desert to recruit and train captured Italian prisoners-of-war, to operate in the Italian mountains as anti-Fascist partisans. Mike Calvert left for Australia to set up his own commando training school and finally, before Christmas, Warren was told he was going back out east to Singapore. A berth had been reserved on HMS *Nesta* which was leaving Liverpool on 2nd January. He would be responsible as GSO(1) for all below the belt operations in the Far East. It was also made plain to him that as Singapore was not even on Churchill's priority list and the Prime Minister, personally, monitored all resources sent there, Warren would have to make do with whatever he could find locally. He was, he was told, on his own.

On board the *Nesta*, in place of his personal equipment, he had with him six Tommy guns, the first to be sent to Singapore; thousands of rounds of ammunition, large stocks of a special light-weight explosive, and other special goodies designed by the boffins in London.

He spent his first six weeks in Singapore trying to interest both the civilian and military authorities in his ideas to prepare for, or even consider the possibility of, a successful Japanese invasion of Malaya. It was all a waste of time and he got nowhere. Technically Japan was not an enemy and in fact was one of the country's best customers. She imported large quantities of rubber and oil from Malaya and the Dutch East Indies. It was accepted that these were needed for her war against China and whilst she was fully engaged there she couldn't consider any further territorial ambitions. What Warren didn't know was that she was becoming increasingly short of raw materials and the foreign exchange to buy them with.

This conflict was in fact costing her dearly and, in an attempt to force the Chinese Government of General Chiang Kai Shek to discuss peace terms, Japan was trying to persuade, or force, the European Colonial countries to cut off aid to China flowing through French Hanoi and along the British Burma Road to the Yunnan.

For at least two years Japanese intelligence had been preparing the ground for one of the biggest land grabs in history using local nationalists to act against their colonial masters. The Japanese slogan, Asia for the Asians, fell on receptive ears in many eastern countries. For instance, in Burma many leading local government officials were pro-Japanese, India was awash with talk of insurrection and continually torn by anti-British riots. Many Indians in Malaya sent money back to mother India for anti-British purposes, especially the Sikhs who were clamouring for Home Rule. In the Dutch East Indies the Dutch colonial government had arrested thousands of leading intellectuals and thrown them into jungle concentration camps to die. Throughout Malaya, Burma and the Dutch East Indies, Japanese agents posing as barbers, photographers and fishermen, fed back a steady and accurate stream of information to Japan. Army engineers, disguised as rubber planters or mining engineers, mapped paths through the jungle and tracks through the plantations, by-passing main roads. One enterprising Japanese officer motored the length of Malaya mapping and counting all the bridges and calculating what materials would be needed to repair them if they were blown by the retreating British army – which they were and their rapid repair was largely due to this officer's efficiency.

In contrast to the enterprising Japanese, British intelligence was more limited. The Ministry of Economic Warfare (MEW) gathered information both on economic factors relating to enemy or would-be enemy countries and their seaborne troop movements. This was gathered together at regional offices throughout the world, such as Singapore and forwarded to Whitehall. The Secret Service (SIS) was operating in the Far East, infiltrating agents into Siam (now Thailand), Indo-China and China but it kept to itself and all its intelligence material was processed to the Foreign Office. The military had two competing intelligence gathering services; one belonged to the Royal Navy – very much the Senior Service – and the other was a combined RAF/Army station but, as Warren discovered, the intelligence services in Singapore hardly spoke to each other never mind exchanged information.

In order to tap into both systems he needed a neutral base safe from inter-service jealousy. One advantage of being a Marine was that he could safely relate to either Army or Navy as the circumstances dictated but his address would be a giveaway. Eventually he decided to open his 'shop-window' in the large, modern, air-conditioned Cathay Building, a government office block in the centre of Singapore. This was close to the busy waterfront and from its roof one could overlook the Island, from Bukit Timah some miles inland to the many islands surrounding the harbour. Apart from the apparent neutrality of his new office, the added advantage was that a few doors from the corridor were the regional offices of the Ministry of Economic Warfare, run by Sir George Sansom, who had oversight of all non-military covert operations in the Far East.

Within a few days Sir George sent a note inviting him for drinks to meet two new arrivals from Britain. Sir George was well aware of his interests in clandestine activities and they had discussed areas of possible co-operation. The newcomers, he discovered, were Val St John Killery and Basil Goodfellow. Both had only recently been recruited by Special Operations Executive (SOE) to develop its presence in Asia. SOE was a new organisation formed in London the previous year to carry out sabotage missions behind enemy lines. A large part of Warren's department, MI(R), was used to create the organisation which belonged to the Foreign Office; what was left remained with the War Office. MI(R) and SOE had parallel responsibilities but Warren's aim was to concentrate on building up native guerrilla units, while SOE's Orient Mission objectives were to put in short stay sabotage groups behind enemy lines.

The arrival of yet another semi-secret organisation in Singapore wasn't well received by those already in post. The view of some senior officers was that, reflecting on Whitehall's policy of avoiding confrontation with Japan, to house an organisation on the Island to carry out blatant anti-Japanese covert operations, was rocking the boat. To make matters worse they were bloody civilians belonging to the SOE which 'everyone knew' was Churchill's pet project which consumed essential resources they badly needed.

It soon became obvious to the new arrivals that they were not wanted and their attempts to recruit individuals from local units were rebuffed or blocked. They were, partly, victims of Whitehall politics. In July 1940 Churchill had drawn together the various secret military organisations, seemingly proliferating in Whitehall. This new body became Special Operations Executive and absorbed parts of MI(R) and some SIS propaganda sections. To these were added large numbers of specially recruited businessmen with contacts throughout the world. Killery and Goodfellow fell into this category, two of the many ICI employees tapped on the shoulder for secret work.

Like Warren, they too came up against the barrier of indifference and suspicion of their motives. There were also, additionally, the tangled threads of Whitehall machinery operating on the island in an uncontrolled manner. When attempting to identify any single authority to promote their aims they discovered, to their horror, that the Dominions, Colonies and India (Offices) as well as the Foreign Office (which they were part of), the Treasury and other government departments were operating in Singapore without any central authority or official communications, one with another. Consequently the arrival of any new organisation such as the Orient Mission, only added to the difficulties.

Each time Killery tried to make a move to develop a facet of his covert operations he ran into some department's protective wall. Departmental responsibilities overlapped and he found officials often making or pursuing policies which were contrary to the aims and policies of organisations in the same building. He soon found to his cost that the continual inter-departmental in-fighting was corseting the Mission's work, so he decided to ignore all other departments' objectives and single-mindedly follow his own aims. This decision was to have unfortunate results some months later when an attempt was made to put a group of Free French agents ashore in Indo-China which was Vichy-controlled. But the responsibility for diplomatic relations with the Vichy French in Indo-China rested with the C in C China Station, who was Admiral Layton. He was no friend of any special operations unit, of any kind, and at that time he was in the middle of delicate negotiations with the Vichy French Governor to come over to the Allied cause. When he discovered what was going on he exploded into anger. Killery had his fingers rapped and the agents, struggling ashore through wind-swept surf in rubber boats, were recalled. This was his only attempt to buck the system.

CHAPTER TWO

Operation Scapula

Before leaving Britain in February 1941 Killery recruited a young Sapper officer, Captain Jim Gavin, to provide the Mission with both military know-how and experience. He was a colourful character, a regular soldier, and like Basil Goodfellow, well known in mountaineering circles. He joined the Royal Engineers fresh from university in 1930 and spent the next nine years becoming an authority on explosives, mountain climbing and yacht racing. When the war broke out in 1939 he immediately volunteered for special operations and in October found himself part of the British Expeditionary Force to Finland. His unit was to diverge into Sweden and 'take out' the iron ore mines supplying Germany. This project was abandoned before they sailed. By this time the Germans had landed in Norway and he was selected as a member of a team to be landed by submarine, blow up the main Oslo railway line and join up with Norwegian guerrilla units.

The party drove to Rosyth in lorries laden with explosives, weapons equipment and special collapsible boats and embarked in HMS *Truant*. It was dark when they left the harbour and the submarine, safe from air attacks, ran on the surface until daybreak when she submerged. In the aft torpedo room Jim Gavin and his team drank the skipper's beer, checked the gear and lounged against the cold, black missiles. They tried to keep out of the way but in the cramped quarters wherever they stationed themselves some member of the crew always pushed past. Somewhere near the enemy-occupied coast the crew's easy-going mood changed and Gavin sensed a tension in the air. They were due to land in about three hours when, suddenly, everything appeared to burst around them. The boat was lifted and flung aside. The lights went out and she dropped, stern first, towards the sea bed. More explosions shook the vessel as she slid away, and eventually, before she struck bottom, the skipper pulled her on to an even keel and stopped. Gavin and his team, convinced that their time had come, lay where they had been flung – clinging to the deck. Eventually the water-tight bulkhead door opened and a shaft of light from a torch stabbed the darkness around them. The light probed the seals and joints, examined the seals around the torpedo tubes and eventually swept the floor to pick out the six pale faces. A voice said, 'Nothing to worry about, old chaps, but I think we had better check the damage back at Rosyth.' Before they could reply the door clanged shut leaving their prison once again in total and utter darkness. The engines hummed into life and a feeling of motion shook the boat. Eventually lights, flickering at first, came on and the skipper appeared through the now open bulkhead door. It seemed they had been attacked by an enemy submarine and although the damage wasn't too serious it was enough to abandon the mission.

Back in Scotland Jim Gavin, Bill Stirling, his brother David, who later formed the SAS, Peter Kemp and three others spent the next ten weeks waiting for orders to take them to Norway. Forgotten by the Army, they lived as guests of the Stirlings, in a large country house outside Stirling. They occupied themselves shooting and hunting, blowing up trees and cliffs for practice, rock climbing and trekking with full packs across the barren hills. Despite frequent telephone calls and letters to London no orders came and eventually in desperation the leader of their party left one morning, on the train, for London.

He reappeared three days later with the news that their organisation had been reformed and merged with a new secret army called Special Operations Executive (SOE). Their new role would be to set up a school to train staff for more schools being opened throughout the country. The new schools would prepare would-be agents for the hazards they might have to face in enemy-occupied countries. The school premises they would have to find themselves. The Stirlings, their relatives and friends owned large estates throughout Scotland and so it wasn't too difficult to find and persuade the owner of a large barren expanse of country around Oban to allow them to set up their school and use the estate for training. The owner was a widow whose husband died in France in the First World War. Her son, who volunteered when war broke out, persuaded his mother that it was her duty to the country to give her home to the war effort. The school was located in a fine old country house overlooking Loch Ailort. Behind the house rose high, forbidding cliffs, which Gavin regularly climbed. About six months after the school opened he learnt that he was being given his own command. Because of the threatening Japanese posture in the Far East it had been decided to send a Mission to Singapore. Part of the back-up would be a school for agents and he had been selected to run it.

Within a few days orders came for him to report to London and in Whitehall he was told that he had been promoted to major and posted to Singapore where he would set up his school to train agents to carry out covert operations to be organised by the recently formed Orient Mission. He and his staff would form part of that Mission. The head of the Mission would be Val St John Killery, who had joined SOE staff from ICI. Also from ICI came Basil Goodfellow, who would act as Killery's deputy. Gavin knew of Goodfellow from their mutual interest in mountaineering. He briefly met them both in London before they left for Singapore. This was SOE's first attempt to set up an overseas station and before they left they were given a hastily typed DIY brief on what was expected of them and how to do it. Neither had any recent military training or experience in clandestine and covert operations. Gavin was expected to supply this. What they did have was experience of the Far East and contacts amongst the business community.

The War Office found him a room in Whitehall, near St James' Park, to work out his war establishment proposals. He had roughly drafted these out on the night train from Fort William and altered them slightly after chatting over the project with Killery. These were now presented to the War Office for approval and in the meanwhile he trawled all units for specialist staff.

One of the first to arrive was a young captain from the Royal Signals, Jack Knott. He recalls being shown into a small, bare room with only a desk and two chairs as furniture. On one side sat a suntanned major in the Royal Engineers. The mysterious interviewing officer smiled and gestured him to sit down. He came straight to the point. 'My name is Major Gavin, Royal Engineers.' He then went on to explain that he was recruiting staff for special operations in the Far East. The work would entail long periods behind enemy lines, would be dangerous and unorthodox. Everyone involved would be volunteers and would need the ability to work by themselves. He closed the first half of the interview by pointing out that because of the secret nature of the work he couldn't give any more information, however, if Knott didn't like the sound of the work he could travel back to Yorkshire by the next train. If, on the other hand, he wished to become part of the new organisation, he could stay and the project would be outlined to him in more detail.

It didn't take him long to consider his position. He had been kicking his heels around the Yorkshire transit camp for nine months, ever since he escaped from occupied France after Dunkirk. He certainly wasn't going to ignore this opportunity to get back into active service. Looking across the table at Gavin he promptly accepted the invitation.

In the second half of the interview he was told that a secret organisation known as SOE was mounting an exercise in the Far East, to be known as the Orient Mission. His job would be to look after the wireless training and signals network. He would be responsible for recruiting his own men and if necessary, beg, borrow or scrounge any equipment he needed. 'The Secret Intelligence Service,' commented Gavin, 'have a wealth of experience in this sort of thing. Pop across and discuss it with them.'

Apart from trawling military units for volunteers, Gavin also tried to poach staff from his old school, particularly Lord Lovat. He wanted him as Chief Instructor. 'Impossible,' said the Head of Training when he heard about it. 'Out of the question,' said the Head of Establishment. Not to be beaten Gavin took his request to the top. But General Gubbins would have none of it either. 'Because a state of war doesn't exist with Japan, the school must maintain a low profile – in fact a secret establishment. Lord Lovat's presence on its staff would have the opposite effect. As a member of the Royal Family his posting to the Far East at this sensitive time would excite the world press and create unwelcome publicity. Lord Lovat, said Gubbins firmly, was to remain in Britain and that was that.

Gavin's disappointment was partially overcome by a letter from an old school chum, Steve Cummins. He had spent his pre-war years in China and exotic sounding places in the Far East. He had come back to Britain to look for the war and, hearing that Jim Gavin was involved in unorthodox warfare, wondered whether he could find a place for him. Within a week he was called to London for an interview, accepted, briefed and on a ship bound for America on the first leg of his journey back to Singapore – as a one man advance party.

On 4th April Jim Gavin heard that the War Office had approved his war establishment and, as he was anxious to start as soon as possible, he could recruit the remainder of his staff locally, in Singapore.

Leaving his team of specialists and their chosen men assembling in Hendon Hall, SOE's country retreat, with orders to join him by August, he flew by Transatlantic Clipper to America and then on to Honolulu, where he arrived about the third week in May. As he stepped from the plane into bright sunlight the heat struck him like that from an oven. The glare seemed to bound off the tarmac and dazzle him as he followed his fellow passengers towards the nearby buildings. Alongside the buildings crowds pressed against the fence waving and shouting to friends as they disembarked from the airliner. Suddenly he found himself almost face to face with Steve Cummins, who, with a broad smile on his face and his arms around two very attractive girls, stood waiting for him to clear the arrival buildings. Outside Cummins took his bags and the two girls formed up either side and escorted him to their car.

Slightly bemused, but rising to the occasion he looked to his friend for an explanation. It seemed that on the voyage from America to the Island they met Steve and heard from him all about the terrible war in Europe. They also heard that he was being joined by his friend, fresh from England, and they had decided it was their 'duty' to give their two new-found friends – and brave British officers – full American hospitality. As his friend stowed his bags in the boot of a large new Cadillac parked at the kerbside, the girls, in pretty, off-the-shoulder summer dresses, climbed into the car. The blonde took the driving seat while the amply bosomed redhead sat in the back seat. Cummins joined the blonde in the front while he sat in the back with his smiling new-found girl friend. He gathered they were off to the girls' place for a swim and lunch alongside the pool and so, giving in to the inevitable, he relaxed and let the events take their course.

They flew into Singapore on 28th May and were met, this time, by a serious-faced private, in an ill-fitting uniform, and a military staff car. After the tight security in Britain one of the first things they noticed was the casual atmosphere surrounding the base. It was afternoon and the troops had the afternoon off for sports or relaxation. All servicemen had their own servants and local natives were brought in to do the normal fatigues.

The car drove to town along a straight, metalled road fringed with palm trees. Occasionally they drove past row upon row of rubber trees forming the many plantations on the island. Until they reached the outskirts of Singapore the roads were almost empty apart from the occasional bullock cart loaded high with hands of bananas or pigs imprisoned in tube-like wicker baskets. In the town the streets became congested with taxis, rickshaws, wood-burning civilian lorries and hundreds of bicycles intermingled with pedestrians. The pavements were thronged with shoppers in front of open fronted shops while alleyways, opening off the streets, were festooned with washing fixed to bamboo poles. The doorways were decorated with colourful paper lanterns and aged, wrinkled Chinamen sitting on many of the doorsteps, smoking pipes, completed the picture.

Eventually they arrived at the Cathay Building, close to the waterfront. In fact Gavin had caught sight of the sea and ships tied up alongside the quay as the car turned off Holland Road, one of the main shopping thoroughfares. The Sikh sentries at the door gave the two officers a smart salute as they strode into the building. After the bright sunlight the corridors were dark but not too dark for Gavin to miss the secretary's attractive smile, and her figure, as he followed her along the corridor leading to Killery's office. He found both Killery and Goodfellow waiting for them and they were introduced to a third officer, Colonel Warren, a smartly turned-out, six foot Royal Marine.

From the discussion that followed it seemed that Killery had come up against a barrier of indifference from both local military and civilian government. It didn't help matters when he discovered that to get anything done he had to negotiate with some nine different local government committees and liaise separately with three service intelligence agencies. Remembering those early days Jim Gavin believed that both Killery and Goodfellow had some difficulty in explaining the purpose and value of their mission. The senior military commanders gave them no help whatsoever and Warren commented later that the two found themselves in a ring of jealousy. When he was trying to smooth the path for the SOE an officer told him to 'send all those bloody SOE back to Britain – and not first class either'. Despite all these rebuffs and lack of co-operation the four-man SOE team struggled to create an embryo organisation.

Killery was anxious that the new school, now officially known as 101 Special Training School, should not in any way be seen to be connected with the Mission. It should remain a secret. He emphasised the point by telling them that this must be the first and last time Gavin, or any of his men, set foot in the Cathay Building. He then handed out a list of secret telephone numbers and instructions on how to make contact with the Mission, using cut-outs. These cut-outs consisted of leaving messages in secret places or meeting total strangers in crowded bookshops, whispering a password and passing notes hidden in newspapers and books. However, the European population in Singapore was small and those involved with the military even smaller so the strangers soon began to recognise each other and when their paths crossed at social functions, made a great play of meeting each other for the first time when mutual friends brought them together. One of the messengers at these clandestine meetings was an attractive secretary from Killery's office, one of the Gambol twins, working for SOE. But unlike his fictional counterpart, James Bond, Major Gavin found these covert operations a handicap.

When the meeting in Killery's office finished, Warren offered to take them both to the site of the proposed school at Pula Uban, an island in the Johore Straits between the Naval Base and the mainland (where eight months later the Japanese infantry stormed ashore in a feint attack to divert attention from the main thrust at the causeway).

The island was clearly visible from the Naval Base and Warren arranged for a Royal Navy launch to take them across. The crew brought the boat gently up to the sands and, as they dropped over the side and waded ashore, Gavin remembers being greeted by clouds of mosquitoes rising from stagnant pools. Above them monkeys screamed from the tree tops and colourful birds glided over their heads and disappeared amongst the trees. They spent about three hours on the island, which was completely useless for their needs. It had very little fresh water, the jungle would need to be extensively cleared and accommodation built. But, more important, there seemed to be a grave risk of malaria from the mosquitoes. At that one moment it became clear that the selection of the island epitomised the considerable lack of interest by the military authorities in SOE activities. Reflecting on the Siting Board's choice thirty years later Warren, in a typical understatement, thought it lacked consideration.

After turning down the Board's offer Gavin borrowed Warren's truck and naval charts and set out to find his own site. This eventually turned out to be Tanjong Balai, often described as an island but really a headland connected to Singapore Island by a long, narrow causeway at the mouth of the Jurong River. It was formerly the home of an Armenian millionaire who made a fortune opening wildcat tin mines. It had a large ornamental bungalow with Chinese-style pavilions. Off-shore were small, jungle-covered islands and the nearby coast was covered in rubber trees and mangrove swamps. Following complaints from the Head of Economic Warfare, Sir George Sansom, the mysterious Warren 'from the War Office' and Killery, the Siting Board was forced to reconsider its offer and quickly agreed that Jim Gavin's new site could be requisitioned. So, on 26th June,

Major Jim Gavin

A view of Singapore from the top of Cathay Building.

Tanjong Balai, home of 101 STS.

Gavin and Cummins and the school's new quartermaster, Lieutenant McGarry, who had recently arrived from England, moved in.

They all started work straight away. Through contacts Warren had made with Special Branch, hand-picked Chinese appeared at the gates to be selected for jobs as cooks and servants. At the same time GHQ issued a trawl notice to all units for guards, drivers and storemen. One of the applicants turned out to be Sapper John Sartin, an explosives expert and one-time bugle boy when Jim Gavin joined his squadron straight from Sandhurst. For a short time in the squadron he had been Gavin's groom so when he heard, on the grape-vine, that the CO at the new school was Gavin, he applied for a transfer. Equally his name was also recognised and his transfer quickly arranged. He was promoted to a sergeant instructor and planned the first course on the use of explosives.

As the volume of activity increased the detailed work was left to Cummins and McGarry, leaving Gavin more time to chase up the contractors and generally oversee the reconstruction. The place bustled with servicemen and civilians. Royal Engineers swarmed over the site, water pipes were laid, sewage and drains were extended, generators installed, cables strung and buildings wired; and all the time bow-legged Chinese, carrying impossibly large loads extended from either ends of long bamboo poles balanced across their shoulders, trotted around the site.

Now that Gavin had arrived, Warren was more confident that SOE could string its plans together, so leaving them to their problems he began to explore opportunities for developing his own guerrilla units. He considered war with Japan inevitable despite noises to the contrary from both the military authorities and civilians.

His enquiries revealed that the Chinese Nationalist Government in Chungking kept a close contact with its people overseas – even to such an extent as having Chinese Government officials or representatives stationed amongst large overseas Chinese communities. He reasoned that if China was fighting a bitter war against the Japanese, logically the local Chinese population would welcome the chance to serve their homeland. When he tentatively broached the suggestion to local government officials they were appalled at his ideas of putting armed 'natives' into well-stocked jungle bases. The answer was a firm 'NO'.

More encouraging news came from Captain Lowe, one of Gavin's team from England, who had recently arrived back from a trip to

Burma. It seemed that the Governor, well aware of the inadequate British military presence in that country, welcomed the idea of marauding guerrilla units. He promised to look for someone to run the organisation. Although no agreement existed between the Dutch and British governments for mutual aid if either one was attacked, they too went along with Warren's ideas and agreed to consider sending a company of locally recruited colonial troops to Malaya, for behind-the-lines operations.

When he arrived back in Singapore from his trip to Java, Warren found the political scene hardening. Some days previously, on 22nd July, a British spokesman in Singapore announced in a radio broadcast that there was no likelihood of British intervention in pro-German, Vichy-governed Indo-China in the event of Japanese pressure on that country for additional military bases. So if Japan had any doubts about Britain's intentions this announcement must have cleared the air, for within six days Japanese transports were disgorging men and equipment into French Indo-China and they swiftly seized airfields and naval bases. The Japanese move created alarm in GHQ and with the Singapore government. The island defence was based on the assumption that if the Japanese did attack, its task force would be launched from Hainan island, some 1,000 miles away, in which case it would be seen, identified as such, and could be wiped out by British air and sea strikes well away from Malayan waters. This new move brought Japanese bombers, based in Indo-China, within a few hours' flying time from Singapore. In addition the possible invasion beaches of Singorra and Patani were now only two days' steaming for Japanese troop transports. In comparison the British Fleet, still in the UK, would take six weeks to sail to its base in Singapore.

Naturally the landings also excited the Free French group in the Cathay Building. They immediately requested facilities to be parachuted into Indo-China. Such facilities hardly existed in Britain and resources of that nature in Singapore were non-existent. The whole idea was treated with wry amusement but the GOC let them down lightly and promised them a place on the first course organised at the new SOE Training School.

The leader of the Free French group, Baron de Langlade, was also head of a large French firm, SOCFIN, which ran thousands of acres of rubber trees throughout Asia. Warren and he shared the same club and one evening sitting on the verandah, sipping long, cool drinks, they discussed the latest development and its possible effects on the local European population. This gave Warren an opportunity to express his views about the lack of co-operation from the civilian population and their 'business must come first' philosophy. De Langlade listened with interest. 'But why don't you telephone X?' he said, mentioning a well known businessman. 'Mention my name and ask him whether he would be prepared to release some of his staff for training.' Warren had previously been turned down by this particular firm but next day, on the telephone, their reluctance evaporated at the mention of de Langlade. Each new contact had a snowballing effect and soon a steady stream of students began to fill Gavin's school.

By the end of July the school grounds were almost bursting with servicemen, students, new buildings, military vehicles and native staff. The Scapula party had arrived from England and these new arrivals brought the establishment up to 150 men. With all his staff now with him apart from two, Major Gavin organised his unit into three sections:

1. The Headquarters Unit which looked after general administration and support services.

2. The Country Sections which were responsible for special operations in the neighbouring countries. His friend Steve Cummins took over Burma and China while Freddy Spencer Chapman, another mountaineer, who was on his way from Australia to take up his new post, would look after Siam and Indo-China.

3. The Recruitment and Liaison were really Warren's affair. He was now providing the school with a mixed bunch of students, including the Free French section which formed the first course. Specially selected men from the Burma Frontier Force and the recently created Burma Levies filled the second course in August. Then until Christmas it was inundated with civil servants from Hong Kong, tin miners from Siam, Swedes from Burma, French, Dutch, a lone American who was later sent to Java, recruited by the OSS and used in the Balkans.

The security at the school was tight and for a long while it certainly remained secret but as more civilians went through the system its existence gradually became known. Students at the school were confined to barracks and the French contingent nicknamed it 'The Convent'. Apart from training in small arms, explosives and wireless, students and staff were taught to sail a wide variety of boats. As large areas around Malaya and Siam were fringed with what was thought to be impenetrable mangrove swamps Gavin decided that his men needed experience in operating in such conditions if they were to teach others. So early one morning eight army officers and Lieutenant Passmore, RN, the only sailor at the school, filed along the wooden jetty sticking out on the seaward side of the school and climbed down into a small native sampan tied up alongside. The sea was choppy as the early morning breeze, chasing the rain clouds across the skies, swept over the headland. A heavy night in Singapore and the rocking motion of the boat didn't do much for the digestion and some felt that this was taking the war too seriously.

The school was surrounded by swamp so the journey didn't take too long and soon they were amongst the stunted trees of the mangrove swamp. The trees stood on multiple roots in dirty brown water, full of rotting vegetation and water snakes. Almost as soon as they entered the gloomy vegetation the boat went aground. Reluctantly everyone eased themselves into the water and pulled it off. Within minutes, as they crept further in, they went aground again. The procedure was simply a disorganised, and unsoldier-like, climb overboard. Gavin decided to smarten the whole thing up. On the command 'aground' everyone would leap quickly overboard, pull the boat off and back in within minutes.

For the next thirty minutes the sampan continually went aground or jammed amongst the roots. Morale reached a low point and as the boat was pulled off for the umpteenth time someone, it might have been Lowe, suggested that if one sat in the bows with the anchor hanging from the front, everyone could pole back when the anchor touched and before the boat went aground. Cold and soaking wet everyone congratulated him and climbed aboard again. Freddy Chapman was given the anchor job and he moved cautiously forward over the mass of tangled legs and bodies until he reached his perch at the bows. Within minutes the boat was touching and on Chapman's command everyone poled backwards except Passmore, who had been daydreaming. He leapt overboard.

The school considered the local military installations fair game and they provided real life training schemes. Needless to say the victims took a dim view and continually complained to GHQ. One night, for instance, a party led by Captain Lowe silently moved through the secondary jungle surrounding a heavily guarded ammunition dump. They cut the barbed wire and eight men, their faces blackened, wriggled through the gap. Avoiding the sentries they placed sections of bamboo, individually wrapped in brown paper and stencilled 'dynamite', at strategic places. Returning through the wire they waited for each other at a pre-selected point in a monsoon ditch that ran along the side of the road close to the camp. Back at the school they waited for the reaction.

They didn't have to wait long, by mid-morning a major alert swept the island as the bamboo bombs were discovered. Shortly afterwards everyone was stood down after red faces had peeled off the brown paper and the hollow bamboo was revealed beneath. Spencer Chapman had finally to admit that the raid was part of the school's training exercise. The victim was not amused, GHQ were not amused, Killery was carpeted and Spencer Chapman had a rocket. Everyone else had a good laugh at the Army's expense. On another occasion – possibly to avoid showing any Service bias – Spencer Chapman, together with a sergeant instructor, penetrated the well guarded Kallong Airfield one night and left a message 'We were here at 2.30 a.m.' – obviously a forerunner of Kilroy.

On 28th July, two days after the school was officially opened, Jack Knott's wireless party arrived from England. When the signal equipment was unpacked Knott remembers finding it quite useless. It didn't stand up to the knocking about it received during the voyage nor could it take the tropical heat. He recalls that equipment suitable for jungle operations was simply non-existent. When he tried to scrounge replacements from local units he soon discovered the rarity value of a wireless set. Some battalions moving north to cover the border with Siam were lucky to have even one.

Before leaving London he had taken Gavin's advice and made contact with SIS (Secret Intelligence Service). The Liaison Officer was Wing Commander Pile, who listened with interest to Knott's problem and eventually supplied him with one of their new lightweight Mark 1's. With it came a titbit of advice that the set worked best from the back seat of a Packard. Later, dutifully and rather proudly, showing his new set to the Procurement Officer, Knott asked for six. Remembering the friendly SIS officer's advice, he also asked for the Packards. The tubby, round-faced officer sitting at the desk went through various shades of red until he burst out – 'You'll get no bloody Packards here – and for that matter no Mark 1's either!' Eventually he was sent a battered 15 cwt truck and well-used wireless equipment.

Three months later, sitting in the recently built bamboo *basha*, a hut with a frame of bamboo and the walls and roof made from palm tree fronds, Knott pondered on the problem of running a wireless course without transmitters. Even the Mark 1 had its drawbacks. Nearby two of his sergeants with long lists of equipment and pencil stubs, methodically went through a mess of headphones, cables, batteries and the battered transmitter before finally placing them into stores. His thoughts were interrupted by the arrival of a rather bossy major who flung open the door and strode in. Seeing Knott he announced himself as Major Rosher 'Secret Service old chap' and dropping his voice slightly, he looked around at the almost bare room with an obvious air of disapproval and added confidentially, 'The Commander asked me to keep a fatherly eye on you'.

The SIS enjoyed a privileged position and had first call on all wireless equipment and operators anywhere in the world, so when he discovered Knott's dilemma he arranged for the school to be supplied with the first Mark 1's to be sent out east and stocks of reasonable equipment. He had a vested interest of course; he wanted the school to supply him with trained wireless operators for his own clandestine work.

Although the Mark 1's were most welcome Knott found them almost useless for clandestine work in the Far East. They had been designed for Europe, in civilised conditions over a short range. To succeed in the enormous distances involved in the east required a careful selection of frequencies and timing of signals using special twin aerials. The Mark 1's needed a mains supply and the only solution the school could find was to adapt them to Stratton and Webb generators. This meant that to use the sets in the jungle, the clumsy generators and gallons of petrol had to be back-packed through mountainous jungle. 'Given all these factors,' mused Jack Knott. 'and the fact that the Mark 1's were not designed for tropical use, it was no wonder that wireless communications often failed in those early days.'

Apart from wireless training it was essential that all instructors should be conversant with all weapons whatever their individual speciality – so one Sunday they decided on some mortar practice.

In the heat of the mid-day sun, on the lawn overlooking the sea and flanked by tall palm trees, the mortar was set and everyone moved in close. The instructor gave a brief speech on the bomb and its capabilities. Kneeling by the tube one of the officers dropped the bomb into the mortar and with a characteristic cough the bomb flew out, deflected off the overhanging branches of a nearby tree, hurtled in and exploded amongst the party. The mortar tube spun away knocking people over like skittles. Others were bowled over by the blast and one was spread-eagled against a palm tree before sliding to the ground. Everyone, badly shaken and shocked, tried to regain their feet except the sergeant instructor who lay dead and Captain Lowe who writhed on the ground clutching his stomach. His thighs and stomach had been ripped open by shrapnel. After pumping him full of morphine and cleaning up his wounds, his friends tried to console him that his damaged crotch would not affect his future love life. That night everyone got drunk.

CHAPTER THREE

Special Operations

Indo-China

The Japanese moves into Indo-China in August 1941 belatedly shocked the military into realizing that it knew next to nothing about Japanese capabilities and weapons. As military intelligence was in short supply and the Free French group was anxious to get into Indo-China it was decided to infiltrate them ashore, along some deserted stretch of coast, to make contact with some of de Langlade's friends. They would take with them both weapons and wireless equipment and prepare the ground for further parties. It was decided that 101 Special Training School would equip and land the party and, in turn, Killery chose Freddy Spencer Chapman, who had arrived at the school from Australia where he had been training Australian Commando teams, to lead the British support team. This would consist of Jack Knott and three other ranks including Sergeant Shufflebottom, a wireless instructor at the school.

The Royal Navy's contribution was a tug boat named *Frosty Moller*; however as this drew too much water they swapped it for a flat-bottomed Yangtse river steamer, the *Wuchang*. This was eventually brought around from the Naval Base and anchored some hundred yards off shore. For the next few days the Anglo-French team practised inflating and loading the collapsible rubber dinghy. Spencer Chapman, with growing dismay, watched the inexperienced handling of the boat and equipment. Each launch threatened to put passengers and stores into the sea until eventually Chapman asked Knott, short, slim and lightweight, to take charge of the shore party and see them safely onto the beach. His actual job was to look after the ship-to-shore communications link as well as organise the overall communications network for the party.

The night before they sailed was spent hiding explosives, arms, radio equipment and home-produced dangerous toys, in the ship's coal bunkers in case they were stopped and searched by Japanese naval patrols. Recalling the event, Knott commented thirty years later that 'Considering the need for the raiding party to melt in with its surroundings nothing would have been more out of place than a Yangtse riverboat manned by Europeans off the coast of Japanese-occupied Indo-China with coal bunkers full of explosives and weapons.'

Slipping her anchor before dawn, the little river steamer crept through the eastern entrance to Singapore Roads and headed out to sea. Almost immediately the flat-bottomed riverboat struck the ocean waves. Momentarily passengers and crew went a shade of green, then pale under the suntan before finally they were all seasick. The roughish trip took almost a week with everyone, apart from Knott and Shufflebottom, confined to their bunks.

All communications had been tested before they left but when the army wireless station at Kranji came on the air with an urgent signal for them their acknowledgement went unheard. Everyone aboard the ship suffered from severe seasick symptoms but despite this Knott and Shufflebottom between bouts of vomiting tried to get their set working. The aerials were re-rigged, the set dried out, crystals changed but all to no avail – they were still mute. The 400 ton vessel continued to roll its way across the Bay of Siam, rising and falling with each sickening wave and Kranji kept up its hourly calls that it had an urgent message for the party. In desperation the urgent message was sent blind and although the atmospherics were poor Knott and Shufflebottom copied it; only to discover that it had been distorted in transmission. Meanwhile the *Wuchang* anchored off the coast and prepared to disembark its passengers leaving the signals personnel to decypher the message. The wind was high and the sea pounded down on to the sandy beach making it impossible to put anyone ashore that day. In the middle of all the arrangements Knott appeared on the bridge with the unscrambled and decyphered message Chapman read it with growing amazement. Briefly it read that unless they had good reason to continue they should return to base.

Chapman called all the officers together to discuss the new development. What particularly puzzled everyone was the reference to 'the need to be there'. The general opinion was that if there had not been a good reason for them to be there in the first place they wouldn't be there now. It was a well known fact exclaimed the French that the British were crazy and didn't this prove it? Eventually everyone agreed that the message didn't make sense and should be ignored. The wind had dropped and by nightfall the surf was expected to subside. The French were anxious to get ashore so the rubber boats were again launched, dropped overboard and packed

with stores. Chapman stood against the ship's rail looking into the
boat when Knott again appeared by his side clutching another message. This one was more positive – 'the landing zone is compromised
– return immediately'. The French were furious and for a moment
they seemed to be about to ignore the order to return to the ship. For
a moment they argued amongst themselves then reluctantly they
began to climb back on board. At that moment Anglo-French relations fell to zero.

In Singapore harsh words were also being exchanged after Admiral Layton, C in C China Station, discovered that SOE were putting
men ashore in Indo-China at the very time he was trying to persuade
the French Governor to come over to the British side. This SOE-de
Gaullist operation threatened to ruin months of secret negotiations
but the party knew nothing of this. When the little steamer eventually appeared unexpectedly one morning and anchored off the pier
near the school, all the staff were delighted. The passengers and
crew, on the other hand, were surprised at the welcome, never realising that they had been assumed captured or even dead. Killery,
already sick, worried excessively about both their safety and possible
diplomatic repercussions at a sensitive time in Anglo-Japanese-
French affairs.

About this time a Free French regular officer arrived from London
to co-ordinate French activities in the Orient. He listened to the mut-
terings about the crazy British and the lack of resources and decided
to move their base from Singapore to Kunming in the Yunnan State
of China. From there they could mount land-based operations into
northern Indo-China without needing to rely on the British.

Siam

Shortly after the abortive Anglo-French seaborne raid, Warren
invited Jim Gavin and Spencer Chapman to dinner at the club. This
was neutral ground in view of secrecy surrounding their activities.
Apart from Indo-China, Chapman also looked after the school operations in Siam and Warren's reason for paying for dinner was to outline a proposed British plan to carry out a pre-emptive strike against
Siam in the event of hostilities with Japan. This entailed occupying
all of southern Siam. 11 Division was already moving troops up to
the border and SOE's role would be to train and infiltrate armed parties across the border ahead of the main force, to seize strategic positions.

Briefly, the plan that evolved fell into four parts. It was anticipated that any Japanese landing along the Malayan Barrier would take place at Signorra, Patani and Khota Bharu – the latter being in north Malaya. The enemy force was expected to move along the well-metalled roads and thrust into north Malaya. It was this force that needed to be delayed long enough for the British 11 Division to cross into Siam and seize the strategic positions to block the advance. SOE was given the tasks of capturing the important Yala crossroads, on the road linking the invasion beaches with Malaya, and also seizing Phukit Island on the west coast of Siam with its vital airstrip. If the enemy captured the airfield it could command the sea routes from Rangoon to Penang and give air cover to its troops advancing into Malaya. It was also decided that SOE would carry out seaborne raids in Siamese fishing ports and seize any enemy shipping hiding there. The artillery support for the latter would be given by a mine-sweeper's (SS *Mata Hari*) four inch gun. The land-based operation was code-named Etonian and the seaborne raids, Betty.

Recruits were found amongst the European mining population in Siam and soon miners and businessmen appeared at the school for training. When they returned they had special stores hidden in car seats, weapons strapped to the underside of their cars and special explosives packed with the normal stores for their businesses or mines. One big problem was how to communicate with the groups when they returned to their civilian occupations. Wireless transmitters were simply unobtainable and the public telephone system was not only insecure but would take hours, even if the system worked.

It was eventually decided to send two of Knott's sergeant wireless operators, with false papers, to Siam. Disguised as deputy mine managers and armed with two valuable wireless sets they would watch the anticipated invasion areas and report back the strength of the enemy landings. They would work to the radio station at Kranji who in turn would alert Radio Malaya. Each SOE group in Siam was issued with an ordinary domestic wireless receiver and each morning the groups tuned into the six o'clock news. If the news of the invasion had been received the announcer would give a coded message hidden in a news item. This would tell the public that a careless army officer in Singapore had lost his brief case and important papers were missing. He would then read out a list of serial numbers of the alleged documents and each reference would be the signal for one of the groups to seize their objective.

At about the time the two sergeants crossed the border GHQ, without informing SOE, sent some thirty officers dressed in mufti into Siam on intelligence gathering missions. This sudden influx of smartly dressed Europeans alerted Siamese counter-intelligence and kept the Japanese agents amused until December when it was time to round them all up.

Malaya

The defence strategy for the Malayan peninsula, in the event of a land-based assault across the Siam border, was for half-trained and badly equipped 11 Division to hold the enemy as long as possible in the border areas, then fall back slowly to Singapore. This could take up to six months and allow ample time for the Royal Navy and rein-forcements from England to arrive to relieve the defenders. Warren wasn't so optimistic. Unlike many in Singapore he didn't underesti-mate the Japanese, either as a soldier or as a field engineer, and wasn't convinced that 11 Division could hold them off for that length of time.

But the withdrawal down the peninsula did offer an ideal oppor-tunity to place guerrilla groups, operating from well-stocked jungle hideouts, in forward areas likely to be over-run by the Japanese. After the tide of battle had swept across the area they could emerge behind the enemy lines and cause mayhem amongst the enemy's lines of communications, its transports and reinforcements. This should cause dislocation of supplies and ease the pressure against the British defenders.

Both Killery and Warren set about selling the idea to senior gov-ernment staff and the military. As early as June and July 1941, Kil-lery put the plan to General Percival, C in C Malaya, but despite his promise of full co-operation, he not only turned it down but failed to notify Killery until October. Eight weeks later the Japanese poured across the border. While Killery fretted for a decision the old Malayan hands made their views obvious to Warren. They consi-dered the problem one of not letting the side down. If coolies and natives were trained for behind-the-lines activities before the war even started, it would be like admitting that the Japanese were superior and this would be bad for native morale. The Chinese also presented a problem. Russian-trained communist organisers had built up a strong underground movement amongst the Chinese com-munity and not only was the Chinese Communist Party banned but Russia, its mentor, was pro-German. Another factor that needed to be considered was that both America and Britain supported Chiang Kai Shek's Kuomintang National Party which was in open conflict with the Chinese Communist Party. So, the argument ran, it was politically dangerous and undesirable to arm and train the Malayan Chinese Community.

As the idea of marauding, armed natives, loose behind enemy lines didn't appeal an alternative plan was produced involving European sabotage groups also operating from well-stocked jungle hideouts behind enemy lines. This idea was also turned down by the civilian authorities who, ignoring the obvious fact that war with Japan was imminent, insisted that the production of tin and rubber should not be impeded and the selection of Europeans from these industries, to be trained by the Orient Mission, would interfere with output. Others argued, and Warren was apt to agree with them, that white men would stand out in the native environment 'like lighthouses in the night'.

It was ironic that while the Orient Mission was meeting resistance to putting guerrillas into the Malayan jungle, a police counter-intelligence unit based in Kuala Lumpur learnt that Japanese agents were being infiltrated across the border. This little known operation was discovered by accident. 3 Corps part of 11 Division manning the border with Siam, was having teething troubles with the terrain. Due to pre-war neglect the army commanders discovered that the maps issued by Divisional Headquarters showed large areas simply marked 'jungle' or 'unsurveyed'. But the border it seemed existed only on paper and was ignored by the local population who, in any case, considered themselves in Siam not Malaya. The border was riddled with unmapped roads and tracks and the villagers thrived on smuggling goods across the border. The job of bringing the maps up to date was given to a recently arrived staff officer acting as G2(I) 3 Corps. He in turn approached the Chief Game Warden for Malaya who quickly recruited five European civilians who knew the border areas. Showing more motivation in five weeks than the military did in five months, this little team, using local headmen began to mark up jungle tracks and forgotten villages. And it was through this little ad-hoc group that Intelligence in Kuala Lumpur discovered that the Japanese had two agents based in the jungle town of Betong, just across the border in Siam, whose job it was to infiltrate pro-Japanese natives recently arrived from the training camp of Hainan Island, into Malaya. Their job was to act as scouts to invading Japanese columns spearheading the thrust into Malaya.

Indo-China and Hong Kong

The arrival of Spencer Chapman at 101 Special Training School for
Australia freed Jim Gavin from the day-to-day administration of the
school whose new role had widened to include the provision of military support to any Ministry of Economic Warfare agents in Indo-
China, China and Hong Kong. In fact the Chinese mainland. After
the nerve-racking experience of trying to put a team of Free French
ashore in July it was decided to have another try but this time making it less obvious. The Free French leader Baron de Langlade,
despite the danger to himself as a well known Gaullist supporter,
agreed to visit Indo-China on a business trip and contact as many
anti-Vichy supporters as possible. Using these as a basis for an
underground cell he would arrange for the Orient Mission to smug-
gle in arms agents and transmitters. Rather than make his connec-
tion with Singapore too obvious he would return via Hong Kong.

Having arranged to meet him there Gavin flew to Hong Kong and
took the opportunity to discuss with MEW's agent, Mr Turner, possible operations on the Chinese mainland; especially in the Treaty
Ports dotted along the coast. Unlike Singapore he found everyone
enthusiastic. The Japanese threat was in their own back garden and
the city was full of European businessmen and their families
evacuated from the Treaty Ports in the face of Japanese intimidation.
Many had lost their homes and possessions and could give first-hand
examples of Japanese atrocities. The rape of Nanking was still fresh
in everyone's minds. The GOC, General Maltby, was keen to help;
businessmen quickly released their staff for covert operational training and volunteers disappeared from view. One volunteer, a
businessman named Kendall, slipped ashore on the Japanese-con-
trolled island of Hainan to develop his own clandestine group. He fed
back information on the Japanese strength and training facilities and
also tried to identify Asians attending the spy school. Through the
local Chinese Communist organisation contact was made with anti-
Japanese groups in the Treaty Ports. The Communists were in fact
the only ones actually fighting the Japanese in China.

Meanwhile Turner introduced Gavin to the commander of a local
TA unit, whose men had volunteered to remain behind and operate
against the enemy lines of communications, following the expected
Japanese attack on the island. General Maltby had long realised that
the New Territories could not be defended and his plan was to fall
back, when attacked, through the mountains and form a defence line
around the island of Hong Kong. The TA volunteers would move off

into the mountains and let the front line roll past them to the sea. They would then monitor road transport, feed back information on the enemy strengths and movements and pinpoint enemy columns forming up for an attack.

The unit's Commanding Officer, Major Hugh Williamson, left for a training course at 101 STS. With him went Petro, MEW's man in Indo-China, who would provide a contact with the de Gaulle underground in Saigon. All the Volunteers, part of the Reconnaissance Unit, were well known businessmen and when Jim Gavin needed a plane to study the terrain one immediately offered to pilot him around in his own private aircraft. In this they flew over the New Territories mapping suitable valleys and caves for bases. The flights were quickly followed up by the army who carried out ground searches of the selected areas. The most suitable locations were stocked with food, ammunition and weapons. When the secret headquarters of the stay-behind party was chosen, Royal Engineers and Royal Signals equipped the base and laid a special telephone line to Brigade HQ. An urgent signal to Spencer Chapman at the school brought more stores and equipment. In a few weeks six hideouts had been built in the mountains, a secret training centre and a peacetime headquarters established.

China

The heads of Propaganda and the Intelligence Sections normally met every Wednesday in the Cathay Building to discuss the most up-to-date intelligence assessments and plan future operations. These meetings were usually chaired by Sir George Sansom and included Killery, Goodfellow and Warren. At one such meeting, from the conference room window behind Sansom's chair, Warren could see the red tiled roofs of the Chinese-style houses below. Beyond, in the harbour, a large Chinese junk with its bat-like sails headed gracefully for the islands on the horizon. Launches scurried around the harbour ignoring a line of lighters bringing passengers off a nearby recently arrived liner. Not a plane or warship to be seen, he mused to himself. The scene was serene and war a long way off it seemed. The loss of Greece and Crete was no more than headlines in the morning newspaper, to be read and forgotten.

Warren stopped his day-dreaming and tried to concentrate on the report Killery was giving about the encouraging developments in Indo-China, Hong Kong and Siam. When Siam was mentioned the Chairman referred to a recent memorandum from the Foreign

Office. The British Ambassador had complained bitterly that SOE's activities along the border were upsetting the delicate political situation in that country and wanted them restrained. The military were also complaining that scarce resources were being channelled to 101 STS.

Someone indignantly compared the Ambassador's views with the current situation; Tokyo had advised its nationals in western colonial countries to return home, enemy shipping and troop transports were daily bringing troops and equipment to Indo-China and local reports were continually mentioning agent activities in Malaya. 'What should we do?' the speaker asked. 'Tie one hand behind our back?' The Chairman calmed the meeting and Killery reported that Steve Cummins had just returned from Burma where, it seemed, the Burmese government was pro-Japanese. In the mountains the hill tribesmen were pressing for home rule and politically the situation seemed unstable.

Overhead the fan slowly whirled around, creaking and swaying slightly on its mounting. Sansom picked up another report from the pile beside him. Warren could see he was perspiring.

On the Chinese mainland the tension was increasing; the Japanese had seized the Treaty Ports of Shanghai, Amoy and Canton and now, in a threatening manner, had put a strong force ashore alongside the British-held mainland of Hong Kong. They were insisting that Britain stopped supplies reaching China through Hong Kong. The Chinese Government had retreated up the Yangtse to Chunking and this city was now being attacked by Japanese bombers, although the American mercenary flyers, the Flying Tigers were defending the city fiercely. The Chinese government, reported Sansom, had some five million soldiers facing the Japanese on a two thousand mile front. Another million were under training. Warren now began to give Sansom his full attention. The Americans had promised the Chinese more planes and a loan of five million dollars. As the Chairman recited his report Warren came to the conclusion that SOE trained Chinese guerrillas, armed with American equipment and operating behind the Japanese lines in China could surely give the Japanese one big headache.

Gradually at the meeting the Chinese plan took shape as each person bounced ideas into the discussion. They were reminded that groups of Australians were being trained by Mike Calvert at the Bush Training Centre at Maymo in Burma. These had been earmarked for operations in China. Eventually it was decided to send a team to China to discuss the possibilities of SOE activities on the Chinese mainland. Logically this would mean setting up a second school, probably in Chungking, using 101 STS staff and resources. It was eventually agreed that Killery and Warren should fly to Chungking to discuss the possibilities.

Warren remembers sitting in his club with Killery. GHQ had sent over their papers and, as they were travelling incognito, they would need a cover story. A long cool drink stood invitingly on the table. They could choose their own identities – who should they be? Someone suggested white slave traders which brought a gleam to Warren's eye. Killery, more staid, decided to be a rubber planter and Warren after more thought simply wrote, 'Gentleman'.

Two days later they were aboard a slow-moving DC 3 heading for China. Apart from themselves and two hard-drinking American Volunteer Force (Flying Tigers) pilots, all the passengers appeared to be Chinese or simply oriental. Warren found himself sitting beside a Chinese general but any attempt at conversation was drowned by the noise of the rattle of every nut and bolt in the plane. The Americans simply ignored everyone and drank their way through bottles of whisky. The Chinese watched them in disgust and Warren, sitting next to the window, watched mile after mile of snow-capped mountains and ridges unfold beneath the plane. Eventually the mountains gave way to a fast rushing river cascading through deep gorges on to a plain covered with paddy fields. In the middle of the plain stood a large walled city with a nearby dirt airstrip. It was Chengtu and the General was told that because of heavy bombing at Chungking the plane was being temporarily diverted there.

As the plane rolled to a stop on the airstrip the general spoke for the first time to Warren, inviting him and his fellow officer to dinner. Killery looked uncomfortable at having his cover blown but Warren smiled and accepted for both of them.

The general introduced himself as they strode across to a waiting car. He was General Ma from Chinese Intelligence and as the plane had been diverted he believed the local 'warlord' – a fellow general – would no doubt welcome the opportunity of treating him, his staff and his British friends, to a lavish dinner – which the local commander did with gushing oriental charm and politeness. As the dinner progressed General Ma talked a little about himself. Not only did he speak perfect English but he was in fact born in Stepney, the son of a Polish immigrant named Moshie Cohen.

He had emigrated to Canada at the age of sixteen in 1889 and, shortly after arriving there, saved a Chinese from being mugged. The grateful victim turned out to be a member of a Chinese secret society committed to the overthrow of the Manchu Empire in China. Intent on adventure Cohen found himself deeply involved with the conspiracy. As the years went by he became involved with training courses for guerrilla activities and later arranged for trained guerrilla leaders to be infiltrated back into China through the Treaty Ports.

When the First World War started he returned to England and joined the Irish Guards and within a few months was in France. There he became responsible for Chinese coolie labour brought in to move supplies to the front. In 1917 he was brought back to England severely wounded and by the time he recovered the war had ended. Back in Canada he rejoined his Chinese associates and organised surplus war weapons to be smuggled into China. Following the collapse of the Manchu Empire and the later formation of the new Chinese Republic, Chiang Kai Shek came to power and appointed him bodyguard to its leader and later instructed him to create a new Chinese Secret Service.

Warren found Ma a person after his own heart and he had every intention of developing this new contact. Unfortunately General Ma was sent to Hong Kong some months later to rescue the widow of Sun Yat Sen, the founder of modern China. She was also Chiang Kai Shek's mother-in-law. Here his luck ran out and he was captured by the Japanese.

When he and Warren returned to the plane they found the Americans still drinking. They also had with them a black holdall which they never let out of their sight. From remarks made by Ma it seemed that one of the pilots was the boyfriend of the South American wife of a senior British diplomat in Chungking; although he was well known to the Chinese for smuggling gold and opium, the American was protected by her patronage.

Eventually the plane reached Chungking and circled the town. The town straddled the wide Yangtse and little houses clung to the side of steep cliffs dropping to the muddy river in the gorge. Troops had burrowed long tunnels into its banks as air raid shelters and the rocks and dirt emptied on to a large mudflat in the middle of the river. This was the new airstrip and it was on to this that the plane dropped, giving the passengers a tremendous view of the cliffs towering above them.

The British Embassy had a car waiting and they were soon driven at a somewhat reckless speed through narrow streets, competing with Chinese-driven American army lorries for gaps between rickshaws and people. Eventually Warren and Killery found themselves seated in the ornate Embassy rooms, in comfortable high-backed chairs overlooking the river. Their host was John Keswick, MEW's man in Chungking and also head of Jardine Matheson, a major business concern in the Far East.

They were briefed on the complex military and political situation and it was pointed out that despite the Japanese incursions China didn't consider itself at war with Japan. In fact, Chiang Kai Shek actually belonged to the same secret society as some of the Japanese leaders. Its objective was simply Asia for the Asians. Even now reports were reaching the Embassy of the Chinese leader's tour of India. Whilst there, as guest of the British, he spoke of his encouragement to anti-British nationalist parties to free India from the British.

China had a large internationally trained army. It was originally created by Russian advisers in the twenties but these were thrown out when it was discovered they were creating communist cells amongst the officer cadets. Chiang Kai Shek himself had been sent to Russia as a young officer for special training. The Russians were replaced by Germans, who in addition to providing the advisers also set up their own spy rings to watch the Japanese and British. The chief Nazi controller of networks had his base in Japanese-occupied Tiensten. The Japanese too had their spy network, they had agents in every major city and even bribed the Chinese generals opposing them at the front to take no effective action. The senior Japanese agent in China enjoyed the protection of the Chinese Secret Service and had his office close to the British Embassy.

The Americans were also involved but their policy was one of even-handedness. This really meant that as long as they continued to make a profit they didn't care who won. American businessmen had a strong Chinese lobby in Washington which pumped in dollar millions, weapons and equipment. This lobby was fiercely anti-British and this influenced the Chinese.

Apart from the European spy networks operating nationwide the Chinese nationalist secret service, largely based on the *Triad* secret society, operated its own intelligence system world wide. It had links with every overseas Chinese community and in every stratum of Chinese society. In addition the Chinese Communist movement, which seemed to be the only one prepared to engage the Japanese columns moving across China, had contacts in every village. Volunteers were known to walk hundreds of miles to Red-held areas for training, then walk back again to form their own guerrilla groups behind the Japanese.

Killery and Warren were undeterred by this briefing and arranged a series of meetings with their Chinese counterparts. To their surprise, they found their offers of help enthusiastically received but after being fêted for two weeks Warren came to the conclusion that the Chinese only wanted their resources and not the men. He had expected to have news of Calvert's Australians but discovered from Keswick that in fact they were marooned at Lashio, on the border with Burma, waiting for Chinese permission to cross over. The Chinese suggested there must have been some mistake and promised to look into the problem.

Although they found the Chinese evasive they didn't suspect the dead hand of the head of the Chinese Secret Service, Tai Li. He was the main barrier and, with some historical justification, was suspicious of British help. As the Americans helped to fund his activities, he always gave them a ready ear. His lack of love for the British was not improved when he visited Hong Kong in 1940. When the British-led police found him on the island they threw him into jail.

Warren remembered Chungking full of Americans singing the fighting qualities of the Chinese, while at the same time selling them lorries and planes. But it was obvious that the generals were nothing more than warlords whose loyalty to Chiang Kai Shek diminished in direct relation to their distance from Chungking.

Lashio, Burma
Lashio was to be the SOE's half-way house to Chungking – a base camp built by Danish volunteers on the border of north Burma and China. Before he left Singapore, Killery asked Jim Gavin to do a practice run along the route to identify any problems likely to occur in moving large groups of men and stores overland from Rangoon. Gavin had only just returned from Hong Kong but within a few days he flew to Rangoon and booked in at the Pedu Club, full of olde worlde charm – Oriental politeness, native waiters, comfortable beds and good food. The harbour was packed with ships of every nation full of war materials for China. The ships queued in The Roads for berths and lighters bustled around full of cargo. Along the waterfront long lines of Indian dockers so thin that one could see the outline of their ribs, snaked in and out of the berthed ships.

Gavin's road transport problems were solved by the British Military Mission responsible for co-ordinating American supplies into

China. Its American counterpart had a large lorry park full of brand new USA vehicles and they were only too pleased for him to ferry one of these partway to the base at Yunnan in China. They also offered their full co-operation when he began to move his men and supplies through Burma.

Apart from a few small units like the Military Mission, this furthest flung outpost of the British Empire was manned by only a company of Gloucesters and forward units of a scratch division moving slowly up to the borders of Siam. The city was completely unprepared for war, it had no civil defence, no air raid shelters and the only ack-ack guns were manned by a small unit of Volunteers from the university.

Leaving the problem of berths and transport with the Military Mission he set off on the first part of the eight hundred mile journey along the fabled Burma Road. His vehicle was the first military lorry to use the route since Churchill had ordered it to be closed because of Japanese threats.

The road from Rangoon took him along well metalled roads, skirted with tall forests or occasionally mile after mile of rice fields. Elephants leisurely plodded along the road with their mahoots on their backs. Slow-moving oxen carts and wood-burning lorries filled the roads whenever he neared a town. As he drove up the hill to Maymo, a British Army garrison town, he could see its landmark – a large white pagoda. The town was full of troops, pretty girls in colourful sarongs and colonial style houses with well trimmed lawns. The town housed the military detention barracks, a military hospital, British Military Headquarters and Mike Calvert's Bush Warfare Training Centre.

Gavin stayed at the rest house and in the cool of the evening, having showered and eaten, he now sat on the verandah enjoying the night and watching the fireflies flitting around amongst the trees. Suddenly at his elbow stood a tall, blond officer. He introduced himself as Lieutenant Sodorbohm, a Dane, from the base camp at Lashio. He had been responsible for creating the base and he had driven down to act as guide for the remainder of the journey. This was a polite way of saying he would be riding shotgun through the next stretch which was bandit country.

The road from Maymo was hard dirt and beaten stone. The metalled road became a pleasant memory. The road was opened in 1939 and now provided China with the only route for supplies since the capture of the Treaty Ports by the Japanese. The Japanese occupa-

tion of French Indo-China closed the French-owned Haiphong to
Yunnan railway and the threat to Hong Kong forced the British to
reduce the flow of strategic goods across the border with China.

About 400 civilian lorries a day used the road, rattling and bouncing their way through occasional narrow streets which clung to the
mountainside. The road was built through some of the wildest countryside in the Shan States. From Mandalay, high cliffs rose out of the
paddy fields and successive mountains rising higher and higher,
could be seen fading into the distance with the road becoming a thin
white line winding its way like a corkscrew into the clouds. The
unfenced mountain road gave a wonderful view of the valleys
thousands of feet below. On about the third day, some twenty miles
from Lashio they reached the Salween River; after a spectacular
drive down a three mile long hill which dropped 10,000 feet from
crest to river.

Apart from the hazard of a breakdown on this route from Maymo
there was also the additional problem of no petrol stations, so every
motorist carried his own supplies. Another hazard was Japanese-led
bandits who gladly followed their military trained leaders in raids on
the traffic or villages and towns along the roads. Native lorry drivers
using the road revised the charges upwards every few miles giving
the owner the option of paying or having his goods left at the side of
the road.

Lashio had become the main centre for all goods entering China
and had all the appearances of a goldrush town straight out of a Hollywood film set. The narrow streets were full of mule trains from the
mountains, pack horses, stray cattle, rickshaws, ancient lorries and
modern cars. Parked cars were stripped in minutes leaving the unfortunate owner to search the well-stocked bazaar for replacements.
Beyond the town was the Chinese border and the only way across
was to pay a hefty bribe to the Chinese border guards.

As they entered the town Sodorbohm guided Gavin through the
streets. They turned left, up a side road, on to the mountain road to
Bhamo. The SOE base camp was about a half mile outside the town,
near the airfield on the Hse Paw road. The airfield was just a
bulldozed dirt strip boasting a few wooden huts at the end of the runway. The SOE stockade was more substantial surrounded by a high
barbed wire fence. Apart from a wooden hut which served as an
office, there were three long stone built huts, with other structures of
wood and bamboo. These were the sleeping quarters and a
cookhouse. A generator provided electricity and piped water was on
tap for the ablutions.

In the camp Gavin found Calvert's Australians, bored and aggressive, making money for themselves working the bazaar. Their quarters were possibly the best equipped in Burma.

Shortly after he arrived Warren and Killery turned up. They had checked out the rest of the route from Chungking. They had found a large number of French at Kunming, in the Yunnan, and many seemed anxious to do something about the Japanese. As far as the China operation was concerned they were reasonably optimistic. The Chinese had promised to look into the reasons for the hold-up at Lashio and had agreed that the Australians should be moved as quickly as possible to within striking distance of Shanghai. They also agreed that some hundred Chinese communist guerrillas could be trained at Calvert's Bush Warfare Training Centre and at the same time they were prepared to accept twelve SOE trained guerrilla leaders. Meanwhile they would make arrangements for a SOE training camp to be built near Chungking.

When the trio eventually arrived back in Singapore at the end of November they found everyone on second degree alert and most of the school's staff in hospital, suffering from swamp fever better known as dengue.

CHAPTER FOUR

SOE Parties Wiped Out

'Where is the Strike South Commander going to set up his headquarters?' asked Hirohito.

'In Saigon,' replied Sugiyama.

'Is there any possibility that we shall spoil the rubber plantations?' [in Malaya]

'I don't know, there may be some damage,' replied Sugiyama, 'but since the roads are narrow we think the best procedure is to advance in small units of a single Regiment led by a few tanks.'

Japan's Imperial Conspiracy

In the few weeks they had been in China the international scene had deteriorated and tension in the Far East increased. The growing Japanese presence in Indo-China was causing concern in GHQ Singapore, and Brooke-Popham, GOC, sought the advice of the Chiefs of Staff in London on whether he should launch 'Matador', the codename for the operation to pre-empt a Japanese strike on Siam. As the policy was to avoid war and compromise whenever possible, the reply he received came as no surprise. He was told that London would need 36 hours' notice of any definite news of any Japanese moves before they could give him a reply. It seemed lost on Whitehall, and Churchill, that Singapore was now only a few hours' flying time from the Japanese bases in Indo-China.

As unconfirmed reports of Japanese troop movements continued to come in, the GOC was reluctant to take the initiative and order the army into Siam to block any possible overland advance by the Japanese. Instead he called up the Volunteers (TA's) as a precautionary measure and ordered a further search for the Japanese fleet, at sea, in the monsoon; somewhere in the China Seas. On the evening of 7th December, a patrolling Hudson bomber spotted the enemy battleships and troop transports but with heavy seas pounding large waves onto the beaches the GOC refused to believe an attack was imminent. The fleet could be a bluff and it could turn north away from Malaya. Still unconvinced he ordered another search.

Warren sat in the Operations Room at GHQ waiting for a meeting of the top brass to finish. Brooke-Popham had called the meeting some hours previously at 10.30 p.m. to discuss the proposed military strike into Siam. The meeting went on into the early hours and it finally confirmed the GOC's decision not to launch Matador. From reports in their possession, the enemy's intentions were uncertain and if they did land at the expected points in Siam, the British troops poised on the border would arrive too late to intervene. That night Matador was cancelled and one SOE survivor, after the war, commented cynically that 'Brooke-Popham was an old woman'.

In the north, along the Siam border, the monsoon rains lashed across the jungle and filled the deserted trenches with water. Along the coast Indian troops manning the beach defences at Khota Bahru huddled under their waterproof capes. Out to sea huge white-topped waves crashed down on the sands and the palm trees, fringing the beach, bent in the winds.

In Siam the miners and their families listened to the rain battering the tin roofs of their bungalows. It would soon be time to switch on the radios for the six o'clock morning news from Singapore. Some families had left but many refused to leave their husbands and fathers – a decision which was to have tragic consequences.

Further north in Singorra, the enemy were already ashore and the Siamese police with Japanese advisors were rounding up suspected British agents. These included the two SOE sergeant wireless operators: one was blown out of his chair by a shotgun when he was discovered at his wireless set trying to contact Kranji; while the second Sergeant Wright, managed to convince the police that he was in fact only a deputy mine manager and was interned and his set never discovered.

In Singapore the meeting of senior commanders broke up and after being briefed on the latest but out-of-date military position Warren walked across the deserted Naval Base to the Mess and went to bed.

At 101 Special Training School, Jim Gavin was fast asleep in the partitioned main bedroom of the millionaire's bungalow he shared with Spencer Chapman. Gavin had spent a romantic evening with the attractive daughter of a squadron leader in the RAF at Seletar. Outside the school was in darkness and in the distance the glow of Singapore's lights could be seen above the tree tops. It was these the

Japanese pilots could see, like homing beacons, while they were still
many miles away, high above the jungles of Johore. As they
approached the island they could see a large ship ablaze with lights
heading for the Naval Base. In the harbour the waterfront was lit up
as dockers unloaded a large freighter. Cars and pedestrians could be
plainly seen in the well lit streets as the bombers picked out their
targets and dropped upon them.

   The first intimation Warren had was when the blast flung him out
of bed as bombs from low flying enemy planes cascaded down
amongst the hangars and wards of the nearby airfield and hospital.
The noise of what sounded like distant thunder woke Jim Gavin and
as he lay in bed it gradually dawned on him that Sing
apore was being bombed and that the war had begun. After rousing
Spencer Chapman from his bed they both stood at the open window
watching the raid. Some military units, thinking the raid was a practice, were slow to react but after a late start the searchlights began to
sweep the skies as the ack-ack filled the night sky with flak. In a
nearby military hospital Jack Knott took advantage of the confusion
and excitement to find his clothes and discharge himself. He was one
of the victims of dengue or swamp fever, which swept the school in
November. That morning on the six o'clock news he heard Radio
Malaya announce to the world that Singapore had been bombed and
Britain was at war with Japan. As soon as the corps commanders in
north Malaya heard the news they besieged GHQ with telephone
calls for orders. It wasn't until eleven hours after the first bombs had
fallen, and the Japanese stormed ashore at Khota Bahru, that 11
Division heard that Matador was cancelled. However, 3 Corps was
to send its Indian troops across the border along the jungle-fringed
Yala Road. Because of the lack of suitable wireless equipment, all
orders from GHQ to its commanders in the field were through the
public telephone system.

   Some years later a semi-official announcement stated that had it
been definitely known that the Japanese convoys were proceeding to
Siam, the British Government might have been induced to allow
Allied troops in the North-West Sector, the 11 Division, to move forward to Singorra before the enemy arrived. Because of concern about
American opinion, the uncertain information available did not jus-
tify the violation of Siam neutrality.

   About the time the Indian troops were being hustled out of their
water-filled trenches to assault the Yala Road, the Chief Game Warden, Mr Shebbeare, who had been supervising the small team of

Europeans mapping the routes into Siam; received instructions to close down his operations. With the benefit of hindsight this force could have provided the army with a worthwhile intelligence service and later a framework of agents for Force 136, SOE's later activities. When his team heard the news one, Pat Noone, joined the Argylls stationed near him; another, Dolman took a Commission in the East Surreys and the SIS claimed Shepherd. The remaining two joined the Volunteers.

The part-time SOE agents in Siam, grouped around their Philco domestic wireless sets, heard the announcer's voice – sometimes fading away – reading out the list of serial numbers – each number relating to a SOE group. When their number was given each group broke open its store of weapons and explosives. On the west coast they seized the airfield and installations on Phukit Island. Another group on board the SS *Mata Hari*, left Penang and sailed 'up-coast' to raid the fishing port of Tonkah. Three Italian freighters had been hiding there from the Royal Navy. When the *Mata Hari* and her raiders appeared the ships were scuttled by the crews. After seizing and holding the town for some four days, the ship's wireless operator picked up a signal from GHQ aborting the mission. It also instructed the skipper to search Phukit Island and other coastal areas, for any SOE survivors who had managed to reach the beaches and bring them off. Some agents used their own initiative when it became clear that Matador had been cancelled and tried to escape back to Malaya – either on foot or in stolen boats.

In some cases it was a race against time between the SOE agents trying to reach their objectives and the Siamese counter-intelligence trying to arrest them. It is uncertain whether the miners at Pinyok knew that Matador was cancelled. When they heard their coded signal coming over the ether that morning they rushed out of the rough, wooden miners' bungalows in the saucer-like valley in the mountains and collected the hidden arms and explosives. Quickly assembling outside the company offices they loaded the stores on to one of the lorries then drove off down the water-filled rutted track – through the tree-lined defile towards the Yala Road. As the lorries bounced and swayed along the muddy track the first lorry came to a sudden halt, throwing everyone standing at the back, off balance. Police and soldiers appeared out of the trees and they were arrested, disarmed and escorted back to their families at the mine. Here everyone was rounded up and imprisoned in the mine's store room.

Meanwhile the Indian troops belonging to 3 Corps had launched themselves across the Siam border and ran into stiff resistance from armed police behind well defended road blocks. The Japanese assembling at Singorra and Patani soon joined in and after some days' heavy fighting the Indian troops were ordered to withdraw back across the border leaving behind their dead and missing. Some of the missing eventually turned up at Pinyok where they joined the miners and their families in the store room prison.

When the Japanese troops passed through Yala a patrol was detailed off to go to Pinyok. They arrived in a civilian lorry and immediately searched the mine's offices and European homes. As they went from bungalow to bungalow they left behind a trail of discarded loot.

The soldiers tramped through the mud and checked the undamaged mine machinery. In the distance the monsoon clouds still hung low on the surrounding hills, clinging like cotton-wool to the tree tops. It had stopped raining by the time the Japanese arrived at the store room. After rubbing the grime from the windows they peered in. The Europeans had little to eat for two days and were starving. After a brief conversation one of the Japanese opened the door while the second threw in two grenades. They bounced in amongst the prisoners, some sleeping, others sitting or comforting the children. The explosion blew out the windows and half lifted the roof from its wooden walls. The door flew off its hinges and landed in the mud. Not waiting for the explosions the Japanese were already in the lorries driving out through the main gates, leaving the dead behind and the badly maimed to look after themselves.

Some hours later villagers and local police began to creep into the camp to loot and found survivors with gaping wounds and some almost limbless dragging themselves through the mud. These survivors and those still alive in the store room were battered to death with pieces of wood or rocks and robbed. One of the badly wounded, a teenage girl, rolled herself under some bushes where she was later found by a native clerk from the mine and nursed back to health. Interned, she survived the war.

Burma

In Burma a middle-aged officer in the Burma Frontier Service, H.N.C. Stephenson, anticipating the Japanese invasion, began to recruit and train his own private army of hill tribesmen. When Warren heard about this he arranged for him to attend the second course at 101 STS. Jim Gavin kept in touch with him when he returned to the Burma Hills and arranged for a regular supply of stores and explosives to his hill camp. The Governor, equally anxious about the country's open frontier with pro-Japanese Siam, ordered him to expand his organisation into a nationwide guerrilla organisation to be known as the Burma Levies. But the war came all too soon – before he could recruit more men than he already had.

When the Japanese landed in Siam, part of the invasion force thrust south into Malaya, the remainder moved north towards the hills of Burma. To meet this move, the British hastily put together under-equipped units and assembled them in and around Rangoon. Stephenson's Levies were already poised in the trees overlooking the border and soon as he received the news of the Japanese invasion of Malaya, his guerrilla column moved into Siam. After a sixty mile journey through thick jungle and mountains it emerged alongside the strategic railway line which would carry any Burma-bound invasion force to the frontier. His force of about thirty men had a mixed assortment of weapons. He had the only Tommy-gun and others had old Italian rifles captured in Africa. Those without 'modern' weapons armed themselves with blow-pipes and bows and arrows.

The railway line ran alongside a tree-covered hill surrounded by mountains. Below, hidden by the trees, a river tumbled over rocks and hurled itself over cliffs to cascade as a waterfall into a large lake. Placing his men in a security ring around the ambush point, Stephenson began wrapping the explosives to the track at various places, to set off a series of explosions. The Siamese border guards, with their Japanese advisers, regularly patrolled this stretch of railway track and it was one of these that suddenly appeared out of the trees. The Levies were soon under heavy rifle fire and before Stephenson could place the detonators, his men were overwhelmed and it was all they could do to extract themselves and fight a rearguard action into the mountains.

Back in Burma he offered his unit to 17 Division, now slowly moving up to the frontier, but the idea of irregular warfare was coolly received by the regular army officers.

Hong Kong
Another SOE-trained unit in action for the first time was Hong Kong's Reconnaissance Unit (TA). After Jim Gavin's reorganisation the unit undertook a recruitment drive and the new recruits were only partially trained when the Japanese threat to the island became a reality. The CO, Captain Williamson, was in Singapore

when the GOC called-up the Territorials and the only officer left was the recently recruited Lieutenant Teasdale. Despite his inexperience he marshalled his men and led them to the well stocked secret caves in the mountains.

As expected, the Japanese launched their long awaited attack through the mountains overwhelming the defenders who carried out a pre-planned fighting withdrawal blocking any attempt by the enemy's 38th Infantry Division to infiltrate its defences. The GOC, General Maltby, was well aware that Hong Kong was expendable and that it couldn't hold out for more than ten days. In a conversation with Warren earlier he had remarked sagely, referring to the lack of help from Singapore, 'When it is all over and they're knocking nails in my coffin – remember my words.'

Teasdale's unit's objective was to gather intelligence for the Command bunker on the island – such as identifying the numbers and strength of advancing enemy units and warning the defenders of any area about to be attacked.

Kendall had been in Macao when the war started and as soon as he heard that the Territorials had been alerted crossed over on the ferry, a large flat-bottomed vessel with three promenade decks and a rear paddle wheel. Normally the ferry was jammed with passengers but the news of the invasion deterred all but those with essential business in Hong Kong. As she neared the island with the Peak and the mountains of China providing a backdrop on the horizon, a large freighter altered course slightly and cut across her wake heading for the open sea. Kendall could read her name quite clearly and recognised her as the *Kung Wo*, a regular visitor to these waters. Another paddleboat hastened out to meet them with the white ensign flying from her mast. The *Ladybird* was a RN riverboat, which in pre-war days spent her life on the Yangtse, sometimes in Chungking or Shanghai; now she fussed around checking all seaborne visitors. The sea around the colony was usually busy but today Kendall noticed more activity than usual with large sea-going junks with their bat-like sails full of passengers heading for Macao. The wealthy Chinese were already leaving.

In Command HQ a red-haired Canadian major brought him up to date with the latest battle situation and arranged transport to take him across to Kowloon and as far forward as possible to join Teasdale.

He crossed the channel to the mainland by RN launch and found an army staff car waiting to take him further. The harbour was packed with Chinese fighting to get on board ferries to the island and the car just pushed people aside as it forced its way through the packed throng. Beyond the sea front the roads cleared and, as they drove on into the hills, they passed empty villages and shared the road with anxious army drivers who seemed to expect screaming Japanese soldiers to leap from behind every rock.

After leaving the driver, who was only too pleased to get back to Kowloon, Kendall spent the next few hours scrambling up the wooded hillside along a narrow trail which sometimes became nothing more than a three feet wide path, on one side a cliff and the other a long drop. Teasdale had posted sentries and one of these had watched his approach through field glasses for some time. Alerted by these reports Teasdale waited to welcome his visitor.

He had stationed his two-man observation teams on all main tracks and roads leading to the sea and two more teams overlooking the defenders' outposts stretching from Gindrinkers Bay in a wide arc around Kowloon. One of the caves was used as Headquarters and before they retreated the Royal Engineers had cleared trees using the wood and planks from the large crates to build tables and two-tiered bunks. A small generator provided the electricity for lighting. Sitting around a table spread with maps and reports Teasdale and Kendall came to the conclusion that the Japanese were forming up for a major assault against the line held by the Scots Guards. The Royal Signals had laid a direct line from the cave to one of the forward positions and using this Kendall cranked the field telephone and waited. The signal was answered by a Japanese officer. The forward line had been evacuated without informing the men in the mountains and with no wireless sets they were completely cut off from the British lines. Their whole purpose for being there was void. Although Teasdale was obviously badly shaken by the news Kendall saw it as another problem to be overcome. It was no time for recriminations. Someone had to slip through the Japanese lines and reach HQ. It was generally assumed that he would do it and he set off down the mountain while he still had some daylight left.

Darkness had fallen by the time he reached the tree line but aided by a bright moon he followed the path, keeping clear of any main tracks. Eventually after bypassing large units of Japanese forming up for the attack, he stumbled into a deserted trench. Shortly afterwards he was discovered by a Scots Guards night patrol and brought in to Company HQ. After being debriefed he was asked to go forward to the front line to point out the dead ground hiding the enemy concentrations. As his party reached the front line the Japanese opened the attack with artillery and small arms fire. The barrage moved over the trenches with enemy infantry following close behind. The front soon dissolved into individual combat, fierce hand-to-hand fighting with no quarter given. One by one each outpost was overrun and the defenders wiped out. Those who surrendered and the wounded were put to death.

Kendall found himself with a small isolated group of survivors who carried out a fighting withdrawal all the way to the seashore. There they stole a sampan and sailed across the channel that night to Hong Kong.

The collapse of the front line was watched by Teasdale through field glasses. Morale was already low when Kendall left but now without a wireless set they were completely cut off. For a while they tried to work as an independent unit mining roads and ambushing enemy convoys. Often these hit and run raids developed into running battles as they retreated back into their mountain lair. The Japanese seemed convinced that they had the support of the local population and retaliated by destroying villages and killing the inhabitants.

Back in the Command bunker, General Maltby gave Kendall the responsibility of building an effective guerrilla group. In addition he should work with the local security forces and isolate some of the hundreds of suspected enemy agents in Hong Kong. Using his contacts with the banned Communist Party he began to set up a skeleton organisation. Another source of help was a one-legged Chinese admiral who was in charge of Chiang Kai Shek's Secret Service on the island. He was aided by General Yee and between them they set about identifying Japanese sympathisers amongst the Chinese population. General Yee had agents everywhere and his organisation began a ruthless suppression of pro-Japanese activity and enemy agents, actual or suspected, were killed. In the turmoil of the two weeks before the surrender it is doubtful whether the police discovered what was really happening.

Another Chinese agent who turned up on his doorstep was General Ma, who was on a secret mission to rescue Chiang Kai Shek's mother-in-law and widow of the founder of modern China, Madam Sun Yat Sen. In latter years she had been living in Hong Kong and now, in the final days before its capture, the Jewish, Cockney, Chinese general was sent on his last mission and all contact was lost.

(*Right*) Captain Michael Low.

(*Below*) Spencer Chapman and Peter Lindsey.

(*Left*) Major Jim Gavin, in command at 101 STS.

(*Below*) Basil Goodfellow (on right).

Another SOE agent working closely with Kendall at this time was Tallon, who had recently returned from Hainan. One evening taking a break from their cloak and dagger activities they borrowed a native sampan from their Chinese friends and limpet mines from the Royal Navy, and silently paddled out into the darkness towards enemy-occupied Kowloon. Out of sight and sound they rested the oars and let the wind and tide take them towards the mainland which loomed as a black mass in the distance. Eventually, aided occasionally by the oars, the little boat drifted in amongst the enemy ships at anchor in Kowloon harbour.

They held the sides of the sampan as it gently rocked in the waves. Peering into the night they began to distinguish the shapes of destroyers and freighters and, with the occasional paddle, the sampan drifted alongside a destroyer. As Tallon walked his hands along the ship's plates and rivets, holding the sampan off the destroyer, Kendall handled a limpet mine like a dinner plate and firmly planted it at sea level where it clung to the ship's side. Above on the deck a sentry hawked phlegm from his throat and spat. They drifted away unnoticed and repeated the performance with the next ship in line. Three ships were treated that night and by the time they paddled their way back to Hong Kong the night sky behind them was lit up with the blast of the explosions. They later learnt that at least one ship had sunk.

The Free French Special Operations Section also had men in Hong Kong. One French agent, a lieutenant, could speak five European languages as well as a number of Asian and African tongues. He had fought in the Spanish Civil War, served with the French Secret Service and was suspected by some of being a Communist agent. He had been sent by de Langlade to set up an intelligence network in Shanghai but the Japanese assault had marooned him in Hong Kong.

Another equally colourful international character working for SOE in Hong Kong was a White Russian named Petro. Until recently he had been in Indo-China spying for MEW. During the First World War he held a commission in the Russian Army but escaped to France following the Russian Revolution. There he joined the French Army where he was again commissioned and took part in the Riff Campaigns. Later he prospected for gold in Mongolia and worked as an engineer in China. In the thirties he took part in the Citroën transcontinental expedition across China and in the period up to November 1941 he was in Saigon checking on the iron-ore shipments being smuggled out of Indo-China. In November he was selected for a course at 101 STS and came away with his third commission in his pocket, this time as second lieutenant in the Punjab Regiment. He travelled back to Hong Kong where he had his home and arrived only a few hours before the Japanese poured across the border.

The two joined the battle with enthusiasm. Towards the end of December the Japanese, in a determined assault, overwhelmed the island's shore defences and forced their way into the city. Battles raged everywhere finally culminating in street fights and pockets of resistance being isolated by enemy forces. The Frenchman was with one such group which was cut-off and defending the power station. They were all members of the Volunteers and, for all his suspected Communist activities, he was with a select company. In command was the Honourable J.J. Paterson, chairman of Jardine Matheson and a senior member of the Legislative Council. In the last war he was mentioned six times in despatches and now held the rank of major. Never far away was the secretary of the Hong Kong Club, and not one to miss a good fight was 70-year-old Tom Pearce, Chairman of J.D. Hutchinson and secretary of the Jockey Club. Trapped with them were 74 staff of the Electric Company and the China Light and Power Company who were all in the Volunteers. Some of them had already fought in Kowloon before escaping to the island.

The unit was stationed at North Point power station to prevent sabotage but had been encircled by enemy seaborne landings. The Middlesex Regiment had been sent in to rescue them but having lost an armoured car and three lorries and many dead the survivors fell back to their own lines. Some were cut off in the attack and escaped down side streets. A few found their way through the encircled lines and stumbled into the power station to join the trapped Volunteers. These were hotly pursued by angry Japanese who, repulsed by the Volunteers, began flinging grenades through the windows which were then caught by the cricket-playing defenders and thrown back.

After the defenders had held out for almost twenty hours the enemy succeeded in setting the building ablaze. Clouds of choking black smoke crept through the building and the fire roared as the roof timbers caught alight, sending giant flames leaping skywards. The defenders reasoned that the only alternative to surrender was to fight their way out and, with Jacosta leading the way, they burst out flinging grenades, firing and yelling. Momentarily the Japanese were taken aback but they soon recovered and fought off their attackers with the bayonet. Some of the Middlesex survivors, badly wounded, fell back into the smouldering ruins to make a last ditch stand. Edward des Vaux died in the break out and only five Volunteers reached a burnt-out lorry in the Kings Road: a pre-arranged assembly point. The Frenchman was not amongst them – but neither was his body ever found.

In another part of the city Petro was driving around in a commandeered Chevrolet, trying to draw the enemy's fire to pinpoint their positions for the gunners. Needless to say he finished up in hospital when his car was wrecked by an explosion. After the surrender he escaped from hospital on crutches and in his pyjamas. He was found by a group of paroled European civilians collecting and identifying the bodies. They found him clothes and food and hid him for a while. His first attempt to leave the island was thwarted by a Japanese beach patrol but on his second attempt he escaped in an open boat and reached Macao where he had friends. They took care of him and later smuggled him into China and he eventually reached Chungking where he joined John Keswick.

Christmas Eve found Kendall trapped in the city where he had been searching for General Ma and Madam Sun Yat Sen. It was very apparent that the defenders couldn't hold out much longer. As far as Whitehall was concerned the colony had been abandoned to the fortunes of war with no prospect of reinforcements or help of any kind. The city was ablaze and thick black smoke rose in columns from various parts of the island. In every direction came sounds of artillery and small arms fire. Houses had collapsed blocking roads, telegraph poles leaned at crazy angles with broken wires looped across houses and pavements. Some roads were pitted with shell holes which gradually filled with water from broken mains and sewers, drowning any wounded sheltering in them. Small groups of soldiers occupied houses or sheltered in doorways, the defence had disintegrated and these buildings now became isolated strong points trying to hold back advancing enemy infantry.

The Royal Navy still had some small motor torpedo boats hidden in creeks to avoid enemy bombers and Kendall was promised berths on one which proposed to try and break through the enemy naval blockade. Two destroyers and a paddleboat had already broken out (the *Li Wo*, a flat-bottomed Yangtse riverboat closely resembling a Mississippi steamer, and the destroyers HMS *Thanet* and *Scout*). Despite the large demand for the remaining places he persuaded his naval friends to allocate berths to the one-legged Chinese admiral

(Chan Chek), Generals Yee and Ma and Tallon. The MTB crept into Aberdeen harbour under the cover of darkness and on Christmas Day she took on board the SOE party with the exception of the Chinese – who were late. When dawn broke the Japanese continued their heavy shelling of the harbour and sea front and the skipper was forced to leave the area and hide amongst the islands off shore. Kendall left word for the Chinese to sail out to them but as the day went on and the situation ashore deteriorated rapidly Naval HQ insisted that the skipper should evacuate the island. Despite this he reluctantly agreed to Kendall's pleas to allow more time for his special passengers. From the haven amongst the islands they watched the colony's final death throes. Explosions were taking place in all parts of the city and enemy planes weaved in and out of the pillars of smoke. As darkness fell, RN HQ were demanding to know whether they had sailed: then – dramatically – the defenders had surrendered and everyone should lay down their arms. Enemy shelling persisted and guns began to range on their island. In the gathering gloom figures began to spread out along the beach near Aberdeen and, expecting a boarding party, the skipper moved his boat out of range and his crew manned the Lewis guns. He had no intention of being taken prisoner at this stage and although technically in breach of the surrender terms he ordered his gunners to spray the beach. A burst of fire sent the figures scattering and the MTB moved in closer for a final burst before heading out to sea. The skipper could wait no longer and Kendall's insistence was endangering the escape.

Answering to the signal for full ahead the MTB swept in with all guns blazing, its bows lifted cutting the waves in arcs as it raced through the water. Heading back out to sea, in almost total darkness, someone spotted a swimmer in the water: the engines were cut back and the person hooked out of the sea with a boat hook. Grabbed by many hands the swimmer was pulled aboard and floundered helplessly on the deck covered by rifles and Kendall's Tommy gun. The swimmer was a young RN cadet who was with a party trying to evade capture and reach the mainland. They also had with them a group of Chinese, who having crashed the car through a Japanese road block, had escaped in a launch which was sunk by enemy gunfire. The survivors reached the shore where they were found by his naval party and pulled out of the water. They had been trying to attract the ship's attention for some hours before they were shot-up and he had volunteered to swim out to them.

A rescue party was immediately sent ashore and the evaders

brought off. The Chinese turned out to be Admiral Chan Chek and his party minus General Ma. Although the search party found General Yee hiding amongst the rocks, the one-legged admiral was nowhere to be found. With every chance of meeting up with the Japanese – and who could tell the difference between a Chinese and a Japanese in the dark? – the young RN officer called off the search and ordered his men back to the boat. Hardly had he done this when a hoarse shout from above told him the admiral had been discovered hiding in a cave at the top of the cliffs. He couldn't move – he was legless. He had stuffed his hollow wooden leg with gold sovereigns for his escape and when the launch sank he had to untie his leg to float ashore; he was also a non-swimmer. In spite of his handicap he reached the shore and had dragged himself up the cliff to hide until he could make contact with any friendly Chinese.

Hidden by the night the skipper took his MTB some miles off shore and guided by the admiral headed for a guerrilla-held village on the mainland – he had insufficient fuel to try and reach any Allied base. Later that night they found a small launch, the *C410*, aground on a small island. It seemed intact water-tight and abandoned but as lines were thrown aboard to pull it off for their own use, a party of RN personnel appeared from amongst the rocks. When the MTB appeared out of the darkness they mistook her for a Japanese vessel and hid. With them was the senior naval officer in the area, Commander Montagu RN who wanted to know why they had been so late in leaving Aberdeen.

The escape party reached the village on 26th December and Admiral Chek went ashore to make contact with the local guerrilla leader. He soon returned with the village elders and enthusiastic guerrillas, packed aboard a junk which sailed alongside the MTB. When the RN parties from the ship went ashore they were welcomed by the villagers who quickly set up a market for trade. The guerrilla leader, who returned with the admiral, agreed to escort the crew through Japanese-occupied territory and across the Chinese front line. But first he asked whether his men could have permission to unbolt the ship's weapons. When this was done, with the help of the crew, the villagers swarmed aboard and stripped every moveable part. Only then did the captain order it to be scuttled to hide it from the Japanese.

Anxious to get away before the Japanese arrived, the escape party left next morning. Their trek across country lasted four days and they were mobbed every time they reached a village. They passed through enemy lines with ease and on the fifth day marched into a fortified position manned by Chinese Government troops.

The welcome by the Chinese troops was less enthusiastic than the one they received from the villagers. Their arrival had complicated the local commander's position with his Japanese counterpart. The British party gained the impression that some agreement had been reached whereby neither party took aggressive action against the other. This cosy arrangement had been disturbed by the arrival of the British and the Japanese commander had lost face by the mass escape through his lines. To overcome this he would probably launch an attack against the Chinese. The Chinese were also concerned by the large number of Communist guerrillas acting as escorts for the British. His problem was that the Communists were considered to be more of an enemy than the Japanese and this was compounded by them escorting foreign devils through his lines.

While the Communists filtered back to the coast the British party was held on the crossing-point until the local commander received permission from Chungking to allow them to proceed further.

In the mountains of Kowloon, above Hong Kong, the morale amongst the Volunteers had reached an all time low. Although they had ample ammunition and rations some were disillusioned by the fall of Hong Kong and felt isolated in the mountains. Lieutenant Teasdale tried to face up to the problem by abandoning patrols and calling a meeting of his men. He explained that the nearest Allied base was Singapore – the patrol was surrounded by at least a division of enemy troops, all well armed and battle seasoned. Balanced against this the Japanese could spend years searching the mountains without ever finding them and the caves were well stocked. But the possibility of anyone knowing they were still alive was remote. He gave his men the option of either staying with him in the mountains or leaving their weapons behind and handing themselves over to the Japanese. Most chose surrender. While they collected their belongings Teasdale and about four others destroyed the camp and set out for Chungking.

Those who surrendered were badly beaten and thrown into prisoner of war camps while Teasdale's party, after trekking across the mountains, were fêted in almost every village. They were fed and provided with bullock carts for the journey and seven days later crossed over into Chinese lines.

CHAPTER FIVE

Fortress Penang?

From his seat in the Lysander Captain Knott could see clouds of black smoke rising in columns from amongst the trees in the distance. Meeting in one large mass it drifted to the left, westwards, towards the sea. The pilot was occupied with his frequent attempts to call up the RAF control at Ipoh, approximately where the smoke was rising but without success.

Knott had discharged himself from hospital at the height of the raid in Singapore and begged a lift from a passing army truck to get to the school. That was yesterday. Hardly had he stepped into his wireless room when Major Rosher burst in behind him and wanted him to go with him to Ipoh. Since September they had become heavily involved with training SIS operators and 'putting them in' along the borders with Siam astride the probable route of the enemy's expected advance into Malaya.

Now as they approached the town Jack Knott remembered seeing the buildings burning and large craters blocking rubble-filled streets. Rescue workers burrowing into collapsed houses looked up and scattered at the sight of the plane. When the aircraft bounced down on the pitted runway a RAF officer scrambled out of a slit trench nearby and ran to meet them. Shouting above the noise of the engine he told them that if they had arrived only a few minutes earlier they would have run smack bang into the Japanese air force.

In what seemed to be a well co-ordinated attack the enemy planes had 'taken out' all the new RAF airfields in north Malaya, destroying large numbers of planes. Despite the need to give 11 Division air cover the RAF withdrew all its remaining planes and personnel to airfields in south Malaya, leaving behind vast quantities of bombs and supplies for the Japanese. Without air cover the hard-pressed defenders were left to the mercy of constant air attacks.

At the outbreak of the war the police in Ipoh rounded up all the Japanese civilians in the town some of whom were undoubtedly in touch with the advancing troops. The internees were imprisoned in a large house in the centre of the town which ironically suffered a direct hit during the air raid. A large number were killed and the survivors were evacuated by lorry to Kuala Lumpur and later sent to India. This incident led to a rumour circulated by fifth columnists that British troops had murdered the internees by boiling them in oil.

Leaving Knott in Ipoh to arrange for the Chinese SIS agents to be passed forward by Richard Broome, a Government officer in the area, Rosher went off on a mysterious visit to Penang. His visit could have been connected with the *Mata Hari* raiders but more likely he was seeking contacts amongst the Malayan Communist Party which had a large membership on the island.

The island of Penang, two miles off the west coast of Malaya, had long been considered by Churchill as an ideal base from which to launch commando-type raids against the enemy's flank as it advanced down the peninsula. The Japanese, aware of its possibilities, considered it a thorn in their side.

In Singapore, Jack Knott's departure only added fuel to Jim Gavin's impatience to get into action. He remembers approaching Killery with the suggestion that a small party from the school, all highly trained in setting booby-traps, with its own transport food and special stores; could work in an independent capacity helping out the hard pressed rearguard in north Malaya. Killery liked the idea and by afternoon Jim Gavin had selected Trappes-Lomax, Brian Passmore and ten other ranks to make up his party. They loaded lorries with weapons, ammunition, explosives and fuses and by evening were rolling across the causeway into Johore.

When the party arrived, without mishap, in Kuala Lumpur the commander of 3 Corps was delighted to see them but had his own ideas how Gavin's party should be used. Penang had long been considered a strong point in the defences and the SOE team should go there and place themselves under the command of the Penang Fortress Commander.

The following day Jim Gavin and his men arrived at Butterworth the ferry point for Penang. The town had been repeatedly hit by air raids. The British fighters parked on the nearby RAF aerodrome had been almost totally destroyed; the Naval Base had been severely damaged and the town was covered in smoke from burning buildings. All the morning, as the SOE trucks neared the town, the road ahead became more congested with natives fleeing from their burning homes, carrying salvaged possessions on bamboo poles or in cheap suitcases.

As the lorries moved slowly through the streets past the burning houses the drivers found their way blocked with debris or roped-off and cratered streets. A simple message hung from the rope – UNEXPLODED BOMBS – KEEP AWAY.

When the lorries finally stopped at the ferry point at Prai Gavin's men could see small RN steamers, flying the white ensign, at anchor in the bay. Across the water was Penang with its reputation as a tropical paradise. Pre-war it was the first sight visitors to the Orient had of the easy-going racial blend and relaxed Malayan way of life.

Penang Island is about the size of the Isle of Wight. Its deep water anchorage helped make it one of the major pre-war stopping places for all the liners and merchant ships on the Orient run. The Japanese turned it into a submarine base.

The SOE had not long to wait for the ferry, a flat-bottomed, open-decked, paddle steamer rust stained with a suggestion that at one time it may have been immaculately white-painted. The two mile trip across the Kra Straits took some thirty minutes and the ferry docked against the 1,200 feet long Swettenham Pier with its trainless railway station and clock tower. Railway passengers buying tickets at Penang boarded the ferry first and joined the train at Butterworth. When the ferry docked the SOE lorries moved off down the ramp, through the crowds packing the pier waiting for the ferry's return journey.

Jim Gavin had visited the island before and now guided the trucks along the waterfront packed with fishing boats sampans and high-decked Chinese junks. Most had large eyes painted on the bows to ward off evil spirits and bring the boats safely back to shore. Alongside the waterfront the lorries drove past *godowns* (warehouses) packed with rubber and tin, left behind at the outbreak of war when the larger merchant ships fled to Singapore. Following Gavin's directions the drivers eventually arrived outside the Eastern Hotel on the hill overlooking Georgetown, the island's capital.

The hotel was popular with the European community and built just below the 2,700 ft summit, the highest point on the island. From its verandahs guests could look down on the hotel's beautiful rose gardens. Beyond lay acres of scrub and jungle full of wild blossoms, inhabited only by tribes of monkeys, small jungle deer, colourful birds and butterflies.

Every day since the outbreak of war Japanese bombers had blitzed Butterworth. The daily raid was about due and everyone seemed to be waiting for the sound of the enemy's planes' engines. Everyone knew the RAF field at Butterworth was the daily target and waited

confidently for the show to begin. The sound of engines brought the
spectators to the windows and crowds into the street. More cautiously the SOE team began to climb from the lorries and spread out.

Suddenly the planes appeared over the top of the hill. Forty-nine
planes followed their leader swooping low over the hotel, sending the
monkeys screaming into the jungle to hide. Before he finally leapt for
cover Jim Gavin noticed the bomb racks open. The bombs tumbled
out to crash around the waterfront and Georgetown's busy commercial centre in Bishops Street, giving the town the doubtful honour of
being the first victim of a Japanese blitzkrieg in World War II. After
dropping their bombs the planes circled the town and came in a second time dropping anti-personnel bombs and sweeping the packed
streets with machine gun fire. The panic amongst the town's 170,000
population was complete. Those in the streets were mown down.
Those indoors were trapped by falling debris crashing around them
as the houses collapsed. In the streets they were cut down by gunfire
as they fled, crashing into each other, trampling the fallen underfoot.

The town with its wooden houses and shops quickly erupted in
flames and the screams of those trapped could be heard plainly by
the SOE men sheltering near the hotel. As they clung to the ground
the soldiers could feel it pulsate beneath them with each explosion.

The raid left Georgetown an inferno. Bodies lay everywhere in the
wreckage of houses and shops, in monsoon ditches and in the sea
amongst the fishing boats. Those still alive and trapped in the burning houses were screaming in terror and agony as the flames barbecued them. The fire station was demolished and all its equipment
destroyed. The police station had been hit and its staff promptly
deserted. All civil organisation had ceased.

In Singapore the monsoon rain swept across the Naval Base,
amongst the cranes and disembowelled ships in the repair docks.
Groups of sailors in capes, with their heads down against the rain,
made their way along the wet roads to the messes. Leaving his billet
that morning Colonel Warren remembers receiving unsettling news
from home. He was in a pensive mood he recollects, pondering at the
lack of apparent positive action by the Allies. He had been present at
Brooke-Popham's conference when it was decided to cancel
Matador. When later that night he went across to the War Room he
discovered the RAF Station at Khota Bahru was under air attack.
The Japanese had landed right on time at the most likely landing
area. He now learnt that Admiral Sir Tom Phillips, the new com-

mander of the Far East Fleet, had taken his two capital ships to sea without air cover.

Walking along the road in the pouring rain he heard a motor cycle approaching and looked around. A dispatch rider was looking for him. Warren read the message which confirmed his worst fears, it simply said that the *Prince of Wales* and the *Repulse* had been sunk and Admiral Phillips was missing.

In three days Japan had gained supremacy in the air, on the sea and, in the next seventy days, was to destroy an empire Britain would never rebuild.

When he eventually arrived at his office Warren was asked to go to Penang. All that was known was Fortress Penang had been 'bombed into impotency'. Nearby Butterworth with its airfield and naval base was under constant air attack. All land lines to the area had been destroyed he was told. He should leave immediately to assess the situation and report back.

The Singapore railway station was crammed with people fleeing 'up country' from the repeated bombing raids on Singapore. Trains arriving from 'up country' brought in bewildered European women and children, carrying all they possessed in bulging suitcases.

When Warren arrived he found the Penang train crowded with nearly two thousand passengers – families, relatives, servants, household goods and animals, surrounded by bettle-nut chewing porters demanding larger tips. As he watched a convoy of army trucks stopped at the station entrance to disgorge recently arrived pink faced soldiers. These formed up in ranks. With their weapons on one shoulder and kit-bags on the other they marched off into the crowds which parted like the Red Sea for Moses.

When Warren found the berth attendant he was told that all the berths were taken. With all the would-be passengers eager to thrust money into the attendant's pockets, it was only too obvious that berths were for sale. Warren's first thought was to 'thump him' but instead he clawed his way back through the crowds, fighting to get on the train, to telephone GHQ for them to intervene.

Later when he had a berth he found that the dining car had been taken off and the only way to get food was to jostle and push to buy refreshments from food vendors on the station platforms. The train normally left at 8.00 p.m. That day it was late. Continuing enemy bombing had destroyed rolling stock, railway stations and track. The normal peacetime, fast, daily service took twelve hours. Twenty-four hours later Warren was still on the train.

When he arrived at Kuala Lumpur all he could gather was that Penang had suffered a severe air raid. The full extent of the damage was unknown. To compound the situation the enemy was across the border and fighting its way into Kroh, only sixty miles north of Penang.

In Penang harbour the crews of locally owned coastal steamers, taken over in 1939 by the Royal Navy, had watched with horror as Georgetown disppeared in a cloud of smoke and flame. All the water-front seemed to be blazing and suffocating clouds from burning rub-ber began to drift out to sea. One minute they watched the bombers at work over the houses; next they saw a second wave of twenty planes sweep over the hill. In seconds the planes were amongst them. Unarmed ferries were blown out of the water with direct hits. Ships' plates burst with near misses. Machine gun bullets rattled across the open decks leaving them littered with dead and wounded. Some crews jumped overboard – others kept their heads and deserted the moment the ferries touched the mainland.

Off shore the little steamers acting as minesweepers fought off the bombers with their sole armament – a four inch gun fitted for surface defence and almost useless against aircraft. The HMS *Sui Ho* was badly damaged and the crew took to the boats: the SS *Kuala* turned on her attackers with an unofficial Lewis gun and brought down one of the planes. The SS *Kampar* was on the point of sinking when her skipper managed to beach her on a mudbank.

When Colonel Warren reached the Prai ferry point next day he found the ferries manned by volunteers from the Harbour Board and Penang Pilots. One of the first ferries in action after the raid was manned by the skipper and native crew from the *Kampar*. After tak-ing to the lifeboats the skipper with his first mate led the crew to the nearby naval base where they helped themselves to oil and stores. They then patched up an abandoned ferry and with the help of a junior naval officer took the ferry back into service.

When his ferry pulled alongside Swettenham Pier, Warren remembers seeing it packed with crying, jostling, fighting, crowds of Malays, Chinese, Indians, Sikhs, Anglo-Burmese, Siamese; Euro-peans – their families and baggage; all making up one panic ridden mob. Near the Clock Tower Warren found a 15 cwt army truck with an Indian driver waiting for him.

The town was almost deserted and fires raged unattended and out of control. As he left the waterfront the roof of a burning *godown* collapsed with a shower of sparks and a mushroom of smoke. The dead lay where they fell and unclaimed. Apart from the occasional looter the only other people about were some soot-blackened soldiers looking for the injured. Warren could hardly distinguish whether they were European or Asian.

At Fortress Headquarters he met the monocled Army Commander, Brigadier Lyons RA, and Jim Gavin. The brigadier was most upset about the attack. He had only three weeks to go before finishing his tour and going home. The commander quickly briefed Warren on the situation. There had been a heavy death toll but no one had yet made a head count. The hospitals were full and the wives of the Volunteers were out manning temporary dressing stations in the streets. The fire station was destroyed together with its equipment and the police had deserted.

'In view of the island's importance what about the Service personnel and its defences?' asked Warren. Apart from the racially mixed Volunteers, he was told, there was only a company of Indian troops fresh from the training camp in Burma; some HQ Admin staff and Major Jim Gavin who had arrived with is men who were now in the streets. The only artillery were two pairs of six-inch guns. The partially completed defence work, similar to a spider's web in design, was mainly in the blueprint stage. An Argyll officer Captain Angus Rose, responsible for its construction, had been transferred to GHQ Singapore in September and not replaced. To say the least, Warren wasn't impressed.

CHAPTER SIX

Fortress Penang – The Evacuation

The following morning Warren was up early and walked around the town and along the burning waterfront assessing the damage. Bodies floated around in the sea and in the harbour the SS *Kampar*, deserted and aground, still flew the white ensign. Apart from Gavin's men Bishops Street was empty. Some of the houses and offices were burning or smouldering, giving off rolling black clouds.

Back at Fortress HQ with Brigadier Lyons he noticed the RN ships in the harbour preparing to sail. When he mentioned this to Lyons the brigadier seemed as surprised as he was. Warren now discovered that very little liaison – if any – existed between the local Army Commander and his opposite number in the RN. Under the circumstances Warren suggested that he should act as a liaison officer, an idea warmly welcomed by Lyons. At Naval HQ Warren found the Commander RN to be the one-time retired harbour master of Port Swettenham, recalled for war service. He explained to Colonel Warren that the RN Singapore had ordered all RN ships to leave.

Following Warren's detailed report to GHQ, another newcomer arrived in Penang, to act as deputy to the senior RN officer. His name was Commander McCalland Alexander RN and Warren understood him to be General, later Field Marshal, Alexander's cousin. Like Warren he quickly assessed the situation and agreed that they should work closely together.

They moved into the nearest office with a telephone, dumped the files and papers on the floor, pulled two desks together and set about trying to bring order to the chaos.

They discovered that all civilian organisation had ceased. The fire station, police station and power station had been destroyed. No one was collecting the unclaimed bodies littering the streets and contaminating the water supply. The only means of speaking to GHQ was by telephone, but all lines to the mainland had been destroyed, although Penang Radio Station was still on the air. The hospitals were packed and in the town Jim Gavin's men had been joined by the Volunteers.

To bring the fortress up to scratch both ack-ack guns and infantry would be needed so as soon as the telephone link was re-established with the mainland Warren got through to GHQ. After giving his situation report he began by asking for more ack-ack guns. This request was immediately turned down. All available guns, he was told, were needed to protect the airfields. The faceless informant in Singapore continued by saying that the Jitra line had broken leaving a large number of British and Indian troops out of touch with their units. 'Don't panic,' he was told. 'The Divisional Commander has reformed his defence line at Guran – thirty miles from Butterworth – which should give sufficient time to evacuate the Penang Garrison.' 'Evacuate?' shouted Warren. 'I thought we were being reinforced!'

Commander Alexander had walked into the office in the middle of the conversation and now raised his eyebrows questioningly. Warren had hardly finished explaining the telephone conversation when an orderly said two civilians wanted to see him. These turned out to be two European doctors, one tall, suntanned and wearing a white topee. They were very concerned about the health situation on the island, they said, presenting a long verbal report finishing with the threat of typhus and cholera in the town.

Warren and Alexander listened with growing incredulity until Warren remembers bursting out, 'What do you think we can do about it? The police have scrammed and I'm sitting here like an oil-man waiting for the gusher to blow. If it wasn't for Gavin and his men and the Volunteers we would be in one hell of a mess.'

By the time he finished he left them in no doubt about the critical position the island was in. Later he took the opportunity of discussing the doctors' visit with Jim Gavin. He suggested that his men and the Indian troops with the help of the Volunteers, could collect and burn the unburied bodies. There was no one else to do it; the town was deserted, recollects Warren.

Leaving the women to look after the wounded, Gavin and Trappes-Lomax organised the troops to collect the dead. One party collected the now stinking and bloated bodies, often covered with flies, and soon a long line of hand-carts, rickshaws and stretchers bearing the dead began to file down Bishops Street. Abandoned cars, bits of wooden houses, tyres, petrol and oil were brought together to create pyres. Finally the bonfires were ignited and the smoke and stench of burning bodies drifted in the wind, through the town and across the straits of Prai.

A rumour reached Fortress HQ that the Japanese had landed on the north of the island. There was nothing he could do about it deliberated Warren. Giving the rumour further consideration he concluded that if the enemy had landed they could have reached Georgetown by now and – as they were nowhere to be seen – he assumed the rumour to be without foundation. His thoughts were interrupted by the orderly. 'Some gentlemen to see you, sir.' Walking in behind him came five Orientals in grubby uniforms followed by a European soldier.

The European introduced the party. His name was Parsons, a miner with the SOE party from Phukit Island. The Chinese – waving his hand at the smiling Oriental gentlemen – were some of his mine's staff who'd helped him seize the installations on Phukit Island. Somehow he missed the evacuation but escaped by stealing a sampan and sailed it to Penang. Overcoming his initial shock Warren introduced them to Major Jim Gavin, whom Parsons had met on his 101 STS Course some weeks earlier. It was agreed that they should join Gavin's men working in the town under the command of Trappes-Lomax. They found him standing near a smoking half burnt out shop on the corner of Bishops Street. He looked tired and ill and complained of severe pains in the back. Leaving Parsons and his Chinese with Brian Passmore, Gavin drove Trappes-Lomax to hospital where it was found he had a temperature of 105 and his illness was later diagnosed as back-bone fever, again also known as dengue.

About lunch time Colonel Warren had a telephone call from GHQ explaining that as there seemed little possibility of 11 Division holding the Guran line, Brigadier Lyons, the Penang Fortress Commander, was being ordered to evacuate all European civilians that night, 13th December. When the news reached Dr L.W. Evans at the hospital he refused to leave his patients. His theatre sister said she wouldn't leave without him. The Salvation Army Commander and the Roman Catholic priest also decided to remain. They had set up a reception centre for refugees some miles outside the town.

When the news reached the Volunteers' wives working in the casualty stations they greeted it with disbelief. When the rumour was confirmed they felt humiliated at leaving their Asian friends behind. Others felt ashamed of admitting to their servants that they were running away. Those working at the hospital and the first aid post were of the same opinion as Dr Evans; they didn't want to leave the injured.

Unaware of the discontent sweeping the European residents Warren and Alexander were frantically searching for means of getting the

European (only) civilians as far as Kuala Lumpur. All they had were a few hours to organise the evacuation. In that time Alexander found a seaworthy ferry and Gavin a train from Prai. Together these should at least send everyone a reasonable distance down the mainland. The next problem they considered was the security of the evacuation area as they fully expected the local population to rush the boats. To avoid such a panic the embarkation instructions were issued verbally for all Europeans to assemble at the pier by 5.00 p.m. Despite their earlier objections, some 300 women and children eventually crowded into the area. At the hospital the windows were packed with Asian patients and nurses who watched with disbelief the long line of stretchers carrying only Europeans to waiting ambulances, lorries and cars. In spite of his high temperature, Trappes-Lomax was one of the stretcher-bearers.

In the darkness, on the pier, the situation was tense. Warren had ordered all abandoned cars to be used as a barricade and manned by volunteers to repulse any last minute rush for the ferry. Everyone around him was tired and irritable and blamed the military for their predicament. In the town looters were helping themselves, stripping the recently evacuated homes and searching for anything left behind in the bungalows and wrecked shops. Finally about 2.00 a.m. the grumbling stopped at the sound of ship's engines. Slowly out of the darkness the ferry appeared. For one moment Warren considered the possibility of the ferry being manned by Japanese but this idea was soon dispelled by the healthy swearing of a five-badger who landed heavily on the pier after jumping from the deck of the ferry.

By the time the sun burst over the trees on the mainland the ferry had reached Prai and all its passengers had transferred to the train for Kuala Lumpur. What wasn't known was that the enemy had broken through at Guran and its light tanks were now racing along the empty roads to Prai to capture Penang.

Back in his office a few hours later Warren remembers GHQ continually on the line demanding the latest information. 'Had the women and children been evacuated?' 'Any sign of the expected Japanese seaborne assault?' 'When did he expect to evacuate the Penang garrison?' During one long telephone call Warren under the table with the mouthpiece of the stemlike black telephone in front of him on the floor, holding his helmet on his head with one hand and the receiver to his ear with the other, shouted at the faceless GHQ desk-bound warrior, 'If you don't hurry up and pass your bloody message I'll not be alive to answer it.' At that moment 27 enemy bombers were making unopposed low level attacks on his HQ and the town. Bullets and bombs seemed to be going in all directions. The room was filled with dust and the fan, creaking away above the table, bounced with each explosion, threatening to come adrift and decapitate the officers.

It could only be a matter of days before the garrison left so Warren asked for the garrison's plans to carry out a scorched earth policy. From the garrison engineer he discovered that none existed. Once more Colonel Warren called in Major Gavin who soon gave him his assessment of the situation. The problem was that after the first enemy raid all the local boats and RN launches had dispersed and were hidden in creeks and coves around the island. As far as the contents of the warehouses were concerned if any record had existed it had probably gone up in smoke during the raids. The OC Fortress Company Major Montressor, had some local knowledge and with his help Gavin and the SOE staff began to prepare the *godowns* and any boats they could find for demolition. He ordered Parsons and his Chinese to leave and report to 101 STS in Singapore; Brian Passmore was told to take a party to Prai and destroy what he could over there. Using long delay fuses Jim Gavin and Montressor prepared the *godowns* for demolition.

Warren, with another party, carried out a systematic search of the waterfront and creeks, laying charges on all the boats they could find. Later in the day he called all the Volunteers together. He told them that the garrison was going to be evacuated and the Volunteers had three options. One – they could leave with the garrison. It was assumed that all the European Volunteers would anyway. Two – those who remained could throw away their uniforms and rejoin their families or finally they could join the civil police until order was re-established by the Japanese. The majority of Asians decided to stay with their families and most had businesses in the town. The Chinese and Eurasian girls manning the telephone exchange or working in military offices were less certain of the treatment they would receive from the Japanese soldiers and some accepted the offer of evacuation.

The evacuation was a political bone being fought over by the military and civil government and eventually a scapegoat would be needed. At a meeting of the Singapore Legislative Council, the Governor, Sir Shenton Thomas, warned of the possible fate of Penang. His warning coincided with the arrival of the evacuees from Penang bringing harrowing tales of air raids looting and funeral pyres. The confusion on the railways didn't help. The normal twelve hour journey spanned two days. One train reached Kuala Lumpur with Europeans evacuated from Perak, now occupied by the Japanese, and was sent back because no one believed the enemy had gained so much ground. The censorship was so strict that one of the ships which eventually escaped from Penang at the last moment, was refused oil and water when it reached the Singapore Naval depot at Keppel Harbour and its skipper told that these should be drawn from the ship's base Penang. General Pownall, who was to replace Brooke-Popham, wrote in his diary that, 'At Penang there seems to have been all sorts of a mess-up from which it is impossible to get any sort of coherent picture.'

Unaware of the political storm breaking in Singapore Brigadier Lyons ordered the evacuation of the garrison. Warren agreed with Major Gavin's proposal that he should take the remaining SOE staff to join Passmore on the mainland. They hoped to carry out another scorched earth plan at Butterworth before the enemy arrived. During the late afternoon the European civilians, the wounded and the garrison slowly withdrew past the smouldering ruins along the cratered waterfront to the pier. The Volunteers acted as rearguard and finally formed a picket line behind a barricade of cars.

In the Chinese Cricket Club its members began to board up the statue of Queen Victoria. Hidden by a casing of plywood it survived the war. The fine old British Residency surrounded by 26 acres of garden, stood empty and bomb-scarred. In the shopping area the looters were running from shop to shop fighting over the spoils. On the pier the garrison occasionally heard Jim Gavin's charges sending the warehouses sky-high, sometimes setting off unexploded bombs.

Alexander had discovered an undamaged, fast, RN launch and crewed it with survivors from the *Repulse* and the *Prince of Wales*. Joined by Warren they now cruised around the harbour sinking small craft with gunfire or well placed hand grenades.

The evacuation began when a small convoy of local steamers and fast RN launches berthed alongside the pier. As they drew near the walking wounded moved forward and the stretcher cases were lifted from their shelters. At that moment, remembers Warren, a squadron of enemy planes flew in low straight for the pier scattering the garrison. The wounded watched helplessly from their stretchers and Warren, a lone figure at the end of the pier, uttered those time-honoured immortal words, 'Bloody hell'. This time it was not their turn and the bombers flew past heading for the mainland.

In the final hours the evacuation was lit by the flames from burning oil dumps close to the pier. On board the *Kuala* Lieutenant-Colonel Max Moore manned a four-inch gun and was busy blasting shells into the undamaged buildings along the waterfront. Before they finally sailed Alexander took over the gun and sent shells into the remaining ferry, sending it to the bottom. The embarkation was finished by 11.00 p.m. and by midnight the convoy including the *Kuala*, *Pangker* and five small naval patrol boats were well out to sea, leaving the burning city to the looters.

When Warren stepped ashore two days later at Keppel Harbour he found press censorship so strict that the loss of Penang was still not admitted although Singapore was full of rumours as to its fate.

Unknowingly Warren and Alexander were walking into a political dogfight between Churchill's representative, Duff Cooper, The Governor, Sir Shenton Thomas, and the military. The Rt Hon Duff Cooper, chairman of the recently formed War Council, was about to announce to the press that Penang had been successfully evacuated. On the other hand, in another part of Singapore, the Governor, Sir Shenton Thomas, called all the leaders of the Asian community together to apologise for Asian civilians being left behind, pointing out that the evacuation was masterminded by the military.

Unaware of these machinations Warren and Alexander presented their report to Admiral Layton, C in C China Station. Outlining the events leading up to the evacuation they pointed out that an estimated 1,000 civilians died in the first raid. The ferry crews deserted and the so-called fortress lacked both defensive works and sufficient troops. Finally they described the destruction of the harbour facilities and the evacuation – only hours before the Japanese landed.

It was obvious to Warren that something seemed to be worrying the admiral who only interrupted to clarify points. When they began to describe the demolitions the admiral demanded to know why fast RN launches were allowed to fall, undamaged, into enemy hands. Despite their assurances that nothing of the sort happened, Layton was not convinced and Alexander, as Naval representative, caught most of the admiral's wrath, Warren recollects. Still convinced that he was right, Admiral Layton included the allegation in a signal to Churchill and the myth was born.

Post-war published material from Japanese sources shows that the scorched earth policy at Penang was anticipated and the Japanese took the precaution of bringing special lightweight collapsible boats from Indo-China. Rowing boats used for the Singorra landings were also lashed to any vehicles travelling south.

The next morning, the 19th, much to Captain Spencer Chapman's surprise, Major Gavin turned up at the school. Following the Penang evacuation his SOE team carried out demolitions around Butterworth destroying installations at the airfield and naval base. Finally, before they left, he laid charges around the Prai power station a prominent landmark, and blew it up. Almost out of supplies and the men suffering from exhaustion, Jim Gavin took the team back to Kuala Lumpur leaving 3 Corps digging new defences along the jungle-fringed Kuala Kangsor River.

When he reported to HQ for fresh orders he found a signal waiting from Killery with instructions for him to report back to Singapore. When he was preparing to leave he spotted a familiar face – his adjutant's Trappes-Lomax, who should have been in Singapore. By way of explanation he commented that he'd 'escaped from the hospital train'. After Jim Gavin left, the team, now under the command of Captain Trappes-Lomax stayed in the forward zone for two more days. When supplies and explosives were exhausted they too returned to Tanjong Balai.

CHAPTER SEVEN

Secret Service (SIS) Stay-behind Parties

Any plans Major Rosher may have had to use Penang and Ipoh as forward bases were abandoned when the enemy thrust engulfed north Malaya. Withdrawing with 3 Corps he also took his unit back to Kuala Lumpur where his Special Branch friends provided him with contacts amongst the Communist underground in the city.

Following the German attack on Russia in June 1941, the Secretary General of the Malayan Communist Party (MCP), Loi Tak offered to provide the British Army with recruits. This offer was turned down by the Governor, Sir Shenton Thomas, which was hardly surprising as the Communists had organised a series of successful strikes which led to civil disturbances.

However, in December, the Governor changed his mind and gave his approval for Special Branch to open discussions with Loi Tak about the future role of the MCP in the war. In his book *The Jungle is Neutral* Freddy Chapman describes the negotiations taking place in a seedy down-town room in China town. One concession Loi Tak wrung from Special Branch was that all Communists held in British jails on the mainland and in Singapore, should be released. Despite being in prison the Communists also had their instructions. When the prison gates opened they joined the Chinese Volunteer Force or reported for training to 101 STS. One of these was twenty-year-old Yeung Kwo who, seven years later, led the guerrillas against the British troops in Selangor, during the post-war emergency.

Whether Special Branch briefed Shenton Thomas on Loi Tak's role is unclear but he was a double agent who had spent many years building a cover for himself. As a young man he studied in Russia before returning to China to become a member of the Communist Shanghai Committee. Later, with Ho Chi Minh, he went to Indo-China to organise the party in Saigon. It was here that he began to work with the French police. Following a series of successful police raids which broke up the Communist organisation in Indo-China he fled the country, probably smuggled out by French counter-intelligence. His co-conspirator, Ho Chi Minh, also escaped and reached Hong Kong but he was arrested and jailed by the British.

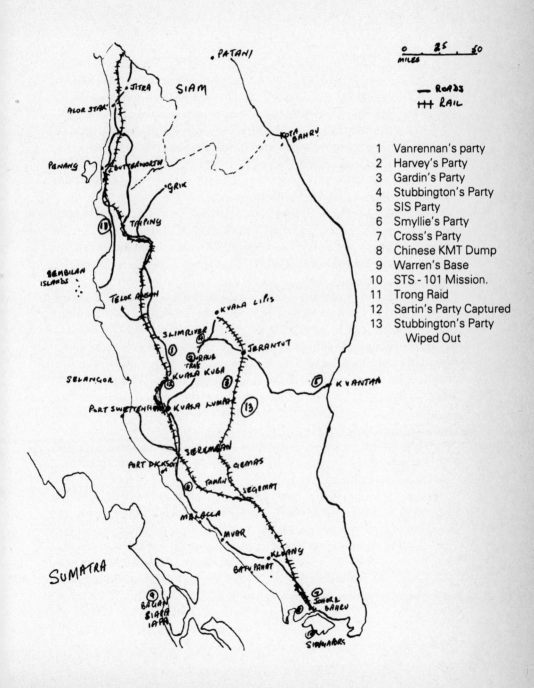

MALAYA.

0   25   50
MILES

— ROADS
╫ RAIL

1 Vanrennan's party
2 Harvey's Party
3 Gardin's Party
4 Stubbington's Party
5 SIS Party
6 Smyllie's Party
7 Cross's Party
8 Chinese KMT Dump
9 Warren's Base
10 STS - 101 Mission.
11 Trong Raid
12 Sartin's Party Captured
13 Stubbington's Party
      Wiped Out

PATANI

SIAM

JITRA

ALOR STAR

KOTA BAHRU

PENANG

BUTTERWORTH

GRIK

TAIPING

SEMBILAN
ISLANDS

TELOK ANSON

KVALA LIPIS

SLIMRIVER

JERANTUT

KUALA KUBA

SELANGOR

KVANTAN

PORT SWETTENHAM

KUALA LUMPUR

SEREMBAN

PORT DICKSON

GEMAS

TAMIN

SEGEMAT

MALACCA

MUAR

KLUANG

BATU PAHAT

SUMATRA

JOHORE
BAHRU

BATAM
SIARA
IARA

SINGAPORE

Loi Tak resurfaced in Singapore and for the next three years took an active part in rebuilding the Malayan Communist Party. As had been the case in French Indo-China many leading Communists were arrested, leaving the way clear for Loi Tak to gradually take over the party leadership.

The concessions he obtained during his war-time discussions with Special Branch strengthened his position at the top. The leaders, who he had previously exposed, had been released and were in his debt; the British wanted to use his underground organisation and had agreed to train Communists in clandestine activities. In Kuala Lumpur the Chinese Communist underground leader in the city, Tan Chen King, received instructions to meet Special Branch and Secret Service representatives while others were to receive their military training with the Volunteers.

Remembering the occasion John Davis, who was about to be recruited by SOE, recalls he was in Singapore at the time: the sole Security Liaison Officer in Singapore. He was responsible for investigating suspected sabotage but felt his job was a waste of time as he had nothing to do. When his boss came in one morning and asked him whether he would be interested in working with the Secret Service he jumped at the chance. Later he was flown to Kuala Lumpur and introduced to Major Rosher.

In the discussions that followed Tan Chen King agreed to co-operate with Rosher's plan to put fifteen Chinese stay-behind parties into Perak and to carry out intelligence gathering missions for the British. With very little time left before the Japanese arrived the SIS requisitioned the Chinese Chunjin School near Kuala Lumpur as a training base and Jim Gavin soon appeared on the scene with weapons and explosives for the new recruits. For his part Tan Chen King assembled over a hundred Communist underground fighters at the school for training.

For the project Rosher had gathered around him a small band of Europeans with mixed skills and experience. There was, for instance, Chinese-speaking John Davis, Captain Knott – who ran the wireless network and Shepherd who joined his team after leaving Shebbeare's SOE border survey organisation. He had only just escaped from Tapah by the skin of his teeth after destroying a large amount of supplies left behind there by the RAF. A civil servant named Barry* briefly appears on the scene and John Davis remem-

---

* He later took over one of the stay-behind parties.

bers him as being a strangely intense sort of chap. Finally there was another civilian named Cole who had many contacts in east Malaya. With the help of this small group Rosher set about giving the Communist recruits a crash course in intelligence work.

When the would-be guerrillas left for Perak they were joined by Knott's two Chinese wireless operators and he was left to poach replacements from the nearby Royal Signals Regiment.

One of the signallers* recalled that the regiment arrived in Kuala Lumpur after retreating from Ipoh. They arrived on Christmas morning and were still unpacking when he was called before the company commander and asked whether he would be prepared to undertake special duties. He recounts that Major Rosher sat on the corner of the CO's desk idly swinging his leg while the OC briefed him. When he agreed to join Rosher he was given fifteen minutes to pack his kit and leave.

Captain Knott had relocated his wireless shack in the grounds of 3 Corps HQ where he was joined by Cross and a second serviceman named Mortimer. Together they were briefed on the unit's function which was to train the Communists and put them as far forward as possible in the enemy's line of advance. The agents would take with them arms, supplies and the occasional wireless transmitter. They would also receive an advance of pay.

The ban Sir Shenton Thomas had placed on the planning of irregular warfare in Malaya left both SIS and SOE with no alternative but to scramble and get things done before the enemy overran the area. Although Rosher's unit was not part of the Orient Mission his approach to clandestine work was similar. If it seemed like a good idea he would go ahead and do it.

In addition to the Chinese Rosher was also putting in European parties mainly on the east coast. One party consisting of two of Knott's sergeants, Regan and Meldrum, were placed near the Kuala Krai to watch and send back reports about the traffic on the east coast railway. Like the Siam party they too never came on the air and met a tragic end. Another likely landing beach on the east coast was at Kuanton but although the Indian Brigade was stationed there the only means of communication was by the public telephone system. If the Japanese did try to seize the town in a seaborne landing it was imperative that GHQ should know the strength of the enemy, so Rosher decided to put in one Chinese group and a European party.

* Read *The Red Jungle* by John Cross DCM.

On Boxing Day, after leaving Sergeants Cross and Mortimer in charge of the wireless network, the SIS party loaded its supplies including weapons and wireless sets; on to the back of a lorry and set out for Kuanton. Rosher took with him Knott, Davis and Shepherd and a party of Chinese. The road over the hills rose steeply and was wet with rain. Somewhere along the road the lorry skidded around a bend and the Indian driver, fighting to control it drove over an embankment. Not a very fortuitous start thought Knott at the time but no one was injured he remembers, although they were all badly shaken. After salvaging the damaged equipment and supplies the party begged a lift back to Kuala Lumpur and started again.

The journey to Kuanton took Rosher's party across the main mountain range to Jeruntut, a small town on the river bank. There was no bridge only a ferry, and the lorries joined a long queue of armoured cars belonging to the Malaya Volunteers on their way to join the Royal Garwal Rifles and the Sikhs defending the beaches and airfield at Kuanton. The ferry was an archaic flat-bottomed craft, manned by slow moving native crew who were totally uninterested in the war and military impatience.

Once across the fast flowing river, Rosher's lorries followed the jungle-fringed lateral road for some hundred miles, through two small, mainly one street towns, of Gambin and Marun; before finally arriving at Kuanton. They spent the next day, the 27th, placing the Chinese agents.

The commander of 22nd Indian Brigade at Kuanton was in a quandary. Somewhere in the 160 miles of undeveloped and mountainous country to the north of the town enemy troops were moving towards him along jungle tracks. He had the dual role of defending the aerodrome and beach but as the planes had now been withdrawn he had nothing to protect. There were rumours that Japanese soldiers, who posed as civilians in the area pre-war, were loose in Trengannau and following up one report from a British planter, one of his patrols captured several of these part-time enemy soldiers. The day Rosher's party rolled into town the commander received instructions that his beach defences were only to be treated as outposts and the guns to be withdrawn across the river bridge. In the next 72 hours GHQ changed the orders three times.

To describe the military situation on the east coast as a mess would be an understatement. After landing at Khota Bahru three weeks earlier the Japanese broke off contact with the British brigade which had retreated along the railway line to Kuala Lipis. Instead they turned south to occupy, in fact, the abandoned, well supplied airfield of Gong Kedah on the northern borders of Trengannau. From there their planes could blitz Kuanton and Kuala Lumpur. The only military force in Trengannau was the Local Defence Force. This unit consisted of one Eurasian and five European officers with 100 Eurasian and Malay NCO's and men. In the first two days of the war the LDF arrested 92 Japanese civilians but within 24 hours the LDF and the police were disbanded and the Japanese released. Amidst growing panic in the state's capital, Kuala Trengannau, the Japanese were issued with arms for self-defence and the Europeans asked to leave. When Rosher heard the rumours just before Christmas he sent Cole across to have a look at the town. After walking over the main range, following survey paths and jungle tracks, he reached Kuala Trengannau and found the town almost deserted: the Europeans gone and their homes looted – but no sign of the Japanese. When he repeated the journey a second time he was captured and disappeared.

After installing his Chinese party Rosher decided on the 29th to take a look at the largest British-owned tin mine in Malaya some miles inland at Sungai Lembing. Apart from wrecking the mine he proposed to take the opportunity of putting in a European stay-behind party. Shortly after they left town reports reached Brigade HQ that Japanese patrols were coming down the Jabor valley only some fifteen miles away. Unaware of this latest intelligence, Rosher took his party north-west along the rough made up dirt roads into the hills. The village and tin mine at Sungai Lembing were about three hours' drive from Kuanton and almost hidden in a jungle-covered valley where the muddy river swung in a wide loop.

Driving through the small collection of native houses they took the track leading to the mine and could see the manager's stone built house on the hillside above the village. As they drew near they noticed it was built on stone pillars surrounded by well kept flower beds and lawns. Walking across the lawns towards them was an attractive, slim woman in her late thirties. At her heels padded two panting bull mastiffs. Her brother, she said, Vin Baker, was nearby at the mine – organising the destruction of the machinery, and she sent a servant to fetch him. A few minutes later Vin Baker came hurrying around the corner of the house to greet his visitors. When later they told him what they were trying to do he suggested they could hide the wireless party in the jungle near the river overlooking the village and mine. Being more than fifty he felt he was too old for that sort of thing but would help them all he could. When he came back later he told them that his underground manager, Bryan Tyson, a New Zealander and his friend Maurice Cottrill, assistant manager from the nearby Sungai Lembing Rubber Estate; had volunteered to stay behind to man the wireless transmitter with Knott's 101 STS trained Chinaman as wireless operator. Their contact with the outside world would be the mine's electrician, a Singhalese named Fornesco.

Leaving Jack Knott and Tyson giving the wireless set a test run from the manager's house, Shepherd and Davis decided to do some Jap spotting at Ula Kenaman, about a day's march from the mine on the Trengannau border. Later in the day Rosher and Vin Baker decided it would be safer if all the European staff and their families left and everyone was ordered to pack up and be prepared to leave next day. The packing was in fact left to the women as all the staff were needed to destroy the mine. All stocks of oil were loaded on to the lorries and driven to the river where they were dumped. The tin waiting to be moved to Kuanton was dropped back down the shaft and wherever possible all the machinery was dismantled.

In the middle of the destruction Vin Baker sought out Captain Jack Knott and found him fiddling with the wireless. 'Would you,' asked Vin, 'shoot my sister's two bull mastiffs?' Reluctantly Knott agreed and followed the downcast Baker to the back of some mine buildings where he found the dogs tied to a post. The dogs sat patiently waiting, panting in the heat of the sun. The heavy monsoon rain of the morning had gone leaving the ground a thick mud which clung to Knott's boots. Unclipping his holster Knott pulled out the revolver, eased off the safety catch and placed the barrel against the dog's head – suddenly everything went quiet – the pumps had stopped to allow the mine to flood. The silence was eerie. The noise of the shot echoed around the mine workings and the bullet tore open the dog's head and so startled its mate that it broke free and raced away as Knott's second bullet nicked it. Leaving Vin Baker standing by the body of the dead bull mastiff Jack Knott, perspiring heavily in a sweat-stained cotton uniform, raced after the second dog hurdling bits of machinery and boxes; taking pot shots on the run.

The next day all European civilians left for Kuanton to join the army's evacuation programme. With them went Rosher and Tyson as escorts. Rumours were widespread amongst the Chinese in the village that the Japanese were advancing along the coast murdering and raping. After following the muddy river downstream the mine party reached a spot at a hairpin bend of the track from where they could see Kuanton in the distance. The town was covered in a haze and small black fly-like objects flew around. Everyone could hear what seemed to be distant thunder. Kuanton was being bombed. The little convoy started up and moved more slowly forward. It soon became obvious the town was under heavy ground attack and Rosher sent the civilians back while he and Tyson tried to reach Allied lines.

In Kuanton the streets were filled with dead from both sides. Shells hurtled in, exploding amongst the houses which caved in and tumbled into the streets. Many which were still standing were on fire and the flames leapt from house to house creating an inferno. Suffocating black clouds rolled along the streets or billowed into the air and from these burst enemy fighters bombing and strafing the Sikh soldiers hiding in doorways or monsoon ditches. Leaving the mine staff to make their way back Tyson and Rosher left the road above the town and cautiously made their way through a rubber plantation, across a deserted *kampong* until they reached the edge of the town. Peering from behind a wall, the side road into town which they had used seemed unguarded so together they raced across and flung themselves into a shell damaged shop – to be followed by what seemed to be thousands of bullets thudding and screaming about their ears. Later when they recovered their nerve they dashed from doorway to doorway, forcing their way through locked doors and over walls until suddenly they fell headlong into a sandbagged position manned by equally frightened young Sikh soldiers.

Eventually they were passed from platoon to platoon until they reached the commander. They were lucky, he said, he was withdrawing his troops across the river by nightfall. If they had arrived a few hours later the town would have been in Japanese hands. Rosher stayed with the defenders and later blew up the bridge. As the staff at the mine and the rest of the SIS group needed to know what was happening Tyson slipped back through the enemy lines and eventually reached the mine which he found deserted. The staff, their wives and children had abandoned all their luggage and had set off on foot along jungle paths in an attempt to reach Jeruntut. After they left the mine manager, Vin Baker, went around disabling the vehicles. When Shepherd and Davis arrived back – without discovering any Japanese – they learnt from Tyson that Kuanton was in enemy hands and the wireless set had a faulty valve. Despite the danger Tyson and Cottrill agreed to remain behind and gather intelligence

until Shepherd and Davis returned with a spare valve. Leaving
Tyson and Cottrill in their hideout the SIS party walked across the
hills to the main road. The next day they were on the deserted metalled road, which they followed until they found the Indian Brigade's
rearguard manning a road block at Marun.

Recalling the journey from the mine Jack Knott was surprised to
'slip back through the lines without difficulty'. Having installed himself in a deserted rubber planter's bungalow he set up his wireless set
and made contact with Kranji. 'Things seemed at their gloomiest,'
he recalls. 'There was no air cover and the 9th and 11th Divisions
were falling back rapidly. I sent my signals to Kranji describing the
state of the country. Most of the town and villages were deserted and
the roads quite free of the refugee problem I found during my first
retreat across France to Dunkirk, with the BEF, the previous year.
There was little evidence in Pahang of resistance by our land forces
but occasionally one came across thirty or so men and a gun astride
the main road but little else.' Major Rosher arrived back in Kuala
Lumpur about 6th January and was immediately recalled to Singapore.

CHAPTER EIGHT

The West Coast Raid

At the Naval Base in Singapore Colonel Warren woke refreshed following his first undisturbed sleep for seven nights. He showered. His sweat-stained smelly uniform, worn continuously since leaving Singapore, had disappeared to the *dhobie*; in its place, neatly laid out on the bed by his batman, were clean white shorts and tunic shirt.

At the office he was told he was going to Kuala Lumpur to join 3 Corps as GSO 1, responsible for all behind-the-lines activities and he should take with him what back-up staff he needed. He knew Rosher was in Kuala Lumpur and Gavin and Trappes-Lomax were somewhere up-country so he telephoned Killery to see whether Freddy Chapman, who was anxious to see some action, was available. He was and Killery agreed to release him and signalled Gavin to return.

When Freddy Chapman heard the news he was delighted but asked one favour of Warren. Army units throughout Negri Sembilan, Selangor and Pahang were collecting groups of Chinese, nominated by Loi Tak and putting them on the train to Singapore. Would Warren asked Chapman delay the start long enough for him to welcome the first Chinese class to the school?

Freddy Spencer Chapman's forte was field craft, although he would modestly claim that it was Calvert who taught him all he knew. Warren also needed an explosives expert so Chapman recommended Sergeant Sartin, one time bugle boy, a Sapper and explosives expert at the school. Within the next few days both Gavin and Trappes-Lomax arrived back and the latter took over the detailed running of the school from Spencer Chapman.

On 22nd December Captain Spencer Chapman welcomed the first batch of 30 Chinese Communist guerrillas led by Rosher's acquaintance Tan Chen King. This affable character was senior guerrilla and course translator.

Leaving Spencer Chapman in one of the Chinese pavilions talking to the recently arrived Communist underground fighters, Sartin drove Chapman's red Ford V8 around to the stores and supervised the loading of special, home-made, long delay fuses, explosives, Tommy guns and supplies. In the office Warren took the opportunity of getting Jim Gavin's views of the situation north of Kuala Lumpur. Finally Chapman appeared in the doorway and they all crammed aboard his car.

The journey to Kuala Lumpur was uneventful, commented Warren, despite enemy aircraft shooting up anything moving on the roads and railways. There was a rumour that enemy bombers caught an ammunition train leaving Ipoh station and the fires were still burning and ammunition exploding twenty-four hours later. This may have been a fifth columnist story but as censoring was so strict the rumour thrived.

One of Warren's first and lasting impressions of Corps Headquarters' staff in Kuala Lumpur was that they lacked any form of defensive spirit. Most were preoccupied with the fear that 'the Japs were coming'. Shortly after he arrived at Headquarters Warren was brought up to date with the military situation. He was shown into a small office with a large map covering the wall. From where he sat he looked out across the parade ground with its flag staff and white painted bricks marking the edge of the square. A Tamil poked around with a hoe weeding shrubs. The enemy had crossed the border and taken the towns of Kroh and Grik, the young staff officer told him; another column had taken Butterworth and Penang and both were now advancing towards the Perak River. The 11 Division's commander had pulled his troops and transport across the only bridge over the river at Kuala Kangsor putting the river between him and the enemy. The officer waved his stick at various points on the map. His shorts had a knife-edge crease and dark sweat patches were beginning to appear across the shoulders of his shirt.

The plan was to keep the enemy north of Kuala Lumpur until the 16th. This would give time for nine convoys to arrive in Singapore carrying Glenn Martin bombers, Hurricanes, Artillery and thousands of Australian British and Indian troops. It was imperative that the airfields at Kuanton and Kuala Lumpur should be denied to the enemy as long as possible, said the young officer.

Sitting in the fan-cooled office Warren listened with growing apprehension. The message was clear. Despite the enemy's lines of communication stretching more than a thousand miles across land and sea, the city was expected to be abandoned in some three weeks.

One of the first things Warren did after the briefing was to signal Trappes-Lomax to hurry the training of the Chinese. At this rate the Japanese would be in Kuala Lumpur before the guerrillas finished their training.

Another arrival at Corps Headquarters that day was a fiery officer from the Argylls, Major Angus Rose who had been in Penang. He'd persuaded the GOC in Singapore to let him have fifty Australians to carry out a seaborne raid on the enemy's lines of communications. The Royal Navy thought it was a good idea and agreed to provide a local steamer, SS *Kudat*, as a depot ship. This steamer arrived at Port Swettenham from Singapore on 23rd December.

When Angus Rose discussed the project with Chapman and Warren, who were responsible for special operations, they suggested that seaborne raids would be more effective if the landing zones and the target areas had been previously reconnoitred. It was pointed out by Freddy Chapman that there was a noticeable lack of reliable information about the enemy's communications its transport, armour and the flow rate of reinforcements. He went on to suggest that he and John Sartin should carry out a reconnaissance of the proposed target area and later make their way to the landing beach to meet and brief the Australian raiders coming ashore at Trong. The proposed landing beach was some forty miles west of Kuala Kangsor. Although both Warren and Angus Rose thought him crazy to undertake this mission Warren nevertheless gave his permission. Chapman and Sartin left by road on Christmas Eve. The Australian raiders sailed on Boxing Day in two fast launches, the *ML 1062* and its sister ship.

On the same day Warren was asked to take some men and investigate a report that the enemy had opened up a wireless station behind the lines on one of the islands in the Semberlin group, off the coast near the little fishing port of Telak Anson. GHQ were unable to spare anyone to go with him so Warren rounded up a group of officers, whom Angus Rose unfairly referred to as adventurers, and borrowed a high speed, heavily armed Fairmiles launch from the Navy. Arming themselves with Tommy guns, Bren guns and grenades, Warren and his men scrambled aboard the Fairmiles and roared out of Port Swettenham, down the Klang river into the Malacca Straits and the open sea. The search party spent the rest of the day going from island to island beating through secondary jungle. They found some badly frightened fishermen who lived on the islands but no Japanese. A little disappointed, Warren took the party to Trong to see how Angus Rose and his Australians were getting on.

Towards the late afternoon he found the two launches at anchor off the estuary near Trong. The Fairmiles cut its engines and cruised alongside the *1062* and an agitated Major Rose climbed aboard to join Warren. As planned, because of their slow speed, the small motor boats to be used to ferry the Australians ashore had been sent ahead. The crews had been instructed to make their way to Trong and hide near the mouth of the river and later rendezvous with Major Rose's Australians. Rose now discovered that two of the boats had been beached on an ebb tide and were high and dry on the mud. If that wasn't bad enough, one of the remaining boats had developed engine trouble, leaving only one available.

Major Rose had a great deal of respect for Colonel Warren, whom he was later to describe as utterly fearless, always immaculately dressed and a hard man. Now sitting under the tropical sun in the late afternoon, Warren listened to Major Rose's problems and gave him the benefit of his experience.

The problem of ferrying the raiders ashore could be overcome by sending one of the Malay speaking rubber planters ashore to hire local boats. Two planters, Frank Vanrennan and Bill Harvey, had come with the party to act as scouts. More important however was that Major Rose was GSO 2 at Corps as well as being responsible for co-ordinating all the aspects of the raid. His raiders were Australians under the command of their own officers and once ashore they ceased to be his responsibility nor could he give them orders. If he did go ashore he ran the risk of capture and as a staff officer with 3 Corps he would be a big prize to the enemy. If captured the enemy would give him a rougher time if they discovered he had worked in GHQ Operations Room and privy to policy and operational decisions. Leaving Rose in no doubt as to the treatment he could expect from the Japanese, Warren left the raiding party about 7.00 p.m. that evening.

The following morning, cruising some miles out in the Straits of Malacca, Warren picked out – through his binoculars – a small native sailing boat some three miles away. Hoping that it might be the enemy trying to slip men ashore he ordered full power and gave chase. The Fairmiles' bows lifted out of the water sending large waves arcing either side. At high speed the launch roared down on the boat with every weapon trained on the victim's passengers. As the launch swept in a wide circle around the boat Warren picked out three, very frightened, white passengers. They turned out to be a planter and his wife together with an attractive teenage daughter.

They heard the Fairmiles approaching while it was some miles away and, thinking it to be manned by the Japanese, were praying that they wouldn't be seen. Under sail they could do nothing but sit

and wait. The planter had spent all his life in Malaya and his plantation was now behind enemy lines. He missed the army evacuation,
lost his home, what little cash he had was spent on buying the boat.
All they had left were the clothes they stood up in and his lifetime's
collection of butterflies. Alan Warren found him quite vague as to his
destination. The planter thought he might try for Sumatra or go
direct to the Nicobar Islands or even tackle the Bay of Bengal to
India. After giving him supplies and a chart Warren cast off.

That night under the cover of darkness Warren took the Fairmiles
back to Trong where next morning he found the *1062* full of tired but
jubilant soldiers.

The raid had got off to a bad start when the Australians became
lost in the mangrove swamps. With the help of their two planter
guides, Vanrennan and Harvey, they eventually extracted themselves and reached the coast road from Trong. Unknown to them the
road was being used by the enemy to by-pass 11 Division at Kuala
Kangsor*. After shooting up a pennant-flying staff car and lorries
packed with enemy troops the Australians decided to withdraw
while they still had the element of surprise in their favour. So much to
Major Rose's indignation the raiders retired under cover of darkness
to Trong. Later using local boats procured by Vanrennan they
reached the *1062*.

Seeing the exhausted Australians falling asleep all over the deck
Warren ordered everyone aboard his own faster vessel, leaving the
1062 to make its own speed back to port. It wasn't until they were well
on their way to Port Swettenham that Warren discovered that
neither Freddy Chapman nor Sartin were on board. Another missing
person was Angus Rose who was left behind fast asleep in the cabin
of the *1062*. The raiders had, however, rescued five British soldiers
being hidden by natives around the town. Two were Argylls who had
served with Angus Rose in India, another was a sergeant in the
Leicesters and the remaining two were battle-fatigued privates from
the East Surreys. All five had walked more than 100 miles through
enemy-held territory helped by the local population until they were
rescued at Trong.

In the meantime Chapman and Sartin, after collecting valuable
information about the Japanese, tried without success to cut their
way through secondary jungle some miles away from the coast.

* Realising it could be cut off 11 Division withdrew on the 26th to a new line at Kampar.

Unable to make progress and running out of time they decided to abandon the Trong meeting place and made their way down the Perak River to the small coastal town of Talek Anson. Unaware of the mounting enemy fury caused by the Australian raid they went down river by boat which they later swapped for bicycles, until they eventually reached the Allied lines on 30th December.

Listening to the soldiers' escape stories Warren was interested to hear that Taiping had become a Japanese assembly area. The soldiers had seen troop concentrations as well as transport armour and planes around the town. If the Australians' success could be repeated at Taiping it might take pressure off Kampar long enough for fresh reinforcements expected any day in Singapore, to be rushed forward to 3 Corps.

Warren's requests for more men, boats and specialists were quickly answered by GHQ. After the repeated defeats in north Malaya the propaganda machine and the world press eagerly seized the Trong raid as an indication that the army was not only fighting back but winning. The Australians were reinforced by 200 Royal Marines who were given a crash course in jungle training. The Royal Navy sent five fast Eureka assault boats to replace the unreliable local launches. In Tanjong Balai Major Gavin was asked to round up a team of specialists who could handle boats and explosives and join Warren in Kuala Lumpur.

On 30th December Colonel Warren was sitting in the back of a camouflaged army staff car, looking immaculate in his Royal Marine uniform. With him was Major Angus Rose. The Marines were parading at Port Swettenham for his inspection. The SS *Kudat* was tied up against the harbour wall and the five American assault boats were sighted off the mouth of the river.

In Port Swettenham all units were on the alert following daily air raids which usually preceded an enemy attack. It was rumoured that the enemy would try a seaborne assault using boats captured at Penang.

As Warren's car reached the harbour he could see the Marines lined up near one of the *godowns*. Beyond them the waterfront suddenly burst into mushrooms of smoke and the Marines, in what seemed slow motion, scattered. The sky in front of Warren's car seemed full of low flying Japanese bombers with bomb racks open. Warren left through one door and Rose went out through the other. The Indian driver had already gone. From the shelter of a wall Warren blazed away with his Tommy gun. All around him the dockside seemed to be erupting with bomb blasts. The abandoned car, now well ventilated with bullet holes, was burning.

After repeated attacks the *Kudat* saturated with holes and burst plates sank to the bottom of the harbour taking with her all the raiders' supplies and expectations. The five fast Eureka assault boats were caught out in the open and were either sunk or beached. Despite the heavy pounding the defenders beat off an attempted landing, forcing the Japanese to revise their plans and land instead further north at Telak Anson. This successful landing, together with Japanese columns advancing towards Kuala Lumpur from Kuanton, threatened to trap 3 Corps in a pincer movement.

CHAPTER NINE

North Malaya Stay-behind Parties

Warren's request for men and supplies reached 101 STS at a time when all the resources were being stretched to the limit. The Army had suddenly woken up to the need for soldiers to have jungle training and be taught the skills to carry out special operations and clamoured for places at the school. The French were still sending students and the Chinese Communist Party was providing batches of thirty underground fighters at a time. There was a rumour that the French were going to China and this seemed reinforced by an increase in their scrounging which included the disappearance of one of Knott's precious Mark 1 sets.

In the middle of this high level of activity came Warren's appeal for assistance. Anxious to help Jim Gavin selected Brian Passmore, Second Lieutenant White, who had been on the Siam raids, and a regular soldier in the Argylls, Sergeant Frisken who would look after the transport. The next few days were spent by the team loading several lorries with arms, weapons, special explosives and equipment. Eventually Gavin and his men drove off for Kuala Lumpur leaving Trappes-Lomax in charge of the school.

The journey was uneventful and if it wasn't for the large number of military personnel about it could have been pre-war. When they arrived in Kuala Lumpur they found that Warren and Chapman had moved in with Colonel Dalley who was responsible for civilian counter-intelligence operations in Malaya. They had converted his home into their base and Gavin discovered Chapman in one of the rooms, with his head buried in a pile of papers and maps, planning sabotage missions behind enemy lines. In another sat Alan Warren in a pensive mood. He had just arrived back from a conference called by General Heath, 3 Corps. At the conference the news was broken that because of enemy pressure, the Kampar line had been given up and 11 Division had retired to the banks of the Slim River, where it was digging in. This brought the enemy to within fifty miles of Kuala Lumpur. If 11 Division could hold its new defence position the Indian Brigade, fighting its way out of Kuanton, could reach Bentong in safety. In turn, this brigade would hold the crossroads and protect 11 Division's right flank to enable 11 Division to fall back on Kuala Lumpur.

The Japanese were also ashore on the division's left flank, on the west coast at Telak Anson. Enemy units held back by the LDF* were pushing inland threatening to cut off the Slim River defenders. Similar raids could be expected at Port Swettenham and Port Selangor. The only reserves the commander had left were eight battalions of LDF. A large number of units belonging to this racially mixed volunteer force had already been disbanded and what was left hardly constituted a battalion. He told Warren and Major Rose that they should forget any plans they had for raiding parties. He wanted the Marines and Australians as reserves for 11 Division.

Addressing the other officers the corps commander told them that all units in Kuala Lumpur should evacuate non-essential supplies, equipment and men. At the same time the services should institute a scorched earth policy to deny the enemy all strategic equipment and installations.

Later when Colonel Warren had brought Major Gavin up to date with the latest position he suggested that Gavin and his men would be very useful to Freddy Chapman, who was in the middle of planning a series of sabotage missions.

The idea had all started on the 30th, the night Spencer Chapman returned from Trong. He spent most of that night with Vanrennan and Harvey, swapping experiences about their exploits behind the lines. By morning they'd put together the basis of a plan to put teams of saboteurs behind the enemy lines. When Warren heard their plans he gave them his full backing, which soon received the corps commander's approval – with one stipulation. They had to find their own men as 3 Corps needed all the rifle power it could find.

Alan Warren now told Spencer Chapman to get on with it as it was his show. The plan was based on the fact that all road and rail communications between north and south Malaya passed through an area fifty miles wide between Kuala Lipis and the Slim River. He proposed that small teams made up of men who knew what they were about should attack the flow of enemy supplies and reinforcements using these lines of communications.

Leaving Colonel Warren the job of looking for volunteers Spencer Chapman tackled the problem of planning, organising and placing

* Local Defence Force.

men and supplies behind the lines in two short weeks. With Vanrennan, Harvey and Sartin to help him he examined the availability of
stores, transport, weapons, locations, recruits and replacements.

Communications had been a recurring problem throughout the
Malayan Campaign and because of the shortage of wireless sets
Spencer Chapman planned to equip each team with domestic radios
and batteries. As senior officer behind the lines Spencer Chapman
would have the only transmitter. To contact his men by radio he
would transmit his messages to the STS station at Kranji. The Singapore Broadcasting Station would then send out his instructions, in
code, during their normal broadcasts.

All he had to start with initially were Sartin, Vanrennan and Harvey. When the commander gave his approval Vanrennan persuaded
another two fellow rubber planters, Richard Graham and Boris
Hembry, to join him. With their arrival Spencer Chapman could
now split his men into two teams.

The first two days of 1942 were spent by Chapman driving hundreds of miles looking for suitable hideouts. In the main range of
hills, running like a spine down the Malayan peninsula, Chapman
called on an old mountaineering acquaintance, the chief game warden for Malaya, Mr Shebbeare. It was he who suggested the first
hideout near Tras, used by Sartin. Shebbeare had previously been
involved with SOE surveying jungle routes into Siam. He volunteered to join Chapman's party in the jungle but later, during the
rapid evacuation of Kuala Lumpur, they lost contact with each
other.

On 1st January Freddy Chapman left Sartin and Harvey at Tras
to develop the proposed hideout, promising to send up supplies and
join them later. The following day he took Vanrennan for a drive
along the coast road and finally finished up alongside the Slim River.
They found a hideout a few miles north of Tanjong Malim. Before
leaving Vanrennan, Chapman promised to contact him before the
16th and in the meantime would send him supplies and equipment.

At this point Jim Gavin arrived in Kuala Lumpur as someone was
later to remark with explosives in one pocket and detonators in the
other. Discussing the plans with Spencer Chapman he learnt that
Chapman proposed to use Tras as a rendezvous point.

The plan was based on the assumption that the British would
launch a counter-attack within three months, using the Australian
division being withdrawn from the Middle East and the anticipated
air support from the Americans. Although the units behind the lines

would act independently they would be co-ordinated to support the expected counter-attack. Each unit would have three months' supply of stores which could be replenished. If things didn't work out as planned and it was decided to evacuate the teams, they could assemble at Tras and make their way to Trong where Vanrennan had made friends with the native fishermen. Using local boats they hoped to make their way to British lines, wherever that might be.

On 3rd January Chapman ordered the latest volunteers, Graham and Hembry, to join Vanrennan at Tanjong Malim. On their way they called in to see two old friends working as Vehicle Park Scouts for 11 Division. Their two friends were responsible for finding new locations for lorry parks each time 11 Division retreated. Over a few drinks Graham and Hembry explained they were part of a secret organisation putting men behind the lines. Their two friends, Chrystal and Robinson, listened with interest. The job seemed more exciting than the one they were involved in. After their friends left for Tanjong Malim, Chrystal and Robinson made some excuse to visit Kuala Lumpur.

At Dalley's bungalow which Warren was using as SOE HQ, he was interviewing a new recruit, 101 STS trained and LDF officer Pat Gardin. He was surprised to be interruped and told that two middle-aged visitors were asking for him by name and they wanted to join his show. As far as he was concerned the operation was secret. When they were shown into his office he learnt that his visitors were Graham's friends. Both World War veterans they had taken the precaution of evacuating their families and were now without domestic ties. Their age didn't worry Warren, what mattered was that they appeared keen. After a quick medical they were passed A1 but the MO thought they were mad to be doing this type of thing at their age. Back at Warren's office they were commissioned and enrolled in Pat Gardin's party. By the end of the day Warren had enrolled two more volunteers for this group. One was a New Zealander, Frank Quayle, an ex-miner from Siam and a demolitions instructor with 101 STS, and the other was Clarke Haywood, a RN officer in the Reserve, who before the war worked for a well known firm of electricians in Kuala Lumpur.

A fourth group was also being formed, this time under the command of another 101 STS trained ex-Siam miner, Captain Stubbington RE. He had taken part in the abortive SOE attempt to seize strategic positions in Siam and when the British army failed to reach them, he and his party escaped encirclement and fled to Malaya.

Following in the wake of the advancing enemy troops they eventually bypassed the fighting and reached Kuala Lumpur where they again made contact with SOE. After spending some weeks in Singapore, at the school, they were brought forward for this mission.

Stubbington was a veteran of the First World War and came to Malaya in the twenties. He had lived and worked mainly around the Raub to Benta Road and it was in this familiar area that he decided to set up his camp.

While Warren was busy recruiting, Chapman was busy preparing a master list of equipment, stores and supplies needed for a prolonged stay in the jungle. Briefly the plan was for each party to be supplied with a copy of the list to which it added its own requirements. The role of quartermaster fell on Jim Gavin who had just delivered a large load of supplies from 101 STS. These were stored in Haywood's bungalow. After checking the lists Gavin set out in his lorry to see what he could scrounge from nearby army supply depots. Whether it was his charm or the fact that the Japanese were less than 100 miles from the city, he found depot officers gave him every assistance. He soon had his lorry loaded with food, clothing, arms, equipment, medical supplies and stores and by good luck he discovered one ordnance depot had large rubber bags, ideal for preserving buried supplies in the jungle.

When each leader of the stay-behind parties chose a site the race was to stock it before the Japanese overran the area. The strained transport pool was organised by Sergeant Frisken who kept his severely taxed vehicles on the road despite constant strafing by enemy aircraft. The lorries were frequently chased by fighters and although three lorries were lost all the drivers arrived back uninjured.

Both Gardin and Stubbington's parties left Kuala Lumpur on 4th January and found the roads jammed with exhausted soldiers of 22 Brigade, packed aboard lorries jammed nose to tail on the Bentong to Kuala Lumpur road. Having fought their way out of Kuanton they had been stationed around Bentong but hardly had they settled down than they were hauled off to support the Local Defence Force who were trying to hold back a Japanese seaborne landing on the west coast at Telak Anson. Into this mêlée rode two separate convoys from SOE.

Gardin found Bentong bursting with troops, some in tents among the rubber trees and other sleeping in trucks or empty and abandoned European colonial style bungalows. The hospital was full of wounded and ambulances were taking the overflow on to Kuala Lumpur: the police station was deserted and the town was almost empty of local civilians. Almost by the hour small parties of European civilians arrived from the east coast. Some had been rescued by the army before it retreated, just plucked out of their homes minutes before the enemy arrived and others had been given sufficient warning and made a more orderly withdrawal, mixed in with the tail of the retreat. These made their way to the rest house hoping for overnight accommodation before continuing their journey to Kuala Lumpur. They were disappointed. The place was already crowded with brigade officers and Gardin's men.

The latter were looked upon with some suspicion. They were not obviously soldiers, mused the battle-weary brigade officers, they each belonged to separate units – RE's, RASC and the like – and they acted furtively especially at night when they left for some nocturnal happenings; in lorries packed with equipment their units had the utmost difficulty in getting.

Gardin's base had been previously looked at and stores had been dumped and hidden in the jungle nearby along the Karak Road. His party left again at night, to avoid detection and careless talk, and spent their time splitting the supplies into small scattered dumps. One morning when they had finished their night's work, they made their way back to the lorry only to discover the wheels bedded down in marshy ground. After spending most of the morning trying to push the lorry, digging out its wheels and laying a carpet of *attap* they finally gave up and breached security. One of them set out and made contact with the nearest army unit with a plea for help.

Stubbington's ill-fated party had set off in two lorries: whereas Gardin and his men turned south to Karak, they headed north towards Bentong. His party consisted of four tin miners, Rand, Pearson and Darby and a Malay Volunteer Shika Bin Lida. They were later joined by another Volunteer, Lieutenant Elkin. He left Warren on the 6th in a car crammed with more supplies and a wireless receiver. Unfortunately eleven miles from Raub he found the bridge destroyed by the retreating soldiers and had to abandon the car. On the other side of the bridge he scrounged a bicycle and loaded it with as much as he could carry and was last seen by the disbelieving Royal Engineers wobbling his way and peddling heavily towards the advancing enemy. In fact they were still many miles away and Elkin perspired his way along empty roads for some hours before he turned off into the jungle without meeting anyone.

As supplies became available the SOE organisation, in Sergeant Frisken's vehicles, ran them forward to the stay-behind parties. One of these runs took place on the 5th with Jim Gavin driving. He had supplies and equipment for Vanrennan's party, just north of Tanjong Malim on the Selangor-Perak border. The town was being used by Brigadier Paris as a supply base and was full of lorry-towed field guns and fresh troops moving up to the new defence line at Slim River. The town was being stripped for action. Most of the local population had fled – which wasn't unusual and those who remained locked themselves behind their doors. With almost all the planters in the 'Volunteers' the Club stood empty. The General Military Hospital was being evacuated but because the railway station had been demolished in an air raid, the stretcher-borne patients were being carried along the track for some miles to a waiting Red Cross train.

After clearing the town Jim Gavin tucked himself on to the tail of a convoy moving north and eventually turned off the main road, up a dirt track which followed the town's long water pipeline, until he found the stay-behind party waiting for him beside the track. Sitting on their haunches nearby was a gang of coolies waiting to do the humping. As soon as he appeared in sight the group broke up and ran towards him and he was soon surrounded by a cheerful, voluble, gesticulating, bettelnut chewing crowd of Tamils. He had hardly stopped before the tailboard was lowered and the supplies heaved out and stacked just inside the jungle. While this was going on Gavin drew Vanrennan aside and brought him up to date with the latest position. He also passed on the news that Spencer Chapman was proposing to join them sometime during the next 48 hours, but not later than the 16th.

In the late afternoon Jim Gavin drove off and the Tamils began to move the remainder of their stores deeper into the jungle. The Tamils kept up their endless chatter and everyone slipped and scrambled along the muddy monsoon-flooded tracks, brushing against the rain-soaked bushes carrying heavy loads. All the time flies and mosquitoes swarmed around the party and leeches, hanging from trees like bunches of fruit, dropped on the unsuspecting victim.

When Jim Gavin arrived back at Dalley's bungalow he found that Captain Broome had arrived with the first batch of 101-trained Chinese guerrillas. Their leader was the very amiable Tan Chen King who, it was said, would cut your throat without hesitation – but in a very friendly way. The school had sent the guerrillas' supplies in large crates and these needed to be broken open and repacked for the Chinese into man-carrying packs.

The guerrillas' escorting officer, Richard Broome, had been a district officer in Ipoh when he was asked to help the SOE put the Chinese into north Malaya. He welcomed the idea and asked whether a very good friend, John Davis, with the police in Singapore – so he thought – could also help out.

By the time the message reached John Davis he was in Segimat about to walk with Shepherd across the main range towards Kuanton. 'We couldn't get a valve for Tyson and Cottrill,' remembers John Davis, 'and we were trying to reach the party with a message recalling them.' Together Davis and Shepherd walked for some three days until they reached the Karatag River. 'Here we found two Kwangsai who were prepared to take a message to Sungai Lembing. I returned to join the SOE but Shepherd insisted on continuing with the Kwangsai for two more days before returning himself.' When Davis arrived back in Singapore he was told to report to 101 STS at Tanjong Balai, a place he knew well from pre-war parties at the house. The message reached Tyson and his little group buried the wireless equipment and set off for Segimat where they expected Rosher to be waiting for them.

In Kuala Lumpur Tan Chen King the guerrilla leader took over one of the rooms in Dalley's bungalow for an office and decorated the walls with pictures of Stalin and Churchill. The Malayan Communist Party known by its initials MCP was originally formed by Ho Che Minh and in more recent years its goal was to drive the British from the Malayan Peninsula and free the people from the slavery of colonialism. It had built up a large secret organisation with its own underground army. This could rely on wide support from the local Chinese communities which would provide the guerrilla fighters with both food and local intelligence. Russia was seen by the local party leaders as the cradle of Communism. That country was now locked in a life and death struggle with Germany which was, coincidentally, an enemy of Britain's – so the anti-British Chinese guerrillas now found themselves allied to the British.

The guerrillas being trained at the Chunjun School had been selected for the Perak Patrol while the Chinese Broome had brought with him from 101 STS had been chosen from recruits who lived in five other Federated States. With pressure building up along the

Slim River front Warren was getting anxious to put the guerrillas into the jungle before a break-through occurred: so the Perak Patrol led by a fanatical Communist Lai Foo, accompanied by his attractive wife, was placed north of the Slim River and Vanrennan's party. Lai Foo came from wealthy parents in Sitiawn, a small coastal town in north Perak.

This patrol was to form the basis of the 5th anti-Japanese Perak Regiment under the command of 'Colonel Itu'. Within a few weeks the patrol had been joined by a further 200 volunteers including another resident from Sitiawn, a fresh faced, 22-year-old Chen Ping, who was soon to become leader of the entire underground army. He later led the same army against the post-war British Administration.

Before a second patrol could be put into the same area the British 11 Division fell back to the Slim River defence line where it was overtaken by the Japanese vanguard and overwhelmed. This defeat gave Perak State to the Japanese and the opportunity was lost to put in more guerrillas. It was decided to put the remainder into the adjoining state, Selangor, which itself was on the point of being overrun.

The second patrol, under the command of Tan Chen King, set up its base at Batu Caves an area well known for its limestone caves and largely populated by Chinese communities. This was to be an ideal recruiting ground for the guerrillas. The next patrol went some sixty miles south of Kuala Lumpur and almost a hundred miles ahead of the Japanese but it only took the enemy some two weeks to cover that distance. They were placed in the tin mining area of Jelebu in Negri Sembilan: another area heavily populated by Chinese. Their leader, a Chinese named Martin, was still in Singapore acting as course translator for the second guerrilla intake at the school. He joined them later after walking some hundred miles through Japanese-occupied countryside.

While Warren was organising a seven day crash course for the guerrillas, Rosher had put in two parties on the east coast and now arrived back in the city to find that GHQ were anxious about his safety. When he radioed his safe arrival he was ordered back to Singapore.

Knott had already been recalled. His departure left Sergeant Cross with the sole responsibility for the station and the network of agents transmitting intelligence from behind enemy lines.

The following morning Warren had a visitor – Sergeant Cross. In the last few days, since Christmas in fact, although it seemed weeks, Cross had provided SOE, mainly Chapman, with wireless contact with Singapore and trained Chinese wireless operators for various undercover activities; now he had a problem as he explained to Colonel Warren. Standing to attention in front of Warren, who sat behind his desk in the bedroom which was now his office, Cross spoke of Rosher's sudden departure and his final order to evacuate the wireless station to Segimat. But Rosher had lost all the unit's transport on his latest mission to Kuanton and in view of the close working relationship between SOE and SIS could they spare him a lorry? In the distance enemy planes were bombing the city and they could hear the thud of the explosions and the bark of anti-aircraft guns. 'Where was Knott?' Cross explained again that all the officers had left for Singapore. Could SOE help him, he pleaded? Warren's silence was caused because, not knowing of the recall, he was considering the reasons for what seemed to be Rosher's undue haste. Waving his hand to Cross he indicated he should stand at ease then used the phone to contact Divisional HQ. Reassured that the city wasn't being evacuated, he replaced the receiver and told the sergeant to see Captain Brasher who dealt with Intelligence matters in HQ and he would look after him. Eventually he scrounged a civilian lorry from the motor pool.

The irony was that less than fifty miles away the Japanese had captured more than 500 army vehicles and ample stocks of petrol.

Spearheaded by light tanks the enemy troops smashed through 11 Division's front line and swept aside the reserve units and seized the bridge over the Slim River. After nineteen hours of heavy fighting the enemy destroyed two British brigades, captured 1,200 prisoners, vehicles, guns, ammunition, medical and food supplies: hundreds of Allied soldiers were killed although some 2,000 were thought to have escaped into the jungle. Some of these began to filter into Tanjong Malim bringing first hand news of the disaster.

Spencer Chapman was seriously ill in bed with malaria when he heard the news. His concern was for Vanrennan's party and although he tried to get a message through, the dispatch rider returned with the report that the Army had blown all the bridges this side of the river to slow the Japanese advance on the city. As he was keen to join his men behind the lines despite his fever, he spent all the next day trying to persuade Jim Gavin to drive him to Tras to join Harvey and Sartin. Gavin reckoned he was too ill to join the stay-behind party but eventually he reluctantly agreed to drive him there in Chapman's car.

The whole situation was against Gavin's better judgement. Chapman was still far from well; no one really knew how far the Japanese had advanced and, in a marvellous piece of understatement, HQ had

said that the military situation was fluid. Before leaving the bungalow they loaded the car's dicky with explosives, weapons, food and
some medical supplies. Driving through the heavily cratered streets,
past wrecked vehicles and bomb damaged houses, they left the urban
area for roads bordered with rubber plantations full of tented Army
camps. All along the road military vehicles were streaming back and
as they approached the next line of defence they drove through an
increasing number of heavily manned road blocks. Every bridge was
a hive of activity as Royal Engineers prepared each one for demolition until finally Gavin, who was driving, ran out of road as a Sapper
officer eloquently put it. His men were about to blow the bridge and
the enemy were expected at any minute. Chapman and Gavin had in
fact driven through the front line and the Engineers were the only
resistance between them and the enemy. It took Gavin all his charm,
talk of a secret mission and finally the fact that he out-ranked his fellow officer that he was allowed over the bridge. He also extracted a
promise that the bridge wouldn't be blown for two hours unless, of
course, the enemy appeared before them. The remainder of the journey to Tras was eerie, nothing moved, no civilians nor vehicles and
thankfully no enemy. When he reached Harvey's party at Sungei
Sempan Chapman's temperature was 103° and Gavin rather unceremoniously unpacked the boot, left Chapman in Harvey's care
wished everyone good luck and raced Chapman's Ford V8 back
along the road to Kuala Lumpur.

Meanwhile, coinciding with their departure from the city the new
Supreme Commander, General Wavell, arrived in Kuala Lumpur to
see, first hand, the situation for himself. After talking with the divisional commanders he found his worst fears confirmed and it was
apparent that what was left of 3 Corps would fall apart if it tried to
repeat the step-by-step retreat as it withdrew through Negri Sembilan. Wavell ordered the Australians to form a defence line across
Johore from Mersing to Malacca and then gave General Heath,
commander of 3 Corps, 72 hours to abandon Kuala Lumpur and fall
back behind the new Australian line. This would mean a retreat of
100 miles in one move, handing over Negri Sembilan without a fight.

When Warren heard the news he immediately made enquiries
about whether his men could take part in the scorched earth policy of
destruction of military installations.

In Gavin's absence the city had been transformed and as he
approached along the main road he could see long, black clouds,
drifting across the city and suburbs dropping oily smuts like snow

flakes. Partly burnt papers and ash added to the pollution as military and civilian administrators made bonfires of their records and files. Elsewhere in the city supply dumps were blown up, railway lines taken apart and rolling stock destroyed. As he drove into the suburbs he found the roads choked with vehicles of every size and description all heading for Seremban, some forty miles away. Motoring across the city and against the traffic flow he saw the slow moving never ending line of vehicles were almost bumper to bumper. Dispatch riders on their motor cycles moved in and out of the traffic made up of fire engines, steam rollers, staff cars, breakdown vehicles, wood burning civilian lorries, and battered army transports – all packed with exhausted soldiers.

Turning off the main road he drove through streets of empty colonial bungalows with their well-kept lawns and flower beds. The only people to be seen were the occasional servants who stayed loyally to look after their masters' possessions. The looters had not yet swept through the district. At Dalley's bungalow Warren merely confirmed the obvious that it was cut and run and the retreat was being covered by what was left of the Local Defence Force under the command of Major Angus Rose. This racially mixed force was being stretched out in a thin line from Port Dickson to Kuala Lumpur and the badly mauled 11 Division was filtering through the undermanned road blocks. They were expecting to be reinforced by some recently arrived Indian troops.

Dalley and his men were moving out the following day, Gavin was told, and Warren and the rest of the party had berths on the last train leaving Kuala Lumpur that night. He had arranged, however, for Gavin, a fellow Sapper from 101 STS, Lieutenant White, and six other ranks to destroy the airfield hurriedly evacuated by the RAF. After being briefed, Jim Gavin now suddenly feeling very hungry, wandered into the kitchen where he found Dalley cooking dinner. He confirmed that his counter-intelligence unit was moving out in the morning but he had a lot of valuables and keepsakes which he didn't want to risk in what could be a fighting withdrawal. Gavin remembered the rubber bags, some still strewn around the grounds. Why not use these to bury what couldn't be carried? Good idea, thought Dalley, and they left the food to cook itself while they collected all the valuables and dug a deep hole in the flower beds by torchlight.

The following day, a Sunday, Gavin, White and the six other ranks drove across the almost empty city to the RAF airfield where they found a squadron leader in charge of 24 airmen trying to crater the runway, opening fuel tanks to waste the oil and cutting telephone cables. The squadron leader seemed a little nervous but reassured by the soldiers' presence. When their convoy swung through the gates he thought they were Japs he told Gavin with an embarrassed smile. While he listened to their plans Gavin's men were already at work laying mines and setting booby-traps, even the toilets had their share. Several long delay fuses left over from the supplies brought up from the school were planted to ensure a daily continuity of explosions. When these were used up they resorted to using camphor balls as detonators, a little idea originated by Gavin at Lochailort. Another idea used for the first time was bullet mines. This ingenious device looked like a slim piece of metal pipe about four inches long and ½ inch in diameter. This was pressed into the ground with one's foot. Into this was placed very carefully a specially adapted .303 rifle bullet a small spring and detonator. The bullet sat with about ¼ inch of its tip protruding above the lip of the pipe and ground. An unsuspecting foot would press the bullet down on the detonator and its owner would walk with a limp for the rest of his life.

Before completing their work the SOE stretched small lengths of trip-wire across paths. One end was attached to the ring of a hand-grenade and when an unsuspecting foot caught on the trip-wire, the grenade pin would be pulled free and – !!

About 3.00 p.m. the squadron leader, who agreed to act as scout, arrived back to report that the enemy had reached the outskirts of the city. In half an hour Gavin and his men concealed all traces of their work and left hurriedly. At the time, Jim Gavin estimated that the Japanese would take three months to clear the airfield but after suffering heavy casualties the Japanese used Australian prisoners of war from Puda prison. They did the job in three days.

Gavin's small convoy of SOE and RAF were probably the last organised body of servicemen to leave Kuala Lumpur. They drove past the dirty white shape of Puda prison, now empty but soon to become the home of hundreds of Australian and British prisoners of war. The railway station was burning and looters roamed the streets, going from shop to shop, taking all they could carry. The streets were littered with discarded loot and abandoned files. Dead and wounded civilians lay around unattended. One dressed in a sari sat hunched against a tree as if asleep. Across her chest was a line of bullet holes. Nearby lay the nude body of a pregnant woman her clothes lost in a nearby bomb blast. Overhead a lone enemy plane patrolled the sky flying in a wide circle above the city.

Leaving the city behind the three lorries drove for hours along deserted roads littered with undamaged vehicles. Most of them had simply run out of petrol and had been left undamaged. While they still had supplies the team dealt with them, leaving behind a series of explosions and burning transport. They were still uncertain how quickly the enemy had followed up the withdrawal or whether it had by-passed the city.

The following day they stopped at a road block near Gemas on the borders of Johore. Unseen in the roadside jungle lay men of the 2/30 AIF*. For a few moments nothing happened then a tall Australian in a bush hat appeared and demanded to know where the hell did they think they were going? When he learnt they were from Kuala Lumpur he said, 'You'd better come and see the Commander – he'd like to know what you saw.' For the next few hours Jim Gavin found himself being passed from one senior officer to the next until he eventually found himself briefing the red-headed, fiery veteran of the First World War, General Bennett, Commander of the AIF.

Only hours before the arrival of the Japanese, they left behind a city in the grip of lawlessness. Warehouses were being broken into and looted. Gangs of looters roamed the streets scattered with broken glass, files and papers. The prison and the mental hospital had been emptied and the police disbanded. Criminal gangs were roaming the streets settling old scores. For 24 hours the city became a civilian battlefield. When the Japanese arrived they settled the problem of looting – they just shot the looters.•

In their desire to get away some British soldiers threw away arms and explosives and the MCP later collected a large amount. Young Chinese and Indian teenagers also collected a large amount on a freelance basis. Within three days of the Japanese occupation a ground swell of resistance began to take place inside the city.

Along the Ipoh road a party of three young Sikhs cut and rolled up large sections of enemy field telephone wire and dumped it into the river. Later two Chinese teenagers armed themselves with discarded British .303's and ambushed and killed a three-man Japanese street patrol. Unfortunately they were caught and beheaded. Throughout the city arms dumps were raided, individual soldiers were sniped at and railway petrol tankers blown up. Near the museum a passing Sikh lobbed a grenade amongst a party of Japanese killing six. A

* Australian Imperial Forces.

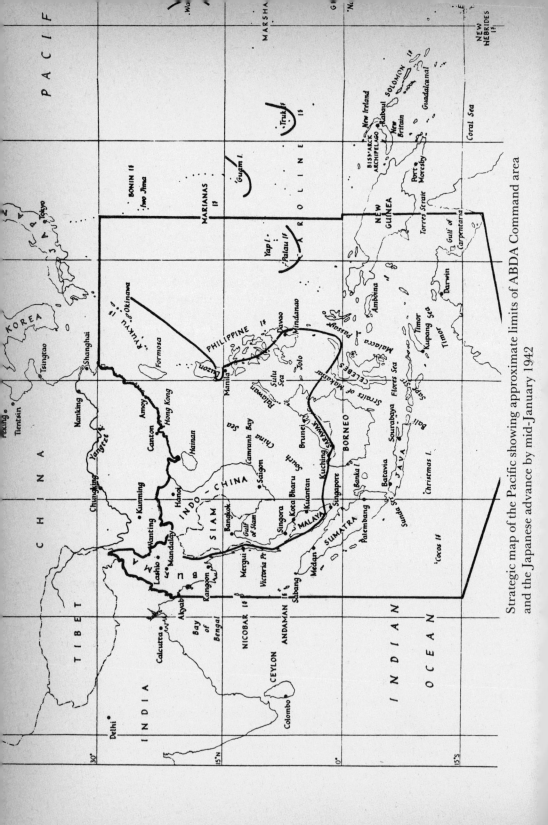

Strategic map of the Pacific showing approximate limits of ABDA Command area and the Japanese advance by mid-January 1942

Chinese cyclist wasn't so lucky: the grenade he threw failed to explode and he was captured. After being tortured he eventually died. The mobilized MCP guerrillas, now calling themselves the Malayan anti-Japanese Army, soon became a catalyst for anti-Japanese feeling. Politically unbiased volunteers went into the jungle and joined up.

This situation was repeated in most large towns in north Malaya. The total effect of this resistance can be judged by the 18th Division's induction.

The Japanese 18th Division which reached Singorra on 20th January was rushed south to join in the last battle for Singapore. Trains full of supplies and packed with troops rattled and swayed their way south. One train finished up a wreck full of barbecued soldiers after being ambushed by the Perak Patrol. Japanese-occupied police stations were also attacked and their arms stolen but the Japanese answer was swift and cruel. Nearby villages were surrounded and the inhabitants rounded up for questioning. Some were beheaded to encourage others to talk, while their women-folk were taken away to army brothels.

Unaware of the hornets' nest being created to the north Spencer Chapman and his party trekked thirty miles through mountainous jungle to Vanrennan's old hideout near Tanjong Malim which they found empty. After resting for a few days and trying to discover what had happened to the party they began to carry out raids against enemy vehicles using the nearby roads. Convoys of captured British lorries parked overnight in lay-bys received the business end of grenade attacks. Lorries travelling through the night were ambushed and sleepy enemy soldiers stumbling from burning vehicles were shot down. When the convoys began to use escorts Chapman changed the targets to trains and the railways. The combined attacks on the enemy's transport system almost strangled the supply route but survivors who had escaped the ambushes now ran into more trouble, this time from Tan Chen King's men.

Well established in Batu Caves he began to recruit large numbers of guerrilla fighters. Using the skills taught by Warren's men his volunteers were trained to use weapons and explosives. Lacking arms, ammunition and clothes the enemy dead were stripped before guerrillas left the scene. One useful addition to his small force was Sergeant Regan who had been brought in by the sympathisers. Regan had been left behind on the River Krai by SIS to carry out an intelligence gathering mission. After losing contact with base, as it withdrew down the peninsula, Regan trekked almost 150 miles through the jungle before being found by the Communists. He now set up a training programme for all the guerrillas and joined them and their raids. Further south enemy supply convoys and reinforcements were ambushed by Martin's patrol in Negri Sembilan and later the survivors found the road bridges blown up by Captain Smyllie's party which had been put into the jungle near Labis in Johore.

As they neared the front line facing Singapore, the journey became a nightmare as they ran into groups of Allied soldiers cut off behind the lines and retreating to Singapore who shot-up anything that moved.

It was not only the Communists who began to form anti-Japanese guerrilla units, supporters of the Chinese Nationalist Government, the KMT, were also launching attacks against Japanese moving through their area and the Sultan of Pahang gave his support to an army of 700 Malays and Indians under the leadership of Yeup Mahiden. Besieged in Singapore and lacking wireless contact with the guerrillas and the stay-behind parties, General Percival was unaware of the growing tide of resistance behind enemy lines and the destruction of enemy supplies. Instead his only option he could envisage was surrender.

CHAPTER TEN

Johore Stay-behind Parties

This chapter outlines three hectic weeks in which the Orient Mission frantically tried to train and put both Chinese guerrillas and European parties into Johore before successive areas were overrun by the enemy.

It is written to give the reader some feeling of the atmosphere of everything happening at once and, to quote Jim Gavin, if it seemed like a good idea they went out and did it.

The school had become the operational base and when Killery left, the offices at Cathay Building became more of a liaison point with other departments. Although Warren was officially the liaison officer between GHQ and the Mission he was now taking a more positive and active role in its direction while, at the same time, recruiting his own small private army.

I

Mid-January 1942

When Killery returned from Chunking at the end of November he had in mind sending Major Jim Gavin back to set up the proposed Special Training School. Captain Jack Knott would go with him to provide wireless training and open up a wireless link with Singapore. The outbreak of war with Japan temporarily set back the planning but by the end of December Killery decided to send a party from 101 STS to China. When he tried to get Knott back from SIS he discovered that Rosher, Knott and a party of Europeans were missing near Kuanton, which was under heavy attack from the Japanese. When he learnt that the town was lost he feared the worst. Eventually much to his relief Knott came on the air from a deserted rubber planter's bungalow, somewhere on the edge of the jungle after slipping through Japanese lines. As soon as he could be reached he was ordered to report to Killery in Singapore. In the meantime Jim Gavin had gone north to join Warren's raiding party against Taiping where the Japanese were concentrating their forces for seaborne attacks along the west coast. Killery wasn't too worried about

Gavin's departure as he expected him back by mid-January. By then the raid should have taken place or failing that the overall plan was to abandon Kuala Lumpur on the 16th.

In the middle of his preparations for the Chunking mission Killery received two pieces of disconcerting news which immediately affected his plans. At a recent meeting between President Roosevelt and Churchill agreement had been reached to form a unified command for SW Pacific. The overall command which included the Philippines was given to General Wavell. The Chinese Nationalist leader General Chiang Kai-Shek was the new Commander in Chief of all land and air forces on the Chinese mainland including Indo-China and Siam. All operations in China would be taken over by a new British Unit, 204 Mission, based in Chunking. MEW's man in China John Keswick and survivors from SOE operations in Hong Kong would join this new body. The situation was compounded when the Chinese demanded that SOE's Mission in China should be commanded by a Chinese general. When Keswick refused he and his men were ordered by the Chinese to pack up and leave. The British Ambassador tried to intervene but Chiang Kai-Shek made himself unavailable.

However the full extent of the China problem wasn't apparent in Singapore and Killery continued with his plans to send a training unit to Chunking.

When Jack Knott returned to Singapore about the second week in January he remembers how ill Killery looked. He'd developed a nervous twitch and looked very tired. Nevertheless he greeted Knott warmly. 'Congratulations – you've been promoted major.' 'Fine,' thought Knott, 'but I'd prefer some bloody good wireless equipment instead.'

Through the open window behind Killery, Knott could see smoke rising from smouldering *godowns* along the waterfront. The harbour was empty except for a large liner recently arrived with hundreds of half-trained reinforcements. It was now embarking women and children. Facing him across the table Killery got down to business straight away. He wanted Knott to get his men together, scrounge what equipment he could lay his hands on and leave as soon as possible for Rangoon. When he arrived he should open up a link with Kranji and also listen out for Spencer Chapman who had gone behind the lines with a wireless transmitter. In the last few days Warren and Gavin had managed to put some half dozen stay-behind parties behind enemy lines and these had been joined by Freddy, now senior British officer behind-the-lines and guerrillas liaison officer. Unfortunately no one told the guerrillas and Freddy's first twelve months were spent trying to establish that fact.*

Recalling this briefing, Knott mentions that he was never warned that he may go to China. Possibly by this time Killery was treating the China operation with more circumspection.

A few short steps down the corridor from Killery's office the Free French Special Operations section led by Baron de Langlade were beginning to pack up and leave for China, which now offered a better base for its operations in Indo-China than Singapore. Its original plans to launch raids against Indo-China had been cancelled because of the increased enemy air and naval activity throughout the China Sea. The SOE was asked to help the French with the travel arrangements and appointed a French-speaking ex-rubber planter, Captain Birnie, as its escort officer. He took with him his wife. All French officers were issued with false papers showing them as British and 101 STS was raided for special explosives, Knott's precious 'suitcase' wireless set and supplies.

About the second week in January Wavell returned from Kuala Lumpur where he had been to see the front line problems for himself. What he saw shocked him. He realised that 11 Division was so exhausted that it would disintegrate if faced with a step-by-step retreat from Kuala Lumpur. He ordered General Bennett to move his Australians forward to form a line from east to west across north Johore. They were to be joined by reinforcements now pouring into Singapore. The battered 11 Division was to pull back through the Australian lines and regroup around Segimat in Johore. Negri Sembilan was to be given up without a fight. He told Percival that if the new line couldn't be held then the mainland was to be abandoned. Before leaving for his new HQ in Java he dictated his plans for the island's defence to Percival.

II

On 18th January when Warren approached Singapore on the last train from Kuala Lumpur he noticed the island was covered in a

---

* This was probably due more to Loi Tak MCP General Secretary than any criticism of SOE contacts. In view of his future liaison with the Japanese and the betrayal of guerrilla leaders in 1942 to the Japanese he may have kept the information to himself.

smoke haze and as the train crossed the causeway he could see oily black clouds mushrooming from the Naval Base which he assumed was the result of an air raid. At the station a long line of ambulances and lorries were drawn up near a platform crowded with nurses. The area was full of tired soldiers, baggage, casualties on stretchers and porters. After pushing his way through the mass of people he eventually begged a lift to the Naval Base on a lorry packed with sailors from the *Repulse* and *Prince of Wales* who had been helping out in Kuala Lumpur. Driving through the outskirts of the town he could see that Singapore had been heavily bombed. There were no air raid shelters for civilians and in the cratered streets Chinese were scrambling amongst the smouldering wreckage of their homes searching for survivors. One school of thought imagined the high water table would flood the trenches while the civilian government believed it would be bad for the morale of the Asians to admit the need for air raid shelters.

At the Naval Base Warren found his colleagues packing. They were leaving with Admiral Layton on board HMS *Dragon* to join Wavell's new ABDA Headquarters in Java. The Base was being evacuated, he was told, and the oil dumps destroyed. Most of the RN ships mainly Australian had already left. All that remained were a few local steamers converted to minesweepers and a small number of destroyers. Warren was astounded: the very reason for the battle on the mainland was to protect the Naval Base. With the Navy gone and the RAF almost destroyed he considered that it was a complete waste to pour in additional men and supplies. As far as he was concerned, 'it was a busted flush'.

Later after he had a shower and a change of uniform he set out for Cathay Building. Before he left his batman told him that in future his Chinese dhobieman wanted everyone to pay cash – the monthly chit system had been stopped. Throughout the island every shopkeeper stopped credit. The grapevine had sent out its early warning of the impending disaster. Because of the increased demands for coins and notes the local mint was ordered to print more.

At sandbagged Cathay Building he found Killery also on the point of leaving. Jim Gavin's friend 'Nixon the Banker' had already left for Java as a one man advance party to set up SOE's new offices at ABDA HQ. After bringing Warren up to date with the latest Chinese position Killery said he wanted Jim Gavin to leave as soon as possible for Rangoon. Warren disagreed. As far as he was concerned it was imperative that the Chinese guerrillas under training at 101 STS should be placed into Johore before the mainland was given up. In Kuala Lumpur Gavin had been Warren's right-hand man, finding supplies and equipment, keeping the transport running and co-ordinating the logistics with Broome and Davis. It was important, Warren believed, for Jim Gavin to stay long enough to give support to the Johore operation. Reluctantly Killery agreed and left for Java leaving Goodfellow, his deputy, in charge of Malayan operations.

III

At Tanjong Balai Trappes-Lomax and his men were concentrating on training and putting in the Chinese and European stay-behind parties. In bomb-scarred Cathay Building Warren and Goodfellow examined the problem of creating supply dumps for the guerrillas. As John Davis soon discovered the main problem was to create the dumps before the Japanese captured the area. The rapid enemy advance, held temporarily by the Australians at Gemas, led to the dumps being lost before the Chinese could take them over. The solution worked out by John Davis was to take one of the guerrillas under training with him when he searched for a suitable site. In this way if the dump fell behind the enemy lines Davis's companion could lead his patrol to the site.

The 11 Division's rearguard had lost contact with the Japanese during the rapid retreat through Negri Sembilan and this gave SOE breathing space to find and stock the next dump. On the 14th, Tampin, a Chinese tin mining town in north Johore, was packed with weary troops and nose to tail traffic all heading south. The one exception was stocky John Davis with a Chinese companion driving north against the traffic. About two miles beyond the town John Davis parked the lorry on the edge of the municipal rubbish dump. In the distance Brewster Buffaloes were attacking advancing enemy columns and the boom of their bombs could be heard echoing around the hills. He remembers finding what looked like a cave in the rubbish and decided to use it to hide the supplies.

It was dark when the Chinese guerrillas from 101 STS finally arrived, escorted by Broome and ferried by SIS and DALCO. The party took over a nearby abandoned rubber planter's bungalow. Talking to the guerrillas that night John Davis recollects that not one of the thirty Chinese had a watch so he gave their leader his.* In the

* He was later killed in Perak.

morning the party split into two patrols and one group led by Martin, the course translator, walked off into the rubber towards Jelebu in Negri Sembilan. The other remained local and took over the dump. Later in Segimat, Sergeant Cross, SIS, one of the drivers who took the Chinese to Tampin met a young DALCO officer who had been with him at the bungalow the previous night. The officer confided in Cross that he'd left Warren's 15 cwt truck behind. He'd just been carpeted by Warren and told to go back and fetch it. Cross volunteered to drive him back.

Tampin had been evacuated and it was dark by the time they reached the bungalow. The lorry stood where it was left a dark shadow against the building. Everything was silent, no cricket noises or croaking frogs, even the monkeys disturbed in the trees remained muted. The only sound came from the crunch of their army boots on the gravel as they searched the lorry for booby-traps. Finally the officer climbed in the cab and told Cross to make his own way back. The lorry's red lights had already disappeared down the estate road by the time Cross had made a three-point turn in the driveway. Driving on his side-lights Cross could pick out rows of rubber trees bordering the track. The main road was empty and dark flanked by towering dark shadows of jungle trees. The moon was not yet up. Putting his foot hard down on the accelerator Cross was becoming anxious to reach the Volunteers' road block. Some hours later he stopped at a signpost only to discover he'd been driving the wrong way and was well into enemy-held countryside. Doing another sharp three-point turn he raced back down the now moonlit road and reached British lines at daybreak without incident.

In January the Malayan Communist Party (MCP) sent out instructions mobilising its underground fighters for training in Singapore. Basil Goodfellow, Killery's deputy, approached Rosher and Colonel Dalley for help to collect the Johore Chinese and take them to the nearest railway stations. When one group* arrived at the school Warren learnt that SIS had sent its only lorry, driven by one of the 101 STS Chinese wireless operators, to tour the nearby Kampongs picking up the Communist trainees. On its way back it had been stopped by an Australian officer who commandeered it for his own men; forcing the Chinese to walk about thirty miles to the nearest station. In spite of this first encounter with the Army the Communists were full of enthusiasm and anxious to learn.

* The third course.

It was originally proposed that the Chinese would receive ten days' training but because of the rapid enemy advance down the peninsula the training period was reduced to five days. The programme was made up of instructions in unarmed combat, expounded by an ex-policeman from Shanghai who seemed to know every dirty trick not in the book, the use of explosives, setting booby-traps and instructions in anti-tank work. Most of Broome's and Davis's time was taken up with searching for and stocking supply dumps as well as escorting patrols to the front leaving little time for training stints. Another Chinese-speaking officer was needed and the Chinese Protectorate, a Malayan Civil Service department which looked after Chinese affairs in the Settlements and Federated States, recommended one of its staff – tall and well built Frank Brewer – who was with the Volunteers* at Sime Road transit camp. After all the red tape had been cleared, Trappes-Lomax sent a colour sergeant over on a motor-cycle to collect him but the Volunteers' Adjutant refused to let him go. He'd lost too many men to the Army and already had too many vacancies. Eventually, after a lot of unpleasantness, Trappes-Lomax sent 'no nonsense' Cochran to find Brewer and bring him to the school. Ignoring the formality of again approaching the adjutant, he tracked Brewer down doing sentry duty at a beach outpost and ordered him to climb into the lorry. Without further trouble Brewer found himself sitting alongside Cochran driving back to 101 STS. Captain Cochran was one of the many characters the school seemed to attract. An old China hand, he'd lost an eye when he and a lady friend were kidnapped by Chinese bandits when serving in north China. Both he and his friend were later ransomed. He was also a qualified parachutist, a rare thing in 1942, having completed his parachute course before anyone realised he only had one eye.

Private Frank Brewer was given a commission and joined a small group of specialist staff including Cochran and Parsons the miner who escaped from Siam and joined Gavin in Penang. Most of the Chinese students were literate and self-educated but not all spoke the Chinese dialects used by the staff at 101 STS. To overcome this problem Frank Brewer recommended a Chinese headmaster, a fellow Volunteer from Penang. The Chinese Protectorate again searched for and found him. He turned up at the school a few days later. Another problem was that no Chinese words existed for some of the sophisticated equipment being used. This had been overcome by

* Escaped from Penang with Warren's party.

mime and gesture. Now the Chinese captain and Frank Brewer spent
each night going through the notes for the following day's lectures
making up new words where none existed.

The Chinese students were very quick and took down copious
notes. They worked twelve hours a day under instruction and then
spent hours at night mugging up their notes. Brewer noted that they
assimilated information at a terrific speed.

Everyone at 101 STS was working at top speed to get the Chinese
ready before the Japanese occupied Johore. With Brian Passmore's
help, Jim Gavin, who had arrived back at the school on the 16th,
went around begging supplies and equipment as well as generally
supervising the logistics. Every day RASC lorries drove into camp
with crates of supplies, food and explosives. These were repacked
with the help of men from RASC Supplies Section, into man-carrying 30 lb packs. These were sealed in tins protected by universal rubber bags. Each pack was designed to last six men two days.

In a similar way arms, spare clothes, equipment and medical
supplies were packed in correct proportions. It was anticipated that
these loads would be dumped in the jungle and the packing must be
strong enough to deter jungle animals and keep out the rain and
dampness. One highlight of the month was Trappes-Lomax's prom-
otion to major but this was rather overshadowed by the continued
absence of news from Spencer Chapman.

One day Trappes-Lomax called Frank Brewer to the office to meet
four Nationalist Chinese, a colonel, major, captain and sergeant.
They were to start up a similar course elsewhere on the island for
Nationalist Chinese. He was asked to show the Chinese around the
school to give them some idea what special training was all about.
Later, after watching unarmed combat, controlled explosions using
home-made booby-traps and weapon training with Tommy guns,
Brewer explained the working of the Mills bomb. The Chinese hand-
grenades had a habit of exploding almost immediately one was pulled off the webbing. To demonstrate the difference Brewer took it
apart and explained the principle of the ten second fuse, keeping a
finger on the pin and demonstrating the throwing action. Finally,
standing on the lawn he threw the grenade over the wall into the
water below which exploded in a satisfying spout of sea water. His
guests nodded and smiled until, taking the pin out, Brewer handed a
grenade to the colonel. The smile froze as the colonel studied the
bomb in his hand and quickly passed it to his major who swiftly passed it to the captain. The captain passed it to the sergeant who

studied it impassively. Brewer almost jumping up and down by this time, urged the Chinese to fling the grenade. Suddenly the sergeant tossed it up into the air and from his now prone position Brewer saw it bounce a foot from his head. Immediately he was on his feet and gave the grenade one big kick which sent it sailing over the four feet high wall, exploding as it hit the sea.

IV

Warren had developed good contacts amongst the Dutch and about this time two Dutch officers appeared at his office. They commanded 150 Dutch native troops with a fierce reputation for jungle fighting. His liaison with the Dutch had paid off and these troops were their contribution to Warren's irregular warfare. He remembers witnessing an impressive ceremony at which the native troops swore loyalty to the British flag. The following day the officers were briefed by Warren and the men issued with safe conduct passes and supplies. After being trucked forward through Johore they assembled at the edge of the tarmac road before disappearing into the jungle. In less than forty-eight hours they walked into an Australian fire-box ambush and, mistaken for Japanese, were wiped out.

In Segimat Rosher's SIS unit was waiting for Tyson and Cottrill making their way cross-country from Kuanton. Rosher was anxious about their non-arrival particularly as pressure against the Australians was increasing. What wasn't known was that the Chinese wireless operator with Tyson had been murdered for his gold while buying supplies for the two Europeans hiding in the jungle. Now without money or guides and short of food and water the two Europeans trekked exhausted and starving through hilly jungle.

When Segimat was finally evacuated on 19th the SOE again drove through the rearguard to put in another stay-behind party, led by a former police officer, Captain T.N. Smyllie. He went into the jungle near Labis.

The same day Churchill, who seemed completely out of touch with the local situation, wrote to his Chief of Staff, General Ismay that 'the entire male population (of Singapore) should be employed upon constructing defence works'. True, but the services, who were still at loggerheads with commercial interests, could only offer local workers less than half the going rate for the job.

The following day in Singapore wave after wave of silver winged bombers, high in the sky and well out of reach of ack-ack, flew leisurely over Singapore. With their bomb bays open they emptied hundreds of tons over the congested city. Without air-raid shelters the Asian civilian population cowered in monsoon ditches. Warren on the roof of the Cathay Building saw nearby Holland Road being straddled with bombs, leaving a petrol tanker on fire and people buried in the monsoon ditches. Some distance away the Chinese quarter disappeared in a cloud of dust and smoke. Alongside the waterfront more warehouses caught on fire, either from direct hits or arsonists.

The enemy planes were using airfields at Kuanton and Kuala Lumur – the one Gavin had hoped to put out of action for three months. Within three days of its capture planes flying from Kuala Lumpur gave Singapore its heaviest raid.

In London 10,000 miles away Churchill told the Chiefs of Staff that a last ditch battle for Singapore was taking place and when the enemy's long range guns came within range of Singapore the island would become indefensible. In the debate that followed the Committee was of the opinion that as many forces as possible should be evacuated and used to beef up the defence of the Dutch East Indies. Churchill however wanted the reinforcements now steaming towards Singapore, to be reallocated to Burma to protect the Burma Road, China's life line. All this was contrary to the agreement with the Australian Government so when Sir Earle Page, the Australian Government's representative in London, heard about it he alerted his Government. They sent a strongly worded protest to Churchill who, despite his misgivings, later instructed Wavell that Singapore should be held to the last man. The fateful decision which abandoned an Army to its fate and was to send thousands of soldiers to their deaths working on the infamous death railway was based on political and not military considerations.

On Thursday the 22nd Warren and Goodfellow travelled by road into Johore to attend a conference of corps and divisional commanders at which Percival outlined the defence plan for Singapore. He envisaged a step-by-step withdrawal from Kluang to Singapore. The withdrawal would take place over three days and each night the rearguard would hold a line at milestone 44 at 32 and 25 before they finally crossed the causeway. The same day, following an enemy thrust along the coast which threatened to trap the Australians at Segimat, Percival ordered north Johore to be abandoned and a 90 miles defence line to be formed from east to west through Kluang.

When he arrived back at Cathay Building Warren ordered John

The Millionaire's House at Tanjong Balai.

Captain Trappes-Lomax in the house.

(*Left*) Captain Trappes-Lomax, Chief Instructor.

(*Below*) Major Jim Gavin and 'Peter' at 101 STS.

Davis to look for a supply dump site near Kluang and Jim Gavin to leave as soon as a flight was available for Rangoon.

Jim Gavin had found time during his nine month stay in Singapore to become friendly with the attractive daughter of the squadron leader based at Seletar. Pre-war Singapore was the ideal place for romance with lovely beaches, swaying palms and warm tropical nights. Now driving into town for their last evening together they watched the crude fingers of light searching the night skies for enemy bombers. Gavin drove carefully as some of the roads were cratered and in the Chinese quarter the streets were filled with debris. From outside the Raffles Hotel one could sometimes hear the deep-throated rumble of artillery blasting away in Johore. The Raffles carried on as normal. Its smart waiters served dinner and the dance orchestra played foxtrots and sambas for uniformed officers and Tuxedoed civilians entertaining their attractive female companions.

That night over dinner, Jim Gavin tried to hide his fears from Barbara. He knew no plans existed for any civilian evacuation and the possibility of the island withstanding a siege was negligible. Both realised that the chances of meeting again were remote and Gavin couldn't help but feel he was deserting her, as they exchanged next of kin's addresses in England and promised to write.

The following morning, Friday the 23rd, he gave Trappes-Lomax his final briefing before walking across the lawn to the waiting lorry. Throwing his small pack in beside the driver he told him to take him back to the Raffles Hotel, being used as an assembly point for airline passengers now that Seletar was under constant attack. Behind the Raffles, near the Synagogue, a long row of fly-covered bodies still waited for someone to claim them. Rapidly decomposing they began to smell.

In the hotel the 'Boys' dressed in spotless white uniforms served drinks to the waiting passengers. The flight was delayed because of another air-raid and Jim Gavin found himself sitting next to the pilot. When he remarked that he was surprised to see so many civilians on the flight the pilot explained that the flying boat was a normal commercial flight but priority was given to military personnel like himself. The pilot seemed tired and fed up and was moaning about the mix up on the passenger list which left one seat empty 'at a time like this'. He went on, 'If you know anyone who could use it you're welcome to it.' Without hesitation Jim Gavin blurted out 'I have – my wife'. The pilot brightened up. 'Well in that case how soon can you get her here?' 'How long have I got?' countered Gavin.

'About ten minutes here or thirty if she can make Seletar,' the pilot shouted after Gavin's retreating figure.

In the hotel foyer, surrounded by potted palms, Jim Gavin fumbled with the telephone and wondered where first to 'phone. At that time in the morning Barbara was normally helping out at the General Military Hospital recently evacuated from Tanjong Malim. Trying her home first a wave of relief swept over him when she answered. His first words without explanation were 'Will you marry me?' There was a long pause. 'Can I think about it?' she asked. 'No,' he replied, 'but if you will I have a seat for you on my flight.' 'How long do I have?' she demanded getting rather frantic. 'As long as it takes Brian Passmore to drive over and pick you up.' By this time Barbara was in a whirl. Could she find her mother? What would her father say? If she couldn't reach them should she leave a note saying – sorry I'm not at home but I've gone to Rangoon to get married! Desperately she asked, 'What can I bring.' 'Nothing,' he replied.

Forty-five minutes later on the jetty at Seletar Jim Gavin anxiously looked at his watch as he paced up and down. The other passengers had already embarked and the pilot standing by his side, told him he could only wait another five minutes. He didn't want to be caught in another raid. The aerodrome had been under constant attack and the flying boats were hidden amongst the off-shore islands. The area was badly hit. Gutted buildings stood deserted blackened with smoke. The grass was heavily cratered but the bomb-damaged roads had been filled in. Scattered around were roped-off holes with unexploded bombs nestling at the bottom. Checking his watch again Gavin finally accepted that Barbara wasn't coming and boarded the launch. At that moment a sports car, with its horn blaring, raced down the road dodging debris and stopped close by with a scream of brakes. Out leapt Barbara, with her hair flying behind her, with a smile on her face. In one hand she clutched a pillow-case with a change of clothes while in the other she held a bottle of champagne.

Because the air space around Malaya was controlled by Japanese fighters, the flight to Rangoon was routed through Java. Somewhere over the Lingga Group of Islands off the coast of south Sumatra the flying boat overflew a little coastal steamer SS *Rajputna* pounding its way towards the Banka Straits. On board were Major Knott and his Signals personnel also on the way to Rangoon. They had left the previous evening. All shipping was banned from leaving or entering Singapore during daylight hours because of the raids.

V

In Singapore Warren read the intelligence reports showing the steady Japanese encirclement of the Malayan barrier. Without meeting any opposition Japanese reinforcements, landing at Singorra, had force-marched across Siam crossed the mountains into Burma and captured Tavoy on the west coast of the peninsula with its harbour and airfield. This effectively cut off any overland route for reinforcements. Another message told him that U Saw, the Burmese Premier, was being accused of negotiating with the Japanese and detained. The enemy were ashore in Borneo, New Britain and New Guinea and there seemed every indication that they were heading for Australia.

Despite reinforcements pouring into Singapore the news from Johore was grim. 45 Brigade was cut off. Later it destroyed its heavy equipment and reserve ammunition and leaving the wounded behind the survivors broke out of the trap and escaped into the jungle. The RAF were searching for 22nd Indian Brigade also cut off and lost in the jungle.* Warren's Chinese guerrillas found about 100 who refused to join them. Later while trying to make their way back to British lines this group was ambushed and the survivors taken prisoner.

There were some 5,000 troops cut off and wandering in the jungle. A party of 1,000 reached Allied lines near the town of Benat. About 1,000 more, including Brigadier Challen, were captured fording a river and some 2,700 were evacuated by sea.

News from the school showed that another Communist patrol had almost finished its training. Warren was anxious to get these behind the lines as soon as possible. More enemy landings along the west coast threatened to cut off Kluang and Warren imposed on DALCO† and SIS to help ferry supplies to Kluang where John Davis was creating a dump near the Mersing Road.

On the 25th Warren arrived to give a hand with a lorry-load of supplies and special home-made fuses brought from the school. The site was some miles beyond Kluang, in an area of undeveloped forest, well known to the Japanese who, pre-war, had mining concessions in

---

* After trekking for four days through the jungle carrying the wounded, Brigadier Painter and his exhausted troops surrendered.

† Dalley Column under the command of Colonel Dalley one time Head of Counter-Intelligence, Kuala Lumpur.

the area. Most of the day was spent portering and burying the stores but by mid-day the native porters were becoming increasingly restless and wanted to return to their Kampongs. Eventually the Tamils were dismissed and paid off. Everyone, tired and perspiring heavily, climbed aboard the empty trucks. The vehicles bumped and swayed along the dirt track on to the jungle-fringed road which that morning was packed with army traffic. Now it was deserted. Leading the way in his 15 cwt Warren eventually came across a burly army sapper laying demolition charges on a bridge. From him he learned that they had spent their day behind enemy lines. Percival, it seemed, had ordered the step-by-step retreat to Singapore after learning that 53rd Indian Brigade couldn't hold out much longer.

When Barry, now running the SIS Unit in Kluang, heard that the town was being evacuated he went looking for Sergeant Cross. The town had been under constant air attack almost all day and by mid-afternoon the streets were being cleared for street fighting. Sandbagged positions were being built at street corners and shops and houses were shuttered. After unsuccessfully searching the empty streets he noticed one of the DALCO trucks moving through the road block leading into town. Waving its driver down he discovered that Cross, who had been with them at the dump that morning, had been driving the last lorry in the convoy. Only when they reached the road block was Cross's vehicle missed. Hearing this Barry ran back to the wireless hut and hustled two operators Mortimer and Wagstaff into a shooting brake. With Barry behind the wheel it raced out of town, past the road block, along the Mersing Road until he came to the bridge. The Royal Engineers confirmed only two vehicles passed through and agreed to allow them not more than an hour before they blew the bridge. After some miles of empty jungle-fringed road they discovered Cross, sitting dejectedly on the running board of his lorry. The shooting brake did a screaming 'U' turn in the middle of the narrow road backed up and before it stopped Mortimer and Wagstaff had leapt out tied a tow-rope to the lorry and disappeared back into the shooting brake as fast as they emerged. No word was spoken. As the tow-rope began to tighten Cross clambered back into the driving seat and the lorry in a series of leaps began to move forward. Behind it Chinese and Tamils who had been pushing the truck for some miles and who were having a drink from a nearby stream raced along the road trying to clamber over the tailboard as the lorry gathered speed.

Shortly after he arrived back from Johore Warren found three dishevelled and unexpected guests waiting for him in his office. Back from the dead, or so it seemed, were Vanrennan, Graham and Hembry. From them Warren learned of the disaster which had overtaken the first stay-behind group.

After Jim Gavin had left them at Tanjong Malim early in January Hembry recalls leaving the stores to be hidden by the local contractor, and his gang of coolies while he, Vanrennan and Graham drove back to the now deserted police station at Tanjong Malim, which they were using as a temporary base. Everywhere, it seemed, the British civil authority dissolved before the advance of the Japanese. They spent the last few hours of 6th January eating a meal and discussing Chapman's non-arrival. This worried them. Every day they had been expecting to see him walking up the track alongside the pipeline, looking for them. Although the Slim River line was expected to hold out for at least two weeks, which would give him ample time to recover from his bout of malaria, this was his operation and they looked forward to going into action with him. A bottle of whisky later they were asleep.

Next morning, before daylight, their sleep was shattered by someone kicking at the door, shouting and swearing and demanding to know who was inside. When Vanrennan opened the door a British officer stepped into the room. He was tired and needed a shave. His uniform was mud-stained. He glared at them. Outside stood his lorry with the engine running. 'What the bloody hell do you think you are doing?' he shouted. Vanrennan wasn't one to be intimidated and carefully explained they were on a secret operation behind enemy lines. Their visitor obviously doubted their sanity before finally announcing, as he left, that the Japanese had overwhelmed the Slim River defences that night and, at that very moment, their tanks were racing down the road towards the town.

In less than ten minutes their vehicle was loaded and heading north towards the enemy. They never felt so isolated. The dark road ahead, flanked by shadowy trees remained empty, no Japanese tanks nor enemy road blocks. Eventually they turned right off the road, up a track, bouncing and swaying in first gear. By now it was daylight and they could see that the track ahead narrowed to a bicycle path. Abandoning the vehicle they walked several hundred yards to the contractor's house. He met them on the path as they approached. He seemed almost in tears; finally they managed to get the story from him. It seemed during the night someone had ran up the path shouting that the Japanese were in Tanjong Malim and were also coming up the track. Everyone was in a state of panic and he, like the others fled into the jungle. When he thought it safe to return he found the stores had been looted. There were no signs of the Japanese or his coolies who could have been responsible. The wireless set, bicycle, rice and tinned food were all gone.

The European party stayed around the area for a further five days still expecting Chapman to appear. Eventually they decided to try and reach the British rearguard which were fast disappearing down the peninsula. When they reached the main road they found Japanese everywhere. Hiding by day and travelling by night they tried to make their way to Port Swettenham where Vanrennan had friends who could supply a boat if the town had been given up by the British. However, within a few days they were picked up by the Japanese and thrown into jail. Recounting the tale to John Davis, Vanrennan told how they escaped that night by the rear of the jail. The village was in darkness except for a shaft of light from the open door of the jail-house. Bathed in light was a Japanese staff car. After creeping across the road Vanrennan's companions were horrified to hear him whisper for them to go on and watched him calmly walk across to the staff car steal its pennant and rejoin them at the edge of the road. In stunned silence they ran off into the darkness putting as many miles as possible between them and the enemy. Eventually the party reached the coast where friends gave them a sampan. This they sailed to Sumatra where they made contact with the Dutch who flew them to Singapore.

The loss of Chapman's transmitter highlighted the shortage of wireless sets in the Far East. Regular army units were short of equipment and a large amount had been lost during the retreat. The only one Warren could easily get his hands on was with Major Barry's SIS unit, now based just across the causeway from Kranji. 'They could almost shout the messages to Kranji,' he commented. After talking it over with Goodfellow they arranged with GHQ for Barry and his men to be transferred to SOE. He and his men were then asked to stay behind with their set in Johore. In less than forty-eight hours Johore was going to be abandoned. After a brief conversation amongst themselves, Barry, Cross, Wagstaff and Mortimer agreed to go into the jungle with the next Communist guerrilla patrol. It would only be for three months. By then a combined American and British counter-attack would be launched to recapture the peninsula. While the three other ranks visited 101 STS for a brief course in sabotage, Barry went with Lieutenant Hunter, acting as guerrilla liaison officer, to look for a supply dump site somewhere near Kota Tingga. Hunter, a New Zealander, had worked with SOE in Siam. Escorting the enemy round-up he made his way over the border and rejoined SOE.

As they drove towards Johore in a small 15 cwt army lorry they passed a continuous line of vehicles nose to tail across the causeway. Every time the line of vehicles stopped the drivers fell asleep at the wheel. Groups of foot-sore infantry fell out at the side of the road and immediately went to sleep – exhausted. Others, red-eyed and grimy, marched alongside the traffic. Ambulances full of wounded and civilian lorries packed with women and children rescued from a train stranded in Johore, moved slowly with the tide of retreat. The ambulances turned into an already overcrowded hospital close to Kranji. 1,600 extra beds had been packed in but these were full. Hundreds of casualties continued to pour in by the hour.

Hunter found a suitable site near the entrance to a pineapple estate outside Kota Tingga. After unloading the supplies they brought with them Hunter left Barry standing guard while he went back for the others. Almost a full day was lost waiting in the traffic jam to get back on to the island. When he reached 101 STS he found Cross's party had gone back to Johore Bahru, near the Sultan's Palace to pick up their gear and equipment. With only a few hours to spare before the causeway was due to be blown Hunter found them in a deserted colonial-style house they were using as their base. Late in the afternoon they met up again with Barry but could find no sign of the Chinese guerrillas. After searching around they found them about a half mile away at a different entrance.

It was dark when the last of the stores had been unloaded and shared amongst the Chinese. After shaking hands with Barry and words of encouragement to Cross, Hunter watched the party shoulder their weapons and packs. In single line the patrol disappeared into the night along the estate road; following up in the rear came four Chinese carrying the wireless set, transmitter and generator.

Some thirty miles to the west two staff from 101 STS, Frank Brewer and Ivor Lyon, were attempting to set up a supply dump for a group of Nationalist Chinese. The previous evening the school had received a request to help this group put in a patrol. When five Chinese turned up with three lorries Brewer asked what had happened to the others. This wasn't the patrol, he was told, but supplies and equipment to stock a dump. A Chinese responsible for selecting the site was waiting for them at the Judge's house in Johore Bahru.

Like Hunter, Brewer and Lyon found the roads choked with traffic but eventually crossing the causeway the Chinese directed them to the house. They found it full of people all trying to get across the Straits but no sign of the Chinese contact man. Leaving his Chinese passengers, in white ducks, searching the area for their contact Brewer wandered around and met an ex-Volunteer, Captain Hawkins, who was now with Colonel Dalley's unit DALCO. The whole military situation was very fluid Hawkins told him and no one really knew where the Japanese were. Carrying out seaborne landings they were popping up everywhere behind the lines.

The causeway was going to be blown that night and Lyon had been warned to be back across by 4.30 p.m. Not proposing to waste any more time he decided to pick a site for the dump somewhere near the town. Following the coast road out of town all they could find were lots of mangrove swamps. The Chinese, now becoming rather desperate, said they wanted to put the dump in the swamp near the road. The spot was only some twelve feet into the swamp; stinking and mosquito-ridden. 'No dice,' said Lyons shaking his head, 'you're not having it there.'

Off they drove again and came across some soldiers moving through a rubber estate. Stopping the lorries Lyon and Brewer in freshly laundered cotton uniforms, Sam Browne belts and polished shoes, made their way through the rubber trees to an unshaven officer in a torn uniform and in need of a bath. Standing amongst his men desperately digging slit trenches he looked aghast at the two approaching officers. 'What's the road like ahead?' asked Lyon. 'Full of Japs but what the hell are you doing here?' he asked. Brewer explained they were trying to put in a Chinese sabotage mission. 'You must be bloody mad – we've just lost a battalion out there' – nodding his head towards the unseen enemy. 'They've been cut off and captured.'

Leaving the officer preparing for the last fight before Singapore the party set off again for about a mile until they found a small copse. After deciding to dump the supplies here the Chinese asked the two European officers to help unload. It was already mid-afternoon, the sun was high and nerves taut. Much against their better judgement the two British officers agreed but this type of work should really be done by coolies or soldiers – not officers. But despite their help the pace of unloading was still too slow for Lyon who was getting more and more angry until finally he pulled out his revolver and threatened to shoot the Chinese if they didn't 'get a bloody move on'.

To add insult to injury they were discovered by a lone Japanese fighter which leisurely circled overhead and they could see the pilot peering out of his cockpit to see what they were doing.

In the late afternoon with the lorry only half unloaded they all stopped to listen to what seemed to be tank tracks wincing their way along the road. Leaving the lorry where it was they scrambled down the bank and melted into the trees. Eventually a lone Bren gun carrier clattered around the bend in the road and moved slowly and cautiously towards the lorry. Its crew were nervous and as it stopped to investigate the lorry Brewer followed by the Chinese stepped into the open. In a tense moment like that, the ability to recognise the difference between a Chinese and a Japanese is important, particularly for the Chinese. Almost immediately Lyon moved into view and the sight of a second European relaxed the crew. When they tried to explain what they were doing there the young officer in command of the carrier 'blew his top' remembered Brewer and ordered them to 'get to hell out of there'. The carrier had been sent forward to discover the enemy's whereabouts which he calculated to be not more than three hundred yards along the road and advancing slowly.

Suitably reprimanded the SOE party quickly covered their partially hidden supply dump, boarded their truck and followed the carrier down the now dark road, through the town with the Argylls lurking in doorways; across the empty causeway watched by Royal Engineers putting final touches to the demolition charges until the carrier moved into the side of the road. Standing up the officer, who was just a dark shadow, waved them on and they sped past towards Jurong.

CHAPTER ELEVEN

February 1942 – Singapore

Referring to his assault to Singapore the Japanese Commander General Yamashita wrote:

'My attack on Singapore was a bluff. I had 30,000 men and was outnumbered by more than three to one. I knew that if I had to fight long for Singapore I would be beaten.'*

Some time after the SOE lorry followed the Bren gun carrier through the deserted streets of Johore Bahru, shadowy figures began to dart from house to house, occasionally stopping to set up a Bren gun point to cover some crossroads. Then as groups of soldiers ran past, they too picked up their weapons and ran to the next firing point. Gradually the Argylls were withdrawn from the town, over the causeway and marched off to some spot in the rubber trees to rest for the night. At 8.00 a.m. the following morning, 1st February, the Royal Engineers who had spent most of the previous few days mining it – blew a 300 foot breach in the 70 foot wide causeway.

The task facing the Japanese looked formidable as General Percival had almost 100,000 troops on the island with more due to arrive. The British had plenty of ammunition and supplies and a large number of Hurricane fighters arriving in crates to be assembled. The Japanese commander on the other hand had only some 60,000 troops, not enough guns nor ammunition and his long line of communication down through Malaya was constantly being cut by guerrilla attacks and sabotage. He believed he needed to strike quickly before the British, Australian and Indian troops' morale, badly shaken by the constant retreats, could be revived.

Across the straits in Singapore a lull had developed. Tired and weary troops camped everywhere and the hospitals were crowded with casualties. Groups of soldiers cut off during the retreat were still making their way through Johore, sneaking through Japanese lines

* 'Defeat in Malaya' by Arthur Swinson in Purnell's *History of the Second World War*. Campaign Book 5.

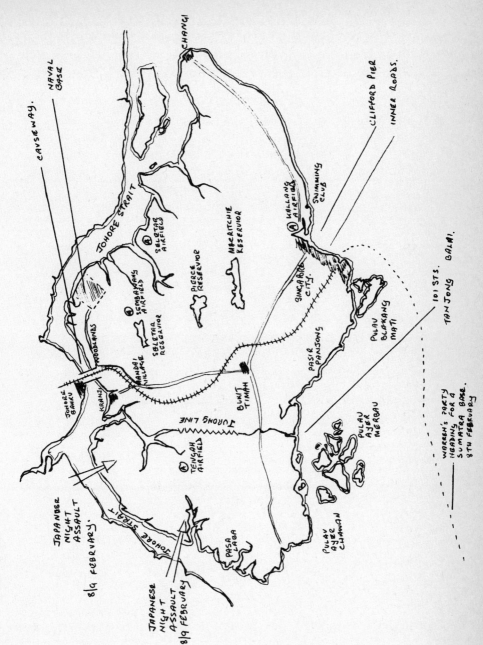

A map of Singapore Island showing the main Japanese thrust on 8/9th February 1942.

and either stealing boats or swimming the straits to reach the island. As both the military and service families began to take stock of the casualties pathetic advertisements began to appear in the local newspapers appealing for news of missing husbands or sons.

Almost as soon as the Japanese arrived at the Johore Straits they began to clear natives from the beach area facing Singapore and started to build a secret road along the seafront to bring forward hundreds of special boats carried, for the purpose, all the way from Indo-China. Every working gun left behind by the British Army and every lorry still mobile were brought along the shell-cratered roads to Johore Bahru.* The enemy field engineers quickly repaired the destroyed railway track and brought up large calibre railway guns from Bangkok.

In the glass-domed tower in the Sultan of Johore's Palace the Japanese Commander, General Yamashita, watched the defenders' preparations for his expected seaborne assault. The Sultan was one of the richest men in the world and a close friend of General Bennett, the Australian Commander, who had often dined with him. But what no one else suspected was that the Sultan was also a close friend of Count Ohtani, the Japanese Emperor's mother's brother-in-law. The Count, coincidentally, was also heavily involved with planning the Malayan invasion and a member of his staff, Colonel Tsuji, took part in a Malayan intelligence operation prior to the outbreak of war. The Sultan's palace was now Japanese Headquarters.

In his office near the waterfront, Warren looked out over the harbour. Since the evacuation of the Naval Base he spent most of his time in the Cathay Building. He was in a circumspect mood – everywhere he looked smoke seemed to be mushrooming up from burning buildings. Even out to sea – beyond the harbour – there was a long trail of black smoke spreading across the horizon. He learned later that the only incoming convoy to try and enter harbour during daylight had been caught by enemy bombers and a large troopship, the *Empress of Asia*, its holds packed with weapons, was on fire from stem to stern. The ship's arrival coincided with GHQ's decision to evacuate service families and thousands of lines-of-communication troops still in Singapore. Two American liners which formed part of the convoy didn't intend to hang about and left the following day after embarking hordes of civilians.

At Tanjong Balai Frank Brewer recalls being asked to report to the

---

* 800 lorries and 300 guns.

school's deputy commander who told him that the school was packing up and would be leaving for Rangoon. Only long service members of staff would be leaving with it. Others would be sent back to their units but he was given the option of either going back to the Volunteers or joining Colonel Dalley's new Chinese unit. Hundreds of Chinese were already flocking to the recruiting offices and with his experience in the Chinese Protectorate his services would be invaluable. He remembers remarking that 'he didn't want to go back to the Volunteers' so he opted for DALCO. 'In that case,' said his deputy commander, 'take that lorry load of stuff you brought back last night with you – it might come in handy.'

When Captain Ivor Lyon arrived back from Johore he changed and went along to the Gordons' Officers Mess for dinner. The following day he was told to report to Warren at Cathay Building. The town was being bombed regularly and he drove through streets filled with debris and burning houses. He found Campbell waiting for him in Warren's office. Warren came straight to the point. 101 STS was closing down and moving out to Rangoon but he and Goodfellow were staying on the island. GHQ were considering setting up a supply route to Sumatra and this, in Warren's opinion, 'could easily become an escape route if Singapore was overwhelmed.' As there was also the possibility of using well stocked island bases as launching off points to carry out raids against the enemy-held coastline, he wanted Campbell and Lyon to set up and run the route.

Warren trusted both men. Major Jock Campbell was a good administrator. Before the war he ran a large rubber plantation in Selangor and provided Warren with a large number of recruits for training at the school when no one else wanted to know. Later when his plantation was overrun he came to Singapore and volunteered for special duties. His companion Ivor Lyon, married to an attractive French wife – now safely on her way to England – was a regular officer in the Gordons. He had served many years out East and was until recently British liaison officer to the Free French now on their way to China. A great deal of his pre-war leisure time had been spent sailing around the islands which he knew like the back of his hand.

Warren pointed out that they would need to select islands and set up bases stocked with food and medical supplies. They should butter up the natives and take the opportunity of forming resistance groups amongst them.

Before they left Warren told them to find someone with medical knowledge to go with them. Lyon knew just the man and later asked

Trappes-Lomax for Sergeant Morris, a Welsh Medical Corps
sergeant at the school, who was both keen and enthusiastic.

Each evening, under the cover of darkness, the Navy took the
opportunity of saving part of its Eastern Fleet. On the 2nd HMAS
Vendetta, rescued from the Naval Base, left under tow with HMAS
Stronghold. With her went the *Hobart*, *Tenedos* and *Maryborough* – all
Australian Navy ships. The little coal-burning HMS *Circa*, a patrol
minesweeper, was recalled to harbour and ordered to discharge her
native crew. These were replaced with sailors from the *Repulse* and
Prince of Wales. Later that evening she took on board a mixed bag of
airmen and Pay Corps clerks complete with records and left that
night in a second convoy with *Medusa* and another minesweeper
known simply as *No 51*. On the 23rd HMAS *Ballarat* and HMAS
Toowooma left to carry out a minesweeping patrol through the Banka
Straits. With them went two smaller vessels, HMS *Gemas* and HMS
Rahman.

Despite this movement of shipping SOE, once again, came up
against the intangible barrier that existed between it and other Service organisations. After receiving Killery's agreement to evacuate
the school Goodfellow ordered Trappes-Lomax to find a ship. His
approach to the Shipping Transport Officer (STO) met with a flat
refusal. SOE would have to take its chance with everyone else. Not
satisfied he left the STO's office on board the engineless hulk HMS
Laburnum berthed in the docks and drove Jim Gavin's car along the
cratered quayside to see for himself. A large 10,000 tons P & O liner,
SS *Talybias*, was tied up alongside the dock wall. The nearby *godowns*
were ablaze and its ship's officers were fighting to stop the flames
reaching the ship already disabled from repeated direct hits during
the air raids. The native dockers had fled leaving the unloading to be
done by recently arrived New Zealand troops. Further along, past
the burning *godowns*, Trappes-Lomax noticed a small steamer tied
up alongside the harbour. He stopped the car and sat for a few
minutes watching for signs of life on board. The ship seemed silent
and empty. Leaving the car he crossed the railway lines running
alongside the dock and strode up the gangplank to the ship's deck.

As he stood assessing the situation he was suddenly confronted by
two fierce-looking ship's officers. One turned out to be the Scots skipper and the other the ship's engineer. The two looked as if they would
take no nonsense so Trappes-Lomax quickly explained that he was
looking for a ship to take his school to Rangoon. The skipper listened
with some amusement. He would 'sail this ship to London, if he

liked, but he didn't have a crew'. By this time they had reached the captain's cabin and Trappes-Lomax was busy extolling the seaman-like qualities of his staff. A bottle of whisky later and the prospect of a crew, even though they seemed to be seaborne soldiers, cheered the dispirited captain. He became more talkative. The ship was called the *Krain*, a Straits Steamship Company vessel. The company seemed to call its ships after rivers. The skipper went on to say that he had sailed the 856 tons SS *Krain* into every port between Rangoon and Bangkok since passing his 'tickets' in Poplar not long after Queen Victoria had died. Since then he had served nearly all his time out East.

Throughout the day the city had been under heavy attack from both the enemy's long range artillery and its bombers. This was part of a softening-up process to encourage General Percival to accept the demand to surrender. All the enemy bombers flew unmolested over the city, in wave after wave, strafing and bombing indiscriminately. Sitting in the captain's cabin they could hear the heavy guns based in Johore range on to the waterfront with the markers. These shells raced across the roof tops with a noise like a passing express train and exploded amongst the *godowns* and ships in the harbour. The little ship shook with each explosion and Trappes-Lomax tried to appear calm and indifferent to the increased bombardment as he sat and listened to the skipper's stories. The whisky consumption increased in direct proportion to the accuracy of the guns.

This escalation of the siege helped thousands of European civilians, now trapped in Singapore to reach a decision to leave. The following day two liners, the troopship *Devonshire* and the French *Felix Rousel*, well known on the Orient run, sailed with more than two thousand passengers aboard. The previous liner which left seven days earlier had sailed half empty. The Governor, Sir Shenton Thomas, had earlier decreed that anyone could leave voluntarily at the Government's expense but he still refused to issue a compulsory evacuation order for fear of upsetting the local native population.

The repercussions of the Penang evacuation could still have been fresh in his mind. Because of the heavy bombing all bookings had been centralized away from the city at the P & O manager's home at Cluny, some miles out of Singapore. His bungalow stood at the top of a long drive. Outside the road was congested with parked cars and a long queue of women and children. Women fainted in the sun, children cried and sobbed and the pathetic line of people disintegrated every time fighters and bombers swept in low. Those lucky enough to get a ticket received a duplicated slip of paper giving sailing instructions. Passengers were asked to take a knife, fork, spoon and sandwiches for the initial part of the journey. A mattress would be provided but no bedding could be expected. With a boarding card, a duplicated sheet of instructions and children clinging to their skirts, the harassed and perspiring mothers made their way back to join the thousands in similar plight queuing up at the waterfront. The would-be passengers were arriving by taxi, rickshaw, some on foot or in their private cars which were later abandoned and either set alight or pushed into the harbour.

Some ships stood off-shore and passengers were ferried out in launches or Harbour Board barges. The two liners with passengers packing the rails steamed away escorted by HMAS *Danae*, HMAS *Yarra* and HMIS *Sutlej*. Amongst the passengers were a large number of Czechs making their way to London to join the Free Czech Forces. The marker buoy was missing from the entrance to the minefields. In its place the Australian destroyer HMAS *Bendigo* acted as a navigational aid. Later she followed them through the swept channel and joined the convoy for Java. Later, about midnight, the last Australian ship in Singapore, HMAS *Woolongong*, was ordered to get away. The missing buoy was never replaced and its omission was to cost many lives in the confusion of the general evacuation.

About the time the convoy was preparing to leave the 101 STS staff at Tanjong Balai was taking the school apart. All the training aids were being dismantled and packed in crates heavily stencilled 'Lashio'. The files and records were burnt on large bonfires. By mid-afternoon on the 5th a small convoy of army lorries left the now deserted school – all the cooks and civilians had been paid off and seconded servicemen returned to their units. At the dockside the crates and stores were winched aboard the *Krain* and as darkness fell the ship cast off and disappeared into the night, leaving Warren, in his whites and Goodfellow in Sam Browne, nothing else to do but walk back to Cathay Building.

All afternoon, while the *Krain* was loading, enemy gunners were flinging shells into the harbour and town. Flying unopposed enemy bombers dropped their bombs at leisure over Chinatown and on any shipping they could find in the harbour. All this had taken its toll on the staff and Sergeant Morris was kept busy patching people up.

In the darkness the ship sailed through a large area of bloated decomposing bodies which bumped gently alongside the hull before disappearing astern. Leaning on the stern rail with his pipe clenched in his mouth, Captain Lyons watched the glow from the burning fires in Singapore lighting up the night sky. The water-front seemed ablaze and fingers of light could be seen leaping above the rooftops especially from the direction of Chinatown.

The first stop next morning was a little island called Puala Moro, near the Durian Straits on the main sea lane to Sumatra. Here Lyons and Morris were put ashore with weapons, stores and medical supplies. The *Krain* remained hidden against the trees for the rest of the day and that night left for Rengat.

In Singapore, apart from the heavy shelling by the Japanese, Sunday the 7th had a certain calm which was to be the lull before the storm. The churches were packed with worshippers; in the Army camps servicemen formed up for church parade. In the centre of the town, near the waterfront, the cathedral was packed and from its grounds overlooking the shimmering sea visitors watched four small steamers preparing to leave an otherwise empty harbour.

Now that 101 STS had been evacuated, Warren's main problem was to get the last of the Chinese guerrillas into Johore. The wireless link operated by Major McMillan from Java would provide SOE with a communications link with the guerrillas in Malaya. Putting the last course behind the lines would obviously have to be a seaborne operation and with help from his RN contacts – 'I just rang them up' said Warren – a small 80 tons diesel driven Chinese coaster was requisitioned to put the guerrillas ashore. The little coaster was called the *Hin Lee* and pre-war sailed up and down the coast trading in and out of riverside villages and fishing harbours. She seemed ideal for the purpose.

Recalling the ship Warren commented that 'When we arrived on board we found her full of rice, sugar, jars of soya bean sauce and other goods guarded by an army of cockroaches who had free run of the ship. She smelled abominably but not so bad as the living quarters where nothing they did overcame the reek of years of poor sanitation.'

Commenting on the proposed seaborne raids he said, 'Davis and Broome were in charge of the Communists who were to be infiltrated into Malaya behind the Jap front to join up with about two hundred and fifty other Chinese who had already been passed through the lines. These men had been trained at a guerrilla school in Singapore to organise and sustain resistance throughout Malaya against the Japanese invader. We also intended, with their help, to organise a two-way line of underground communication from Singapore to

Malaya through Sumatra. The two planters were on their way north
to join up with one of the seven British sabotage groups – known by
the unfortunate, but nevertheless correct as it turned out, name of
left-behind parties. They had been put into the jungle during the
Army's withdrawal down the peninsula to co-operate with the
Chinese against the Japanese lines of communications.'

The *Hin Lee* was crewed by two RN officers, Brian Passmore and
Lind, two survivors from the *Prince of Wales* and *Repulse* who took
charge of the engine room and a corporal in the Gordons. Davis and
Broome brought with them a Chinese boy and a Malay policeman
who had worked with them in civilian life. Despite the air raids and
shelling a succession of lorries from the school brought explosives
arms and ammunition, stores and supplies to the dockside. While
firemen sprayed water on a burning building less than fifty yards
from the launch, staff from the school unloaded the supplies and carried them aboard. Within twenty-four hours the cargo was loaded
and trimmed, the vessel crewed and ready for sea. At the last
moment a discussion arose as to who was in command of the *Hin Lee*.
Both the RN officers were of equal rank. Remembering the incident
John Davis recalls Warren on his haunches bending down to talk to
Passmore whose head jutted out of a porthole below the level of the
dock. In a judgement of Solomon, Warren was telling him that
although Lind was only Wavy Navy he did have more days' seniority
so should be in command however, as he (Passmore) had more sea
service he should take the launch to sea.

Passmore nodded and his head disappeared back into the cabin.
Someone, perhaps Lind, on deck near the stern gave Warren a smart
salute as the vessel, with great thrashing of the propellers, pulled
away from the dockside and nosed its way through the haze that
covered the harbour.

Warren watched them go and wished he could be with them.

As the *Hin Lee* crept away in the early evening, the haze from the
burning city became night and, under the cover of darkness, it
headed for the open sea beyond the minefield. The rumble of enemy
artillery could be clearly heard and the sound was punctuated by
sudden flashes of exploding shells which crashed into the burning
waterfront. While astern the city glowed with fires, the way ahead
was black – not a light nor shape to navigate by. As they cruised
around in the darkness Davis sensed something was wrong and discovered that Lind couldn't find the marker buoy at the entrance to
the swept channel through the minefield.

The following day Warren lunched at the Singapore Club with Angus Rose and Captain Terriant RN. All three had been involved in the Trong Raid and Rose had commanded the Volunteers who had acted as hard pressed rear-guard when 3 Corps retreated from Kuala Lumpur. This was to be their last get-together before Rose left on the *Empire Star* for Java. After a good meal, with wine followed by brandy, Warren said good-bye and made his way back to his office in the Cathay Building where he was more than surprised to find Lind and Passmore waiting for him. They wanted more information about the minefield – there was no marker buoy for the swept channel. While they discussed the next move John Davis took the opportunity to slip away to his home and collect his kit – a precaution maybe. When he returned about two hours later he found Warren on board the *Hin Lee*. He had taken charge and would go with them.

Throughout the day the bombardment gathered intensity and enemy shells pounded the Australians and Chinese volunteers holding the beach around Kranji. Although the British gunners replied they didn't get into an artillery duel, preferring to conserve the ammunition. As darkness fell the enemy fire concentrated on the forward positions, tearing apart the barbed wires and killing and maiming the troops cowering in the trenches. Pill-boxes caved in and telephone wires to the rear snapped as the barrage crept inland to cut a swathe through the support troops dug-in in the rear. Alongside the Johore Straits the defenders, thankful that someone else was on the receiving end, slowly lifted their heads above the parapets and peered into the darkness: from the mud-flats in front of them dark shapes began to appear as enemy launches emptied screaming invaders ashore. Using some 300 specially made launches brought from Indo-China together with local boats propelled by lorry engines, the Japanese sent in wave after wave of fighting troops – overwhelming the Australians in fierce hand-to-hand fighting.

In the creeks and mud-flats between the Australian positions and Kranji, Dalley's Chinese, under the command of Captain Harte Barry, one-time miner and instructor at 101 STS, were ordered to dig-in and sit out the shelling. Like Brewer when 101 STS left he opted to join Dalforce. His company now found themselves up against a Japanese machine gun battalion whose objective was to seize the other end of the broken causeway. With shotguns and sporting rifles and finally hand-to-hand the Chinese fought back. The wounded, propped up with the rifles, fought until they died. They were blown up, shot up and when the ammunition ran out the enemy carved them up. There were no Chinese survivors and only one British officer and five British other ranks escaped to tell the tale. The Japanese had thrown in four thousand well trained troops on the first wave. These were quickly followed by reinforcements with mortars and heavy weapons. By dawn they had broken through the Australians and reached Tengah airfield.

After leaving harbour Warren took the *Hin Lee* into the Malacca Straits to hide at daybreak near the Sumatra shoreline. The noise of battle and firework display along the beach defences told its own story. The night was black, remembers Warren, and full of stars while the moon threatened to climb above the hills and light up the sea. Above the noise of ship's engines Warren's keen hearing picking up a new sound. There was another vessel around somewhere. Eventually he picked out a long sleek shape travelling at speed on his seaward side. The outline of the *Hin Lee* was lost against the shadow of the shore and the unknown vessel sped by the disappeared astern. He never knew what it was. As both Japanese submarines and troop transports were active in the area the fright served as a reminder to everyone to keep on their toes.

February: Sumatra, the escape route

Campbell was put ashore at Rengat on 8th February about the time Warren was taking the *Hin Lee* through the minefields. He was met at the quayside by the Dutch Controlleur, a colonial administrator similar to the British District Commissioner. With his help Campbell planned the expected movement of supplies and men along the proposed escape route. Apart from the logistics Campbell also looked at the problem of overland transport to Padang and the long sea journey from Lyon's camp.

Rengat was a decently planned little town built on a straight stretch of river with a rather imposing waterfront. The journey from there to Padang was some two hundred and fifty miles along tortuous roads through jungle and over the mountains. The Dutchman agreed to provide Campbell with lorries and buses and made arrangements with his counterparts along the proposed route for two overnight stops at Telok and the railhead town of Swanleato.

Later Campbell set off downstream in a borrowed launch to look for two more staging areas, this time between Rengat and Lyon's camp, some two or three days' journey away. His first choice had to be Tambilihan, a small riverside town some forty miles downstream and already regularly used by coastal ships. The town boasted a wooden jetty and nearby *godowns* which Campbell noted could provide shelter if needed. Apart from the Assistant Controlleur's office the town also had a small dispensary – a native-type cottage hospital with one ward and no doctor. The town was built around a large open market with a plentiful supply of fresh fruit and food.

After leaving Tambilihan Campbell cruised down river past sampans and river folk about their day-to-day business untouched by war. There was plenty of contrast along the river, mangrove swamps, jungle full of colourful birds screeching overhead, beds of flowers floating on the river – pretty but a potential hazard for the propellers of unsuspecting launches. Near the river mouth he stayed the night at Pridi-raja, a small fishing village sprawling along the river bank. At this point the river began to change from a muddy brown as it flowed into the estuary bisected with islands and shallow channels.

Thirty miles from the estuary, on Puala Moro, Lyon and Morris built a large *attap* hut near the cliffs some 200 feet above sea level. All the supplies had been unloaded on the banks of a muddy inlet which was to serve as their waterfront. The wind had changed and the monsoon rains driven by strong winds, swirled across the sea and over the island turning the track to the hut from the beach into a muddy helter-skelter. All the stores were humped up to the hut and amongst these they found large ration packs made up at the school. Each pack, expected to last twenty men two days, contained ship's biscuits, corned beef and whisky.

After bringing the stores up Lyon left Morris stacking the boxes around the sides of the hut while he set out in a small sailing dinghy to nearby islands to seek the help of local headsmen. In their own languages he explained to each one that he wanted their co-operation in directing any Europeans in the area to his new camp at Puala Moro.

Every night after supper of bully beef and whisky, Lyon would sit in the darkness outside the hut, puffing at his pipe and listening to the thunder of guns from Singapore. On the horizon gun-flashes lit up the sky like far away lightning. Expecting the Japanese to infiltrate along the island chain, Lyon and Morris took turns to stand guard. In the darkness every nocturnal sound gave flight to the imagination but the noises usually turned out to be nothing more alarming than some wild animal crashing through the jungle or birds and bats weaving their way through the trees above the camp.

Most of the ships which left Singapore before the 10th reached

Java but despite being ordered to sail at night and hide during the day, some captains left it too late and were caught and bombed by early rising Japanese pilots. From the cliff top Lyon and Morris watched a steady stream of ships running the gauntlet. Under heavy attack the little ships fought their attackers with small deck-mounted guns and Bren while the larger ships used their speed and firepower to dodge the planes.

The military in Singapore had begun to backload both stores and men. Two local ships, the *Darvil* and *Kinta*, carried 1,000 servicemen including 2/3rd Australian Motor Transport Company to the Dutch East Indies. The Australians had been in the front line ever since the Japanese had come over the border in north Malaya. The *Sin Aik Lee* sailed without passengers but her engine room was manned by a leading seaman and four stokers from the Australian destroyer *Woolongong*. With her went a small steamer, the *Ban Hong Long*. Faced with a fresh wave of casualties the already overcrowded hospitals took the opportunity of transferring their patients to the Red Cross ship *Wu Sai* tied up alongside the harbour wall. She crept out of Singapore on the 9th crammed with wounded and nurses.

Almost as soon as they set up camp Lyon and Morris began to deal with survivors, a role they were completely unequipped for. Some were in a pitiful condition suffering wounds or bad sunburn from floating around in the water in life-jackets. A field dressing station had been set up by Sergeant Morris who, for the next 72 hours worked almost single-handed until relieved by shipwrecked nurses. He found himself dealing with bullet and bomb wounds, casualties speared by large chunks of wood torn from the ships by bombs; he tried to comfort children screaming with pain and shock and laid out the dead in the jungle beyond the small clearing. More than 1,000 escapers and survivors were helped before they evacuated the island on the 17th, two days after the fall of Singapore.

CHAPTER TWELVE

February 1942 – Sumatra

The fall of Singapore destroyed any plans Warren had for re-establishing contact with his European stay-behind parties and Chinese guerrillas in Malaya. News of this set-back, the first of a succession, reached him when he arrived at General Overaakers' military headquarters at Labohanbilak, a small seaport on the east coast of Sumatra. The general was an old friend of Warren's and Dutch Military Commander in North Sumatra – it was 150 of his best native troops that the Australians massacred, accidentally, in Johore a few weeks earlier.

When Warren learnt that Singapore had surrendered the previous day, on the 15th, he was badly shaken. Although he half expected this to happen he was still shocked that the island's defences collapsed in only fifteen days instead of the expected three months.

The second piece of bad news was that Wavell had abandoned Sumatra after Banka Straits and Palembang had been seized by a combined enemy sea and airborne assault. The two events now effectively put his party hundreds of miles behind enemy lines without hope of securing much needed supplies for Malaya, once the Dutch in the town had surrendered. Overaakers didn't intend to give up without a fight but this decision was later to cost him his life.

Since leaving Singapore on the 8th, Warren had set up a temporary base at Suiapiapi, a small fishing village on the main island of a group in the Malacca Straits known as the Aroahs. From here, some fifty miles from the Sumatran coast, Warren had hoped to carry out secret landings along the enemy-held west coast of Malaya. He had sold the stock of sugar, found on the launch, and with the proceeds hired three junks and their native crews to take his men and the guerrillas to Malaya. After taking on board supplies for three months, bicycles, a wireless set, explosives and weapons, the three native boats set out for Malaya some 100 miles away.

Anxious to make contact with Spencer Chapman, Vanrennan and Graham took one junk, separated from the others and headed north for Port Selangor where they had local contacts. Broome, Davis and

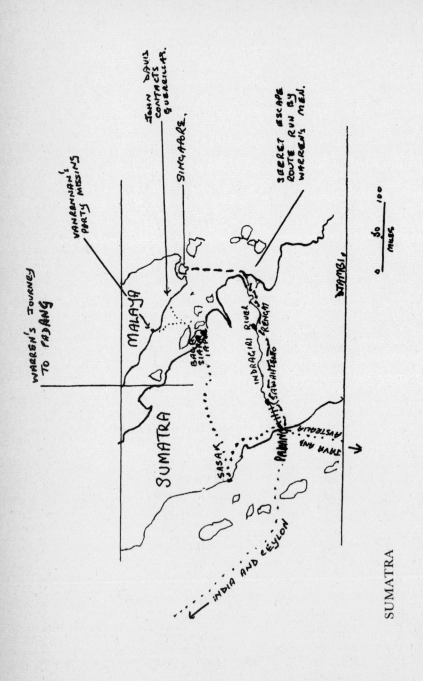

SUMATRA

the guerrillas steered for Sapan, further south along the Malayan west coast.

The Dutch Controlleur on the islands had been a great help, remembers Warren, but seemed completely unconcerned about the war situation. On Warren's last night in the village he brushed aside his warnings telling Warren that 'fat men cannot fuss'. Then taking out his banjo he entertained his guest with renderings of Sari Mari and other old Boer and Dutch folk songs, their singing fortified with large quantities of whisky. Next day the Dutchman came to see them off and Warren recollects watching his rather lonely figure on the pier, until it was almost indistinguishable from the background of native houses.

On the 16th Warren and his party arrived at General Overaakers' HQ and, taking up the story, Warren remembers he was horrified to hear that Singapore had fallen the previous day. 'While we were waiting for Davis and Broome we took stock of the position [probably referring to Overraker, Passmore, Lind and himself]. We thought that an Allied stand would be made at Java and debated our chances of steaming the *Hin Lee* eastwards to Batavia or some other port. This entailed a trip of about eight hundred miles, all of it in waters dominated by Jap warships and aircraft and including many 'dive bomb alleys'. Our prospects seemed to be thin and would get progressively worse as the days passed.

'Colombo, another alternative, was over thirteen hundred miles across the Indian Ocean and the *Hin Lee* was not nearly seaworthy enough for a trip of that nature. She would do about four knots and her old diesel had a depressing habit of fading out without warning. Compressed air had to be used to restart her and our supplies of this were running out.

'Another destination could be Burma, using the Nicobar and Andaman Islands as stepping stones. This seemed a better proposition although the distance was about the same and the Japs might be sitting in the islands.

'We decided to stock up with oil and air in case the trip became a necessity and to this end sent the ship about twenty miles up-stream to a large rubber factory where we were told supplies might be available. This would also get her out of the way of Jap planes, which we had already seen nosing around and expected to be the object of their attention.

'I eventually managed to get through by wireless to Bandoeng, Java, and received instructions from GHQ to make for Padang, over three hundred miles distant on the south-west coast of Sumatra.'

The reason for GHQ's request became easier to understand when Warren received a letter from a Colonel Field at GHQ. The Dutch at Padang had appealed for help to handle the thousands of British and Australian troops who had arrived after escaping from Singapore. Pried wanted Warren to go across and assess the situation there.

Lind had gone up-river with the launch so Passmore was sent to Padang by car to examine the problem. Meanwhile Overaakers, anxious to block the river, wanted Warren to part with the *Hin Lee*. But Warren wasn't prepared to do anything until both Broome and Passmore returned. Coincidentally, they both arrived back at Dutch HQ the same day, 24th February.

Passmore's encouraging news was that the Australian Colonel Broadbent had arrived in Padang and had helped with the reception facilities. He had now left for Java, taking with him some 150 Australians and leaving Brigadier Paris in charge of the town. He had with him about 100 Argylls, including a number who had escaped from north Malaya. Although the town was packed with servicemen and refugees, some ships were calling there to pick them up for either Colombo or Java.

The report Broome brought back was equally optimistic. He had arrived back at Suiapiapi on the 20th and, finding Warren gone, left Davis behind to wait for Vanrennan. The journey to Sapan had taken about three days and was uneventful apart from running ashore on a mudbank almost within shouting distance of the Malayan coast. They had to wait a half-day for wind and tide to lift them off. The lack of surveillance on the part of the Japanese was probably due to the final battle for Singapore, then taking place, and enemy preparations for the invasion of north Sumatra. Once ashore the guerrillas soon made contact with their local underground and John Davis recalls they all gathered in a local coffee shop in the village to have a conference. Unaware of the latest set-back, Davis and Broome confidently agreed to pass in wireless sets, more arms and explosives. Everyone was very enthusiastic and Davis brought back one of the underground fighters* to Suiapiapi to show him the base so that he could go back and set up a courier service with Sumatra.

Meanwhile in Labohanbilak, General Overaakers was fortifying the town. The troops were on full alert, buildings were sandbagged for street fighting and road blocks set up on all roads leading to the

---

* Tan Chen King.

town. Bazaar gossip had already warned the residents to expect a Japanese invasion and the Dutch preparations convinced them that it was time to leave. Within a few days the population had fled to the jungle villages. Overaakers, still needing Warren's launch, agreed to swop it for three cars. One was left behind for Broome. The other two, packed with Warren and his crew, set off to Padang along a road crowded with refugees. Warren remembers looking down at the river and seeing Dutch engineers swarming over the *Hin Lee* coverting her into a block ship.

When Richard Broome reached Suiapiapi on the 26th, he found Vanrennan's junk had returned without him. He learnt from John Davis that Vanrennan had told the crew to anchor off-shore and wait for them. The following day while they were at anchor, fishing, a Japanese in a launch became suspicious and wanted to know what they were doing there. Taking fright the crew returned home without Vanrennan and Graham.

Despite their foreboding about leaving Vanrennan stranded in Malaya, Davis and Broome complied with Warren's orders and reached Padang five days later. John Davis remembers staying one night at a small town called Seanta, in mid-Sumatra, amongst the jungle and hills. As always the Dutch were very hospitable and that night threw a party for their guests. Their mood, recollects Davis, was – let's be merry for tomorrow who knows? Their morale was not low but resigned – they knew that in the morning the British officers would be gone and they would have to stay and face the music.

CHAPTER THIRTEEN

A New Headquarters in Java

General Wavell had lost his Desert command after falling out with Churchill and arrived in Java to create a new, combined American, British, Dutch and Australian command to become known as ABDA. He was faced with the impossible task of pulling together the defence plans of four previously separate commands which included not only the defence plans for the ground forces but air and naval units as well. He had no headquarters staff but needed to create everything from scratch, even where to locate his new headquarters. Although Britain and Australia considered Singapore to be the cornerstone of the defence structure America considered it too close to Indo-China and within Japanese strike capabilities. Eventually in January Wavell decided to place his headquarters in Java close to the island's administrative capital of Bandung, some sixty miles from Java's capital of Batavia.

For four weeks, until Java became encircled by the Japanese, Wavell's new staff began to filter in from every corner of his new command. Among these were Admiral Layton and the British Special Operations Chiefs, Sir George Sansom and Val St John Killery, leaving the Orient Mission's operations to Goodfellow and Warren.

Operationally this move put Killery at a disadvantage as, until the surrender, Singapore remained the hub of all clandestine activities. Detached from that centre he was to take no further positive part in the events which were to follow and only watch with growing concern the loss, bit by bit, of his Mission.

Only a few weeks previously he, like many others, had expected America to send reinforcements to Java and using Singapore as a launching-off point, recover Malaya, using the stay-behind parties in support of any advance. But swift island-hopping moves by enemy naval units and troop transports outflanked the Malayan Barrier, cutting any possible supply route from America. The enemy first seized Borneo, with its strategic airfields. This enabled the Japanese to intercept all convoys using the Banka Straits, the main shipping lane from Java to Singapore. Almost encircled, Singapore was being strangled but interest in its survival waned as the Japanese seized Amboina – the second largest naval base in the Dutch East Indies – then New Guinea and Timor; by-passing Java and bringing Australia within range of Japanese bombers. Not only did these moves bring Australia within striking distance of enemy bombers but the rapid deployment of enemy naval units to Timor threatened the Allied escape route.

These moves also had a serious effect on SOE thinking and planning. All its resources were in Singapore and its objectives geared to fighting north of Singapore. There was nothing in Borneo nor the Dutch East Indies. The Orient Mission needed a new base and Rangoon or Chungking seemed the most obvious locations as it could only be a matter of time before all the Dutch East Indies and even Australia were overrun.

The French had already decided to move and were on their way to Rangoon, heading for Kumming, China: where they were to build a base for infiltrating Indo-China. The 101 STS China party were stranded in Rangoon; this detachment was promised to China by Killery to set up the nationalist guerrilla school. The Signals Unit under the command of Major Knott, had also arrived in Rangoon and set up its listening post for Spencer Chapman, not having been told that Vanrennan's wireless set had been stolen and the mission abandoned. All that remained in Singapore was the school and its staff, training Chinese Communist guerrillas from Malaya. As the situation became worse every day Goodfellow was told to move the unit out as soon as practicable.

Communications between Java and Singapore were cumbersome and delayed and Val Killery began to rely on news from contacts arriving from Singapore, who made their way to his office in Bandung. One of these was Major McMillan, who arrived in Java after his Radio Intercept Unit was closed down at Kranji. He brought the news that Goodfellow had managed to put a second wireless set behind the lines manned by ex-SIS wireless operators, under the command of Major Barry. Before Sergeant Cross had left to go into the jungle, McMillan gave him a wireless plan working to him in Java. If that link failed, Sergeant Cross was to establish communications with Knott in Rangoon: obviously no one considered the possibility of Rangoon being captured. He also brought the news that the No 1 Stay-behind Party (Vanrennan's) had reached Singapore, including the information that Spencer Chapman's wireless set had been stolen.

The following day McMillan began calling Sergeant Cross using GHQ wireless. And 500 miles away in a little bamboo hut, near the edge of the jungle, with rain dripping down through the *attap* roof, Cross sat by the receiver listening to McMillan's signals. His own transmitter was somewhere with the guerrillas who were back-packing it for him. The four man party Hunter left at the entrance to the pineapple plantation found themselves surrounded by a suitcase-type transmitter and receiver, a second, larger, transmitter and receiver, a charging engine with six batteries and eight gallons of petrol, five gallons of oil, two boxes of spares, tools, food, arms and ammunition, explosives, cooking pots and blankets. Sufficient portering for some hundred helpers. All Barry had was three men. However, despite having their own weapons and supplies to carry the Chinese Communist patrol volunteered to help them out. Moving from camp to camp, the loads, and the guerrillas, became dispersed and the equipment arrived piecemeal at Berry's radio shack manned by Cross.

Another arrival at Bandung HQ was Jim Gavin with, to everyone's surprise, his girlfriend Barbara, announcing to all their decision to get married. Killery wasn't happy with the news and complained to Gavin about 'getting married at a time like this'. Soon after landing at Batavia, Jim Gavin recollects Barbara and he cramming themselves into a public telephone box and telephoning the British Consulate. When he asked the Consulate to marry them he was told 'Don't be so bloody daft, I'm burning all my papers and leaving as soon as possible'. The Dutch were more sympathetic – 'to get married today, Saturday, will cost sixty guilders,' he was told. Sixty guilders! That was all the money they had. With the 'phone tucked under his chin he emptied his pockets of money on to a ledge, Barbara did the same with her purse, and they began to count their small change. Hearing the commotion the friendly Dutchman continued, 'If you get married tomorrow it will cost you only five guilders.' They quickly agreed and found a nearby hotel and booked two separate rooms. In the hotel they met an American reporter who, when he heard they were getting married, organised and paid for their reception.

When the newly married couple arrived at the flight desk on Monday 1st February, a Dutch airport official very apologetically told Gavin that his wife didn't have the necessary travel documents and – more to the point – there was only one seat reserved for him. Killery couldn't help. All the flights to Rangoon and Australia were now reserved for VIPs; the Consulate wouldn't help, so reluctantly Jim Gavin left Barbara behind with all the money he had. Before leaving he telephoned the British Consulate and left him in no doubt about his parentage. He added that he was leaving his wife behind and he would hold him personally responsible for her safety.

News reaching Wavell continued to be bad especially from Singapore. He wasn't optimistic that the island's beach defences along the Johore Straits could withstand an enemy assault. His views were justified when a heavy bombardment commenced on the 4th and signalled the prelude to a seaborne assault across the straits. As enemy guns began pounding the harbour, causing heavy casualties, enemy planes flew unmolested overhead, attacking targets on the island and fleeing ships packed with both servicemen and civilians. These ships were forced to hide amongst the islands during the day and continue their voyage during the night. When they were finally out of range of Johore-based planes, they found themselves under attack from planes flying from the recently captured airfields in Borneo. These raids caused many casualties; ships were sunk and some simply disappeared without trace. What survivors there were eventually used SOE's escape route run by Campbell and Lyon. Ships that reached Java found its main port, Batavia, crowded with more shipping because there was insufficient coal and oil to bunker them to Australia or India. The town was packed with refugees from Singapore and servicemen disembarking from the escape ships were marched off to inland transit camps. The RAF especially had a large camp in the centre of Java.

About the 5th Killery received a message from Goodfellow advising him that a ship had been found to evacuate specialists from 101 STS and that Warren had put together two armed parties which he proposed to put behind enemy lines. One party, made up of Vanrennan and Graham, would search for Spencer Chapman – missing somewhere north of Kuala Lumpur in the jungle – while the second group which consisted of Chinese Communist guerrillas from the last course at the school, would infiltrate inland and join up with existing groups in the jungle.

An unexpected visitor for the second time was Jim Gavin who should have, by this time, reached Rangoon. It seemed that the plane flew as far as the Nicobar Islands, a small group between Sumatra and Burma, where the pilot intended to refuel. The plane circled the island, requesting permission to land, but the ground control didn't reply. Suspecting the islands had been seized by the Japanese, the pilot returned to Java. Barbara was delighted, but Killery less so.

News from Singapore continued to be grim. The Japanese had launched their expected attack and in bitter hand-to-hand fighting amongst the island's beach defences, the Australian defenders were overwhelmed and the enemy pushed ashore and attempted to seize the airfield. Wavell flew there himself to obtain first-hand information from General Percival. When he returned he cabled Churchill that the battle for Singapore was not going well, morale was not good and finished by adding that he had given Percival orders that there must be no thought of surrender and everyone must continue fighting right up to the end. This message hid from Churchill the desperate situation which in fact existed. Large numbers of troops, particularly Australians, were roaming around its streets in gangs, looting and drinking and forcing their way on board escape ships at gun point. The hospitals were crammed with casualties and thousands of Europeans filled the waterfront, scrambling for a place on what might be the last ships to leave Singapore.

What Wavell, Percival and Killery didn't know, because no one had been prepared to let SOE have sufficient wireless transmitters, was that Spencer Chapman's stay-behind parties and the Chinese guerrillas were repeatedly cutting the enemy's supply routes which had already caused a supply shortage for the troops assaulting Singapore. If this had been known, and SOE given more support from the local military, reinforcements could have been infiltrated behind the lines. This would have blunted the enemy attack on Singapore and its capture.

Wavell hardly had time to send off his cable to Churchill when news arrived in the middle of the week that enemy naval units escorting troop transports were sailing around Borneo. They were expected to turn west and, cutting across the sea lane between Java and Singapore, seize Banka Island and the oil port of Palembang. For once the intelligence assessment was correct. Preceded by ample air cover the invasion fleet arrived off Banka on the 11th, cutting the only sea route to Singapore. The following day the Japanese assaulted Palembang.

Every day the situation became worse for Wavell's command. On the 13th Wavell repeated to Percival that he must fight to the end 'but when everything humanly possible has been done some bold and determined personnel may be able to escape to Sumatra'. Later

Jim Gavin and his team 'blow' the power station at Prai.

The bridge at Fraser Hill demolished after Jim Gavin crossed back into British lines.

Brian Passmore and two sergeants from the school.

Colonel Warren RM with Lieutenant Passmore RN, settling a discussion as to which RN officer was in command of the launch. Singapore, 7th February 1942.

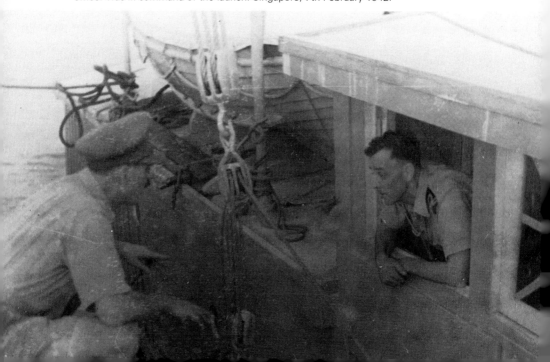

that day when he studied the latest reports from Palembang he ordered all British units in Sumatra to withdraw to Java. This meant that Sumatra was to be given up without a fight, leaving the Dutch troops alone to face the Japanese.

The next day, in Singapore, Percival wanted to surrender. The island was encircled and there was no hope of either supplies or reinforcements. Wavell insisted he must continue to inflict maximum damage on the enemy as long as possible. In London Churchill was having second thoughts about the hopeless mess he had placed the army in. In a signal to Wavell he wrote 'it would be wrong to enforce needless slaughter'. When he received this Wavell signalled to Percival that 'when he was satisfied that he could no longer inflict losses and damage on the enemy' he left it to his discretion to cease resistance.

By the 15th the ABDA Command was disintegrating. Percival surrendered to the Japanese and Wavell ordered Sumatra to be finally abandoned. Alarmed, the Chiefs of Staff in Whitehall told Wavell that Java must be defended at all costs as the Dutch East Indies was the only barrier before Australia. Their concern was much too late; with everything falling apart around him he replied that with the loss of south Sumatra the defences of the area had broken down and it was not a question of prolonging the defences but what could be saved.

Officers arriving in Java on the last ships to leave Singapore found the military headquarters near Bandung in turmoil. Everywhere it seemed bonfires were burning files and records, sending clouds of charred paper floating above the government offices and barrack blocks. To avoid wasting time when the order to move arrived staff were sorting out their personal kit into essential and non-essential items and personnel who had arrived independently from Singapore recognised the signs and made their way across to the west coast to find a boat to take them across the Indian Ocean. All available seats on aircraft were reserved for VIPs and flights to Rangoon were suspended when it was learnt that the Japanese were closing in on that city.

Amongst those still arriving from Singapore was Major Angus Rose. Killery wasn't in the best of spirits and the reports he was receiving did nothing to improve them. He had difficulty in communicating with Goodfellow during the last days of the battle for the island and no one knew what had happened to him.

Gavin was released from his liaison duties with the Dutch and told to make his own way to Burma by any available means. Begging a lift in an American army truck, he and Barbara reached Batavia and booked into a hotel. The chances of finding a berth seemed hopeless as thousands were in a similar position, roaming the harbour looking for a ship leaving for – anywhere.

Major Angus Rose joined two SOE officers, Egerton Mott and Nixon the Banker, in trying to enthuse the Dutch in clandestine operations. The general opinion was that the Dutch lacked fighting spirit but it was also recognised the odds were stacked against them – even the British had been outfought in Malaya. Others also lacked this fighting spirit and it was apparent that many of the Allies in Bandung were anxious to leave before they too were captured.

All the Dutch had to defend Java's 800 miles of coastline were 25,000 Regular, but mainly native Dutch, troops, 8,000 Australians, including a large number who had escaped from Singapore, a squadron of light tanks manned by the 3rd Hussars and a Texan artillery company equipped with old French 75's. Like the Malayan Communist Party the nationalist underground in Java volunteered to fight alongside the Dutch but this offer only caused alarm amongst the Dutch authorities. There was an ever present fear of a native uprising and pre-war thousands of nationalists, university students, teachers, professional people and trade unionists had been arrested in an attempt to wipe out the nationalistic aspirations. They were left to rot in jungle concentration camps in New Guinea.

Sumatra had been abandoned by the military but civil government still functioned and life continued as a pre-war existence except that Dutch administrators waited hourly for the Japanese to arrive. In Padang the authorities were caught by surprise as each train from the mountains brought in hundreds of servicemen and increasing numbers of European civilians from Singapore.

Before he left to carry out his seaborne raids, Warren had arranged for two of his men to set up an escape route from Singapore, through the Durian Straits to Sumatra. Using the small inland port of Rengat on the east coast, specialists and officers selected by GHQ would be passed overland to Padang where, it was planned, Royal Navy ships would evacuate them to India. This the Dutch expected but instead they complained to Java, gangs of leaderless and undisciplined British and Australian troops were arriving by the trainload and the civil authorities couldn't cope. They appealed to the British to send along someone who could take command. With everyone intent on escape from Java when the time came, the prospect of going north into what seemed to be a no-man's land to take command of a demoralised rabble from Singapore was a daunting task.

Unfortunately for Warren he came ashore about now at a small fishing village and made his way to the local Dutch military headquarters to make contact with Bandung for news and instructions. By this time the Orient Mission had effectively ceased to exist as a co-ordinated command. Killery had left by air for Australia and nothing more was heard from him. Jim Gavin and his wife were marooned in Batavia frantically looking for any vessel to take them. All contact with Burma and the Malayan operations had been lost and there only remained Egerton Mott in Bandung as anchor man. He had recently arrived from London on an inspection tour. So when the news circulated in GHQ that a Colonel Warren, on special operations, had turned up in north Sumatra, he was the ideal person to deal with the Padang problem. A Colonel Field wrote briefly explaining the position and sent him instructions to proceed to Padang and report the position he found there.

In Tanjong Priok, the port for Batavia, the harbour authorities were trying to clear all shipping. Any with sufficient fuel to reach any Allied port were ordered to leave. The congestion was so bad that even naval ships had difficulties in getting sufficient fuel. In their hotel near the waterfront Jim Gavin and Barbara sat in the bar discussing the deteriorating position. The situation was fairly hopeless and the most recent news spoke of more enemy landings, this time on Bali and the Celebes.

Looking around the room for a waiter he noticed a gang of soldiers pushing their way into the crowded room. Some had beards, their uniforms were grimy and, from the smell, they could do with a bath. They all carried weapons and looked trouble. Who recognised who first Gavin doesn't remember, but the next moment he was surrounded by Trappes-Lomax and his men.

'What are you doing here?' they wanted to know. He countered with another question: 'How did you get here?'

Lomax told him that he had a coastal steamer tied up at the harbour.

'Don't go away,' shouted Gavin over his shoulder as he turned and hurried out of the bar to collect their kit from the hotel room.

Later, on board the coaster he was briefed by Trappes-Lomax about the chaos that led up to the surrender of Singapore. A few days after he left the Sappers blew the causeway and that simple act, if nothing else, seemed to bring home to the European population that the end was near. It created a feeling of isolation, of being trapped, and the urge to escape gathered momentum and everything began to fall apart. Only Goodfellow was left in Singapore, everyone else was either aboard the *Krain* or had returned to their previous units. Reflecting on SOE business there was a lot to do in Java and three of the staff Trappes-Lomax, Lowe and Hembry were told to report to Mott in Bandung, leaving Gavin in charge of the *Krain*.

CHAPTER FOURTEEN

The Abandoned Stay-behind Parties

Members of the stay-behind party in Hong Kong had the option of either surrendering or escaping across the Chinese mainland to Chungking. Those in Malaya had no easy option. Apart from the ill-fated SIS Kuanton party, SOE are known to have placed four groups north of Kuala Lumpur and at least two in Johore. The Vanrennan party was the seventh and, finding the junk had deserted them, they made their way inland; possibly trying to find Spencer Chapman. For about four weeks they left behind them a trail of destruction and sabotage in an area packed with enemy troops and transports. At first, suspecting the local guerrillas, the Japanese swept away whole villages for interrogation. Following the successful ambush of a train and discovering that Vanrennan's party was involved, the Japanese announced that if they didn't give themselves up they would execute the hostages. To avoid further bloodshed they surrendered on about 25th March.

After being beaten and questioned, Vanrennan and Graham turned up at Puda Prison. They were dragged from the lorry, roughly handled by the guards, searched and thrust through the doors into a small courtyard, designed by the British as an exercise yard for thirty prisoners. It was packed with 700 Dutch, Australian and British troops, all of them captured in combat or shortly after-wards and they lacked everything – no soap, towels, they ate with their fingers from old hub caps or bed-pans. The smell from this large group of unwashed met them as they stumbled into the courtyard but the overpowering stench came from the open latrines dug by the troops in the corner of the yard. The wounded were jammed into a small room, 10 × 6 feet, without medical attention or drugs and they lay in their own filth, covered in flies.

Every day working parties left the prison to clear minefields and booby-traps and it was about the time that Vanrennan arrived, that prisoners were put to work at a large underground ammunition dump left untouched when the British army evacuated Kuala Lumpur. One day, in an underground chamber, Vanrennan forced open a box and found it full of gelignite; in another gallery were boxes of hand-grenades. For one brief moment the guard was distracted and one grenade disappeared under Vanrennan's hat.

Back at the prison everyone was searched – 'Empty your pockets, lift up your arms, bend over – next – '. The hat was ignored. 'Under Vanrennan's inspired leadership,'* comments one of the prisoners who survived the war, 'the prisoners were taught the value of cold-blooded bluffing.' All those with headgear wore a hatful of explosives back to Puda. In the underground dump men queued to urinate in case after case of mortar bombs – molten pitch was poured down gun barrels and one enterprising Sapper set two booby-traps in the tunnels, sufficient to blow the dump and half of Kuala Lumpur to smithereens. His fellow prisoners' enthusiasm was dampened when he admitted that he couldn't remember in which tunnel he set his traps.

About the time the arms smuggling was at its height Vanrennan was joined by his old friend Harvey and two more stay-behind men, Gardner and John Sartin from No 2 Party. They had been captured near Kuala Kuba. From them he learnt that Spencer Chapman was alive and well. He had joined No 2 Party after the collapse of the Slim River defence line, which stopped him reaching Vanrennan. He arrived in a bad state, with a high temperature and still suffering the after effects of malaria. Despite his condition he insisted that they try to contact Vanrennan's No 1 Party and led them on a twelve day, cross-country march through the mountainous jungle until they eventually arrived, at about the end of January, at the now empty camp. When Chapman questioned the Chinese contractor who had previously helped him establish the hideout, he discovered that after losing all their stores Vanrennan's party set off for Kuala Lumpur. After they had gone however, the contractor had searched the area to see what they had left behind and found where some of their stolen supplies were hidden. When Chapman later examined this cache he discovered that all that was left was a large supply of explosives but – more important – no wireless transmitter.

The Chinaman now agreed to help again and took Chapman's party to his own secret jungle hideout where they would be safe from prying eyes. After resting for some days the party used this as their base for sabotage raids. Researching into the success of these it has been concluded that they destroyed some fifteen bridges, ambushed

* Russell Braddon – *The Naked Island*.

road convoys and damaged at least fifty vehicles, as well as cutting the main railway line in about sixty places which derailed seven or eight trains. Apart from killing or injuring some 1,500 troops their activities forced the enemy to use much needed manpower, better employed on the assault on Singapore, to carry out searches as well as guard bridges and roads. At one time the Japanese were forced to stop using both road and railway which caused a shortage of much needed supplies and reinforcements during the crucial and final stages of the battle which led to General Percival surrendering the city.

They heard the news of the fall of Singapore one morning while they rested following a successful night raid. With growing disbelief they heard from their Chinaman that Percival had surrendered all Allied forces there. At first they dismissed the news as rumour but later when they re-examined their position they concluded that if it were correct then the expected counter-attack by the Americans was now out of the question and apart from GHQ, Java – some 800 miles through enemy-occupied areas – their escape must be to India. This meant calling in all the four stay-behind parties but before Chapman could implement that action two members of No 3 Party, who had been sent to find him, walked into camp. This party, he discovered, had not yet been able to start operations and when they finally heard that Singapore had fallen they put themselves on half rations. This was discouraging news and possibly re-emphasised Chapman's decision to evacuate his men and train more effective groups, in India, to carry out the sabotage work in Malaya.

Over the next six weeks he made arrangements for the move which included cycling one night to Sungai Gow where No 3 Party had their base. Here he discussed the proposed plans and bought five more, rather rickety, bicycles for the escape. The other problem was the whereabouts of No 4 Party, under the command of Lieutenant Stubbington. Sartin was sent to locate them with a letter from Chapman telling them of the plans. Although he found the area he was told by a Chinese that the camp was near a number of Malay villages whose inhabitants couldn't be trusted. The contact agreed to carry the message to Stubbington's camp but he never reappeared and, fearing the worst, Sartin returned to base where he was joined by members of No 3 Party.

Chapman now had sufficient bicycles for each member of the eight-man party and on to these were loaded rations, ground-sheets, weapons and their personal belongings. The journey was expected to take some six weeks and he hoped they could pick up extra rations from the guerrillas. The group was separated into two sections for the journey which was to prove a disaster. The bicycles, well past their prime, collapsed, riders crashed and others became lost. One night, somewhere near Kuala Kuba, Chapman's group rode through an enemy road-block before the astonished and half-asleep guards could stop them. The second group, following on a few days later, were not so fortunate. When they emerged out of the darkness at a road-block they were surrounded by angry guards who, after knocking them about and interrogating them, sent them by truck to Kuala Lumpur for further questioning. They were incarcerated in Puda Prison where Vanrennan was also being held.

Stubbington's party had been betrayed by the local Malays and when the Japanese attacked their camp they were forced to abandon all their supplies before they fled into the jungle with their weapons. Following tracks which avoided main roads and villages, they made their way across the jungle-covered hills to Jeruntut, on the Pahang River. During the night they stole a boat and navigated down this swift flowing river until disaster overtook them a second time when the boat struck a rock in the darkness and capsized. Fortunately no lives were lost and when they dragged themselves ashore they still had the revolvers but had lost their personal kit and weapons in the raging torrent. When they dried themselves out they again set out, following the river towards the coast.

On the day Warren was facing the enemy, 17th March, their luck ran out when they were once more betrayed by local Malays and ambushed by the Japanese. In the unequal fight that followed Stubbington, Rand and Darby were killed and Elkin and Pearson captured. The two survivors were badly beaten by their captors before being forced to dig their own graves. When the impatient guards considered the shallow graves deep enough they were ordered out of the pits, bound and lined up alongside the graves. While they were silently making their peace with their Maker someone suggested they should first be questioned. So, still bound, they were again beaten before being dragged across the clearing and thrown on board the back of a captured British army lorry and driven to Gemas, then on to Puda Prison.

Although the Japanese possibly didn't realise the fact that they had almost 50% of the stay-behind parties in Puda, they did discover a safe conduct pass signed by Warren amongst the prisoners' possessions. This led to a search of all camps for officers of that name.

While the other captured SOE staff adopted a low profile, Vanrennan decided it was time to leave. For some weeks he had gathered around him a group of like-minded individuals. They were all suntanned and gradually acquired sarongs, shirts and native shirts. As they could also speak Malay or Tamil they felt confident that they could, in a pinch, pass themselves off as natives. To make themselves as independent as possible they also put aside rice balls from the meagre ration. For good measure, and one which was possibly to seal their fate, they also hid grenades amongst their clothes to defend themselves.

The side door from the courtyard had been receiving their attention for some days and one night they just walked quietly through and disappeared into the night. The next morning their absence was covered by the rowdy Australians and to all intents and purposes they should have had at least twelve hours' start before their absence was noticed. However at noon the main gates opened and the badly shaken and shackled escapers were herded through at bayonet point. Evidently during the night the local population had three times tried to seize them and had also alerted the Japanese garrison. Eventually the escapers found themselves surrounded by a well-armed, large, enemy patrol. The Japanese Prison Commandant was not amused to discover nine prisoners missing, especially as the dawn role call had been correct. During the search following their arrest the grenades were found and the guards demanded to know where they had come from. Fortunately this questioning was overheard by the British Duty Officer so that when the guards swept through the prison searching each cell, they were three minutes behind two British officers with a large sack who collected every piece of explosive in the prison. They dumped the sack down the well thirty seconds before the posse of bad-tempered searchers swept into the courtyard.

The escapers were kept heavily shackled for two days and refused food and water or visits to the latrines. They were then dragged out and taken away in lorries to Kuala Lumpur cemetery where they were given long handled spades and ordered to dig their own graves. Later that day, soaked in sweat from the digging and covered with their own filth from the prison cell, Vanrennan, Harvey and Graham who had shared so many adventures, together with Gardin, Bell (an Australian), Jan (a young Dutch Wildebeeste pilot) and three others were executed. A ninth member of the party in Bentong hospital with a broken leg was also executed when the break was healed.

South Johore: Captain Smyllie's Party

News that Warren had set up a base at Labohanbilak reached Captain Smyllie operating with a small party of mainly Danes near Labin, close to the Johore border with Negri Sembilan. Like Spencer Chapman he had been left behind with a large cache of explosives. He'd spent a fruitful five weeks behind the line destroying trains and bridges and, as a spot of light relief, ambushed enemy lorries rushing troops to Singapore for the final battle. The Japanese were having a bad time trying to reinforce their front line troops. After Chapman and the Slim River patrol had dealt with them, they ran up against Tan Chen King's guerrillas. Once clear of these they needed to cross Smyllie's territory.

Like the other Europeans left behind he must have been badly shaken by the news that Singapore had surrendered, followed three weeks later by the Dutch surrender in Java. The news the guerrillas brought him, that Warren was in Sumatra, offered him both the chance of more supplies and reinforcements and, most of all, the opportunity to leave. Like Tan Chen King, he too made the journey by boat to Sumatra only to find the town in Japanese hands. He returned to Malaya and is believed to have died, on his birthday, some four weeks later.

SIS East Coast Parties

The 101 STS wireless operators left at Kuala Krai in December, Sergeants Regan and Meldrum, were soon faced with the same problem which haunted all Knott's attempts to establish a viable communications system in Malaya – the sets didn't work. Their job was to gather military intelligence and transmit the information back to Kranji and although the transmitters were tested before the soldiers were left behind, their sets malfunctioned as soon as Knott left. While they attempted to trace the fault the area was overrun and within days they were 100 miles behind the lines. Their position was useless so they buried the wireless set and burnt the codes before trying to catch up with the retreating British army. In the weeks that followed their money ran out and both were completely exhausted. They avoided roads and large towns and villages and relied upon the local population for help. Finally Meldrum died, probably of exhaustion and lack of food, leaving Regan to continue the journey to Kuala Lumpur. About the end of January the Chinese family hiding him explained that the city was captured and took him to Tan Chen

King. He too must have hoped that Chapman would have provided him with the opportunity to contact his unit again.

Kuanton Stay-behind Party

About a hundred and thirty miles away the SIS volunteers from Kuanton, Cottrill and Tyson,* were being hidden by an old Chinese couple. Exhausted and starving, they had eventually reached Segimat only to find it in enemy hands. Here they were befriended by the old couple until they were fit enough to travel south to Singapore. Enemy planes doing a victory roll over Segimat brought the news that Singapore had fallen and like all the other stay-behind parties they too pondered on their next move. Should they stick it out until the war finished or try to escape by sea – but to where? Their immediate problems were solved when a gang of local bandits decided to become guerrillas and invited them to join.

Johore

In central Johore Major Barry wouldn't accept that he and his men had been abandoned. Because of a succession of defeats, the loss of Singapore, Java and Rangoon, Barry had lost touch with all the control stations McMillan (SOE's wireless officer) had set up following the earlier loss of contact with Spencer Chapman.

Barry's party, the last one put into the jungle before Johore was given up, had set up its base deep in the jungle alongside the Sungei Pengeli river, a little distance from a large tree trunk which had fallen across the stream and now acted as a footbridge for the guerrillas. The Communists built the British party an *attap* hut using two large trees, at either end as roof supports. This became their living quarters and the wireless shack and for the first few weeks they would sit up each night, when the reception was at its best, to listen out for first Java and later Rangoon stations. When they heard that Rangoon had been evacuated and the British army was retreating towards India, their hopes of rescue began to fade. Discussing it thirty years later Knott's view was that although his Rangoon station had kept a listening watch for them as it withdrew across Burma with the rearguard he doubted whether the set left behind in Malaya had sufficient power to reach any Allied radio station.

Hopeful in his ignorance Barry continued to sit up with the wire-

* Tyson died of pneumonia twelve months later.

less operator, long after the others had gone to bed, searching the wavelengths for a friendly station. While they were doing this by the flickering light of a home-made lamp fuelled by palm oil, some forty miles away Davis and Broome were infiltrating the last Communist guerrilla patrol into Malaya.

Apart from Warren in Sumatra – who was also without a wireless set – the sudden collapse of Allied resistance along the Malayan Barrier left the stay-behind parties in Malaya leaderless. Even if a natural leader had emerged from amongst them, they had no way of communicating with each other. If Warren had known that McMillan was in Java with Barry's signal plan he could have, initially, used General Overaakers' wireless station to establish contact, first with Barry then through him the other parties and the MCP guerrillas. However he didn't have the signal plan and despite their hopes and efforts the Johore party failed to make contact with any friendly station.

CHAPTER FIFTEEN

Padang

Warren and his men drove into Padang about 26th February 1942 having left Broome and Davis behind to wait for Vanrennan's return – not knowing that by this time he had already been captured. Taking up the story Colonel Warren remembered Padang as a pleasant little town of about 60,000 inhabitants, well laid out and built, for the most part, in Dutch colonial style. Huge yellow camphor trees lines the streets. A small creek ran down to the seafront where long sandy beaches, backed by coconut palms, met huge rollers that had travelled unimpeded from the Antarctic.

'Padang,' he wrote in his recollections,

> was the terminus of an escape route I had laid on from Singapore, run by three of my men, Major Campbell, Captain Lyons and Sergeant Morris. This route paid good dividends. A few thousand men had already passed along it to Emmerhaven, Padang's port, by the time I arrived.
>
> Some days before Singapore surrendered, specially selected officers and technical troops had been evacuated to Java and Sumatra. On 13th, 'Black Friday' – many small ships and craft left carrying civilian women and nurses. This action was taken on the advice from England following the behaviour of the Japs after the fall of Hong Kong. Practically every ship was bombed and sunk and the casualties had been heavy. After 15th (the day Singapore surrendered) large numbers of troops made their way to Sumatra by devious routes and reached Padang.

Because of this Warren expected the town to be full of troops but the streets were largely empty except for a few Dutch civilians and local natives. He was told that the British troops were on board a ship in the docks.

The docks and harbour were a grim sight from being systematically bombed by the Japanese. A large number of buildings had been destroyed and the masts of half submerged ships sunk during the raids showed above the water near the entrance to the harbour. Warren found General Paris, late commander of one of the Indian divisions, aboard a Dutch vessel, the SS *Rooseboom*. He had with him

about 90 Argylls, all that was left of 2nd Battalion and some 500 civilians and servicemen, including the usual quota of deserters. The
companionways were jammed with people while others camped out
on deck for the four day journey to Ceylon. The Argylls had mounted
Bren guns on the bridge and bows and kept a wary eye open for air
attacks. General Paris told Warren that the sea links to Java were
almost severed and his only hope was to find a ship for India or
Ceylon.

While on board with General Paris Warren heard that the Australian Commander, General Bennett, had arrived in Padang after
escaping from Singapore. The news annoyed Paris, who commented
that he wouldn't give *him* any help or money to get away. However,
military planes were still flying between Padang and Java and next
morning Warren learnt from Bennett's British ADC, that GHQ Java
had sent a plane for the general and his party. Another VIP passing
through that evening by air was the Dutch Admiral Helfrich, who
had commanded the Allied fleet in the Java sea battles. He was on his
way to Colombo.

Everything in the town seemed disciplined and business-like so
Warren decided, once again, to try and mount clandestine opera-
tions using Padang as a base. Bennett's aide agreed to take a letter to
GHQ requesting a wireless set and arms* for Warren's men.

The *Rooseboom* sailed on the 28th, delayed a few hours by the news
that another train full of escapers had arrived at Padang. Soon lorries
filled with nurses, wives, children, soldiers and businessmen drove
onto the dockside. Some half naked, others in rags gathered in small
groups before brisk, officious army officers ordered them up the
gangplanks. Those already on board lined the ship's rails looking for
friends.

Among the new arrivals were survivors from a triple ship disaster
near the island of Pom Pom when hundreds were drowned. Others
like Lieutenant-Colonel Acworth, Indian Army, AAQMG with 11
Division and who had seen more than his share of the Malayan debâcle, had been specially selected to leave and had safely reached the
escape route. Another Malayan survivor was Sergeant Gibson, an
Argyll, who escaped from north Malaya after trekking 200 miles
through mountainous jungle followed by a sea escape for another 200
miles through mountainous jungle followed by a sea escape for
another 200 miles in an open native boat down the Sumatran coast.

* See Appendix.

General Paris's batman, Private Hardy, had also reached Padang. He had been in action almost continually since day one, retreating step-by-step down the peninsula and had been on the Malayan side of the causeway when it was about to be blown up by the Royal Engineers. Possibly the last man across, he kept the Engineers waiting as he strolled over. When ordered to run he calmly pointed out 'a Jap was only a Jap' and continued his amble across. Also on board Warren noticed was Mr Nunn, head of Public Works in Singapore. He had been shipwrecked on Pom Pom and rescued at the last minute before the Japanese occupied Djambi – a town used by the rescue boats.

After the ship sailed, Lieutenant Passmore RN and Colonel Warren RM walked back alongside the dock, littered with twisted derricks and burnt out *godowns*, to Padang. At that point they both assumed that most of the Singapore escapers had been evacuated, in which case there would be very little work for them at Padang, leaving them free to continue with their plans to ferry men and supplies into Malaya.

As they approached the now empty British Headquarters they found an Australian soldier sitting on its steps, with an almighty hangover, complaining about being left behind.

> *Extract from Warren's diary:*
> March 1st 1941. Padang
> Yesterday *Rooseboom* sailed with more than 500 people on board. Since then hundreds more flooded into town.

As soon as the servicemen heard that a British colonel was 'in charge' they sought Warren out. The civilians he quickly referred to the British Consul and the Salvation Army. He directed the service personnel to the Dutch Military, explaining that he was on a special mission and would be leaving soon. The Dutch didn't see it that way. Wasn't he the Senior British Officer in Sumatra? Wasn't he sent to Padang by Colonel Field at GHQ? Didn't he draw thousands of guilders on behalf of HM Government? 'Then', said the Dutch Commander patiently, 'would he do something about soldiers stealing from the traders, frightening the fishermen and molesting the women?'

Back at the Enderaach Club, which now served as British HQ a young officer stopped him. 'Excuse me, sir, can you do something about the sewers at the school – they're all choked with paper?'

The Dutch had turned the school into billets for the escapers. The sanitation followed the Dutch habit, like the Chinese, of using a bottle of water for sanitary purposes. The arrival of the paper-using British troops in overcrowded conditions soon led to a complete breakdown in the sewage disposal as tons of paper clogged the sewers, Warren remembers. 'New arrivals were greeted with the sight of a long line of water-filled buckets which offered some relief but the problem was never solved as the Dutch could offer no solution and the Royal Engineers found it impossible to clear the blockage.'

Whether he approved or not, Warren became well and truly involved with reception facilities in the town.

Later in the day an excited NCO rushed in – not bothering to salute – but Warren promptly reminded him. Two destroyers belonging to Admiral Helfrich's west coast fleet were tying up in the harbour. The crowded office emptied and Warren joined the Dutch Commander on the waterfront. The two ships took off 700 and soon after they left HMAS *Hobart* steamed in to refuel, taking with her another 512.

The ships had hardly left when another train arrived with 500 more survivors and escapers.

March 2nd

The Dutch told Warren that the port authorities in Batavia had ordered all shipping with sufficient fuel to leave. The lucky ones* slipped through the Sunda Straits only hours before the enemy invasion fleet arrived. The Allied East Coast Fleet had all been sunk including HMS *Exeter*, a cruiser, which had taken part in the hunting of the German pocket battleship *Graf Spee*.

The enemy had seized the RAF airfield overlooking the Sunda Straits and air flights to Java had ceased.

Wavell had disbanded ABDA Command and left for India.

Because of the uncertain situation the Dutch didn't know whether they could expect any more shipping to arrive at Padang. Moreover ships fleeing from Java for Australia, packed with servicemen and civilians, including many from Singapore, had run into the Japanese fleet returning from an attack on Darwin, Australia. Many Allied ships were sunk and reports were coming in indicating that those still afloat were being bombed or hunted down by submarines.

---

* Including the SS *Krain* with Major Jim Gavin, Orient Mission, and 101 STS staff aboard.

This was desperate news, compounded by the arrival of two more trains from Sawantleoha packed with servicemen and civilians. It soon became apparent to Warren that it wasn't just a problem of dealing with a few hundred that had missed the boat – the tailend Charlies – but the escape route was still packed with hundreds more.

Everyone had been held up by floods, and now the water level had dropped the evacuation had recommenced. Most of the official escapers had been evacuated. What was now left were shipwrecked survivors and individual escapers.

In his diary Warren wrote:

A few small parties under the command of good young officers were arriving, still retaining their arms but, for the most part, it was a pretty sorry picture. Most of the troops had lost everything they had and many were practically naked or had no footwear.

Of his own men running the escape route:

The Dutch said they were somewhere along the trail and there was a pretty good mess in some places. In the days that followed survivors began to come in and in co-operation with the Dutch I set about the task of accommodating and feeding them, pending the arrival of a ship to evacuate everyone.

Referring to the pressure the Dutch were under in those last days of the Empire, Warren commented that:

They deserved a tribute for their co-operation and forbearance. They had up till then seen nothing of the war or the demoralization that follows defeat and disaster. There was a lot they couldn't understand and much we could not explain. Certainly there was little in the situation for *us* to be proud of. But they did everything they could and, in the main, refrained from insults and recrimination.

With the help of the Dutch Warren set up a billeting system and reception arrangements. Each train was met by doctors and nurses – survivors themselves – with lorries and ambulances. All the wounded were in carriages clearly marked with a Red Cross at the rear of the train. All soldiers were lined up alongside the train and marched into town. The women and nurses were taken to a large requisitioned, house where a tall, bearded RN officer (Passmore?) added their names to his list. Generally the civilians were put up at the hotel while the nurses found accommodation at the hospital or the nearby convent.

The troops were marched to a school which now served as a barracks where they were met by Sergeant Road-night, a fellow escaper who stayed behind to help Warren. The officers amongst the new arrivals found accommodation at the hotel and others were given command of groups of soldiers and billeted in the school. A few refused this responsibility, complaining that it would interfere with their own escape plans. It was not uncommon, Warren commented, for the NCO in charge of a group at the school to report to him in the morning that the officer had 'done a bunk in the night – sir'. Because of this independent attitude of some of the officers, Warren became aware of a growing disrespect for authority amongst the other ranks which eventually led him to his fateful decision on 10th March to stay with the men when the Japanese overran the town.

Not all the officers shirked their responsibilities: a small number who remained with their men after the surrender and organised their escape from Singapore remained in command after they reached Padang. Nevertheless, reports reaching Warren from the Dutch authorities spoke of theft, rape and soldiers selling their weapons for food and money. The attitude amongst the individual escapers was every man for himself. To add to his worries Warren was told of a growing hostility towards the survivors by the native population whose revolt against the Dutch some fifteen years earlier was still fresh in everyone's mind.

The Dutch opened a used clothes centre in Padang where the women and children could select each a dress, blouse, skirt, stockings, shoes and underwear. While some of the men were lucky enough to scrounge an issue of Dutch uniforms, most still wandered around the town, figures of fun, in native skirts. Each day Warren drew thousands of guilders from the Dutch to pay officers and military nurses ten guilders and civilians nurses and soldiers five guilders. He remembered cynically that almost as soon as he was released from the POW camp on the River Kwai three years later he received an urgent communication from the Treasury asking for a full and detailed account of how the money was spent together with the signatures of the recipients.

A large group of nurses had assembled in Padang and almost as soon as they arrived they set about looking after the sick and wounded who were now arriving in the town in ever increasing numbers as the camps across Sumatra, emptied. Warren commented that after a bath and a hair-do and a clean frock from the Dutch shop, they usually turned up next morning at the hospital in fine spirits.

In contrast to the misery of the escape route, Major Broome and Captain John Davis drove in comfort along well metalled roads. John Davis recollected that the journey from Labinholek, on the east coast, was 'uneventful'. Very little activity had been seen and the towns were untouched by war. They reached Padang on the 2nd and made their way to the Enderaach Club where they found Warren. He was using it as British Military Headquarters and the Mess for some fifty officers. Their news that Vanrennan and Graham were missing must have been another blow to his plans to try and re-establish contact with Chapman and the stay-behind parties. Whatever his feelings, his problems were more immediate and he ordered them to drive across to the railway station and meet the train. They were to collect a wounded Indian Army officer who had won the VC at Kuanton. They were to look after him and make sure everything was done to make him comfortable.

They had parked their car outside the Club behind a long line of native horse-drawn gharries. As they drove in earlier they had noticed some outside the Town Hall and later saw others outside the school and hospital. They learnt from the Duty Sergeant that Warren was expecting a large British India liner, the SS *Chilka*, to arrive at any time and evacuate all British military and civilian personnel. Because the ship would need a quick turn-around, he had hired fleets of gharries and stationed them around the town. Everyone knew their gharry points – 'a bit like lifeboat drill' explained the sergeant.

Extract from Warren's diary:
March 5th 1941. Padang

 1,200 ton cargo boat from Batavia left Padang yesterday with 36 officers and 66 men on board. Amongst them were a crowd of Gunners who had sailed a Chinese junk from Singapore, hours after its surrender. Not a seaman amongst them, they managed to get as far as St John's Island (beyond the Singapore Roads) before they ran aground. They were later rescued by native fishermen and passed on to Major Campbell's rescue boats operating out of Rengat.

The cargo boat still had on board bombs for the RAF at Java. When she arrived at Batavia she was ordered to leave immediately without unloading her cargo.

Shortly after she left a smaller vessel arrived bound for Colombo. Her captain agreed to take fifty passengers but insisted on no women. By this time all the men who had left Singapore with Warren had arrived in Padang, including the NCO's and the men who crewed the *Hin Lee*, so he ordered all the other ranks to leave and filled the ship with men billeted in the school. Early next morning the ship sailed and two days later the look-out spotted a life-raft in the water with two Javanese seamen clinging to it. They were, at the time, the only known survivors of the *Rooseboom*. Unseen somewhere to the south drifting with the current was the ship's only seaworthy lifeboat with 150 survivors clinging to its side or standing shoulder to shoulder in the boat. Around her survivors, seven deep, clung to each other's shoulders taking turns to stand in the boat. Brigadier Paris and a large number of Argylls, trapped on board and torpedoed *Rooseboom*, went down with her. Nunn managed to push his wife through the porthole before the ship sank beneath the waves, taking him with it, trapped in his cabin. Colonel Acworth climbed over the ship's rails and dropped into the sea which seemed to be full of swimmers. The plunge took him below the surface and as he sank he became aware, in a detached way, of hundreds of air bubbles rushing past his face. When he judged his momentum slackening he kicked out for the surface where he trod water. The ship had gone and the night was filled with shouts as friends and families tried to make contact with one another. Some distance away, against the dark shades of the horizon, he could make out the black shape of a ship's lifeboat and with leisurely overarm strokes he began to swim towards it.

The lifeboat drifted for forty days before finally being washed ashore on an island close to Padang. There were only four survivors. One was Doris Lim, a Chinese girl and one-time British agent in north China. She had worked with Intelligence at the Cathay Building and, although Chinese, had been given an evacuation pass at the last minute – probably one of the three hundred allocated for civilians. This enabled her to leave on the *Kung Wo*, which was later bombed and sunk with a large loss of life off Pom Pom. The following day she was seen by another escaping vessel and rescued suffering from exposure and severe sunburn. Soon after landing at Batavia she found a berth on the *Rooseboom* bound for India. Another survivor was Sergeant Gibson, the Argyll, who had led his men 200 miles across Malaya after the debâcle at Slim River – to the escape route based at Rengat. The two remaining survivors were two crazed Javanese seamen.

Unaware of the loss of the *Rooseboom* Warren was told that the Royal Navy ship he had expected to evacuate his men had been recalled without explanation. This was possibly due to the Japanese Navy steaming towards Ceylon and the Indian Ocean becoming the happy hunting grounds for enemy bombers and submarines. Despite this, another vessel, the SS *Chilka*, sailed on the same rescue mission and the Dutch told Warren that this ship was large enough to take everyone.

Although fully involved with administrating the refugees arriving daily, he was still anxious to revert to his independent role. He had given up expecting news or help from Allied HQ at Bandung, Java, and he realised that any behind-the-lines activity by him and his men could only be done with the co-operation of the local Dutch military authorities. One opportunity to extract himself from the mess he now found himself in was offered by Campbell who had recently arrived by car from Rengat. He told Warren that a more senior colonel, named Dillon, was in charge of the last group of servicemen and civilians making its way along the escape route. At the moment the group was stranded by floods at Telok. When he eventually arrived in Padang with his 500 escapers maybe Warren could hand over his administrative authority to him!

Sitting behind his paper strewn desk Warren studied a new arrival, an Artillery officer, wearing a green felt hat. Like most, his clothes were in rags. Despite this he still retained a military bearing and saluted smartly. In a well spoken voice he introduced himself as Captain Rowley. From Campbell's report Warren knew that Rowley* had given up his chance to escape when he volunteered to skipper one of the rescue boats at Rengat. He was probably responsible for saving some 600 people, including women and children. One of the last to leave Rengat, he passed through Colonel Dillon's camp at Ayer Molak. Preferring to act independently, he left without permission, taking with him a mixed party of servicemen. These he led to Padang ahead of the main party, thus missing the floods.

The young captain was anxious for news of his gunners. He had organised his battery's escape by junk when news of the surrender reached him. Warren was able to tell him that they had sailed a few days earlier. A little more curt than usual, Colonel Warren warned Captain Rowley that he should forget any ideas he may have of stealing a native boat. Signing for his ten guilders, Rowley saluted and

* Baron Langford.

left, feeling a little as if he had been carpeted by his old headmaster. Warren realised that a resourceful officer like Rowley would make every attempt to leave.

The Dutch were being plagued by groups of penniless soldiers searching up and down the coast for boats. The Chief of Police was also on Warren's back, complaining that the troops were drinking heavily and openly copulating with the native girls in the fields close to the General Post Office, almost in sight of the Town Hall where most of the recently arrived European women were now billeted.

8th March
The Dutch military commander sent Warren a message that enemy troops were landing at Labinholek near the scene of SOE's recent east coast activities.

'Here was crisis,' wrote Warren.

He felt it was going to be a bad day. His shirt was stuck to his back with sweat. He needed a shower but he needed a drink more than a shower. He found he was getting irritated more quickly over trivial matters and the prospect of a long cold lager appealed to him. Later in the crowded bar he watched a smartly dressed young Dutch officer push his way towards him.

'Sir, I have bad news for you.'

For a moment Warren allowed himself the luxury of the thought, 'How much bloody worse can it get?' As he tried to read the Dutchman's face he was told:

'General der Pooten has surrendered Java.'

No guts, thought Warren bitterly.

'There is more – the liner you were expecting, it has been sunk.'

The young Dutch officer told him that a lifeboat from the SS *Chilka* under the command of its first officer, had sailed into Emmerhaven and had brought news that the ship had been torpedoed off Nais, one of the islands screening Padang. It was later learnt that the skipper, in another boat, also reached one of the islands and took on fresh water and fruit. He then set a compass bearing for Ceylon which he reached, two weeks later, having sailed 1,000 miles.

In the hotel's dining room, the Commandant's wife burst into tears when her husband joined her and broke the news. The crowded dining room went silent as her husband, with his arm around her, left the hotel.

Warren spent the next few hours in the Commandant's office, with both he and the Chief of Police, trying to establish how the surrender of Java would affect Sumatra and what was the military intention of the Dutch troops.

The Commandant told him that a strong enemy force was moving down from Medan, in the north, and it could be only a matter of days before it reached Padang. Warren reflected that he could smell defeat in the air. The Japanese occupied most of Sumatra had captured Palembang; occupied Djambi and Labinholek on the east coast and were pouring troops ashore at Medan. The Royal Navy had fled and Wavell had abandoned Java – as far as the Dutch were concerned – all they wanted was a smooth hand-over to the Japanese. Warren listened to the long list of reasons for not fighting with growing dismay and once again suggested that his men take to the jungle and organise resistance but this was brushed aside.

About the time Warren was trying to inject some fighting spirit into the Dutch a group of British sailors, survivors from the *Repulse* and the *Prince of Wales*, tried to seize a Dutch steamer tied up at the harbour. Following this unsuccessful attempt the Dutch mounted machine-guns along the waterfront and placed sentries on the ships. As a further precaution, the Commandant told Warren he was closing the harbour mouth with a boom trapping some dozen ships. Although some were capable of evacuating all the British military and civilian personnel, the Dutch pointed out that the vessels would be needed by the Japanese to communicate with the islands. As for the other vessels – the spokesman shrugged his shoulders – their skippers and crews refused to put to sea because of the submarine menace and the news of heavy losses amongst the ships fleeing from Java.

Outside, on the steps of the Commandant's office, Warren paused and reflected on the day's news. The streets were empty and sheets of rain beat down on the road filling the monsoon ditches. It was dark by the time he reached his dimly lit office. The storm made the shutters rattle and bounce on their hinges and the overhead fan, slowly moving, creaked its way around, sending a draught of cold air to rustle the papers on his desk.

Warren wasn't totally unprepared for the position he now found himself in. When he first arrived in Padang, Warren commented that he 'acquired a native sailing *prahau* and got her ready for sea. If any vessel had come into Emmerhaven, Padang's port it had been my intention to evacuate everyone, leaving the prahau behind as some small comfort and means of escape for those who might arrive after we had left. She was about 30 tons provisioned, which included a

spare canvas. She was named the *Sederhana Johannes* – the *Lucky John*.
The original intention was to use the boat for seaborne raids behind
enemy lines but as the weeks went by it gradually became accepted
as an escape boat.'

He had given Lieutenant Lind RN the job of provisioning her but
as his men gradually drifted in from the east coast they all contri-
buted something.

The boat weighed about 30 tons and had been used for coastal
trading. The hold was covered over to provide cabin space. Warren
had checked it out that morning and noticed how well provisioned
she was. Stacked on board were bags of rice, coconuts, army issue
tins of corned-beef and coffee. Water was stowed in large earthen-
ware jars and he noticed five bottles of whisky packed firmly in the
hold. Armaments consisted of two Lewis guns, Campbell's Tommy
guns, rifles and pistols together with ample ammunition. Passmore
and Lind had scrounged navigational charts and instruments;
Sergeant Morris RAMC, had found medicine while someone else had
produced mattresses and blankets. Her old native crew had taken his
men around the islands to familiarise them with the art of sailing a
prahau.

When Warren was told that the Dutch were closing the harbour
with a boom he ordered the *prahau* to anchor some five miles beyond
the harbour and hide amongst the lush islands marking the entrance
to Emmerhaven.

Alone in his office with the storm* raging outside, Warren,
sprawled in a cane chair, pondered on the situation he was in.

The whole thing had got out of hand. He was the authority on
organising body blows against the enemy's lines of communication
and here he was, sitting amongst administrative chaos, dealing with
refugees while the enemy was racing down the road to capture the lot
of them. Warren remembered the wind buffeting the building and
seeming to threaten to lift the roof off the club. He eased himself out
of the chair and sat at his desk. 'I decided,' he said, 'that if the *prahau*
was to get away she would have to sail immediately. Japanese planes
were overhead continuously but so far, since his arrival, had taken no
offensive action against the town.'

'The task of selecting the personnel to leave was not easy,' wrote
Warren, 'and the only qualification was their value to the war effort.
This sounds pompous but it was nevertheless true.'

* Known as Sumatras.

The first eight names were his own staff including the 'boys' belonging to Davis and Broome. He appointed Lind as captain of the *prahau* and to help sail the boat he chose three Naval officers, Geoff Brooke, who had helped Warren in the Penang evacuation, and two Royal Navy Volunteer Reserve officers, Richard Cox and Holly Holwell – both from the *Triang*. When their vessel sank they each had sailed a packed lifeboat as far as Dabo on Lingga and then remained behind to help Commander Alexander organise the search and rescue fleet of small boats. These local fishing boats scoured the surrounding islands for shipwrecked survivors. He later added a Merchant Navy officer, Garth Gorham. The remaining four places he gave to the Army. He selected the Japanese interpreter, Clark, who 'lost' his Japanese prisoners when his ship sank after being bombed escaping from Singapore; Dr Davies, Malayan Command Dermatologist, and the two officers rescued by Ernest Gordon as they rowed their way to Sumatra. He had two places left including the one he had reserved for himself.

It was decision time and he wrote in his diary: 'I wrote a message telling the young Artillery officer, who evacuated his Battery from Singapore, to join me.' When Captain Rowley arrived Warren broke the news that there was a place on the boat for him – and added – 'There's also room for one of your officers.' Warren had made up his mind. He would remain and look after the leaderless troops still pouring into Padang.

II
The Fall of Padang

March 9th

Another full day for Warren administrating the troops and civilians struggling in. Another train arrived almost full of casualties, under the care of an Australian doctor, Lieutenant-Colonel Coates. The Dutch were overwhelmed with the human wreckage he'd brought with him from the charnel houses at Dabo, Tambilihan and Rengat. Fifty of his patients were limbless. Often without drugs and under primitive conditions, Coates was forced to carry out complicated surgery. As the passengers disembarked from the train they lined up alongside the track. Those fit enough to walk were marched the two miles into town. The casualties were carried to waiting ambulances and the women taken to the Town Hall. The nurses climbed aboard lorries and were driven to a large house where twelve hours earlier Warren had said goodbye to his men.

Climbing down from the lorry the nurses lined up along the verandah. Darkness had fallen and the chill of the evening began to make them shiver. A tall, bearded, army officer stepped out from a dimly lit doorway and began to record the girls' names and what hospitals they were from. The girls, he thought, were a dishevelled bunch. Most were dirty and motley dressed. Some wore only a bra and sarong, one – who had lost all her clothes in a shipwreck – had scrounged an army khaki shirt but no underwear and now half sat on a tall stool. The exception was one rather matriarchal figure, fully dressed, with a large hat, who kept a firm grip on a suitcase. He discovered she wasn't in fact a nurse and arranged for her to be driven to the Town Hall with the remainder of the civilians. The nurses were taken to the local convent which the nuns had opened up for them. The civilian nurses were found accommodation by the British Consul.

After seeing the parties secure for the night, Colonel Dillon and Commander Alexander, who had arrived on the train, made their way to the Oranji Hotel in the centre of the town. Colonel Coates joined them later. Alexander was delighted to discover Warren in charge and commented about the irony of another Penang-type situation.

Later when Colonel Coates arrived they sat in the bar, in high-backed plush seats, listening to Warren's far from optimistic briefing. As far as he was concerned it was 'a busted flush'. They all agreed that it was useless for all three to remain but Coates followed up the point by saying that he needed to remain with the wounded: Alexander adopted the same attitude and said that he couldn't leave his party behind after shepherding them all the way from Dabo.

Later that night about 2.00 a.m. Warren awoke to the sound of what seemed to be heavy bombing nor more than a mile away. Cracks raced up the wall and plaster fell in large lumps around the room onto the awakening 300 officers now sharing the club. Ordering everyone to lie down, he rammed his tin hat firmly on his head and strode to the door with his pistol in his hand. He recalled that, 'It seemed that the enemy had arrived and had opened up on the town.' From the gateway he could see terrified European women, some naked or in their underwear, running screaming with fright from the convent school to shelter in the monsoon ditches or air-raid trenches.

Apart from the women everywhere seemed relatively calm. The gharries were still parked outside but although the horses were troublesome the drivers sat half asleep calming them with a firm hand and a gentle 'cluck cluck'. The drivers looked at him impassively. In answer to his questions they replied that the mountains were volcanic and the noise was only an earthquake.

The following day more nurses began to arrive at his office. One was Janet Lim, a Chinese nurse from the Otham Road Temporary Hospital. She was also in one of the ships sunk at Pom Pom. She reached the island and was later rescued by the *Krain* captained by Bill Reynolds,* and taken to the escape route. As each arrived, Warren would chat to them gently, getting them to talk out their horrors at sea and the violence and misery of the overland trek. He learnt from them that although some of the natives had mocked their condition, the Chinese and the Dutch helped with food, clothes and transport.

On the other hand, they also spoke of soldiers taking food and women at gunpoint and seizing the only available transport, in some cases, for themselves.

As far as the civilian nurses were concerned he found that snobbery and racial problems had added to the worries. Some European women had tried to insist that Asian nurses and native wives of soldiers and businessmen who stayed behind with the Volunteer Defence Force in Singapore should take their place at the rear of any queue – behind the Europeans – for food, bathrooms or transportation. On many occasions the nurses spoke of starving British soldiers selling their rifles and of women selling their jewellery at the bazaar, for food or money.

'The Asian nurses seemed bewildered by it all,' commented Warren, and confused when he asked them kindly whether they would prefer to go to Australia or India, when the boat came in. They would look at him with their big brown eyes, almost in tears, and explain that their homes were in Malaya.

After lunch Warren arranged another meeting of the four senior officers in the bar of the hotel. It was obvious that it was only a matter of time before the Dutch 'handed them over to the Japs'. They all agreed it was pointless for all four 'to go into the bag' but equally someone must remain to look after the troops. Coates had firmly made up his mind and repeated his decision to stay at the hospital with the wounded. Alexander still refused to abandon his party and he would take his chance with theirs. Dillon had no special responsi-

* He is credited to having rescued some 2,000 survivors scattered amongst the islands around Singapore.

bility: Warren, who had all the contacts with the Dutch and was recognised as the Senior British Officer in Padang, couldn't help
speculating that had Dillon arrived twenty-four hours earlier he
would now be the SBO, leaving him free to leave on the *prahau* which
was now well on its way to Ceylon.

As Dillon was free of any commitment they all agreed he should
leave as soon as possible and Warren would fund the escape. After
replenishing their drinks they considered the problem and Warren
remembered that he had seen two large junks at anchor at Sasak, a
small fishing village about 60 miles north of Padang. He and
Passmore had looked the place over as a possible base for covert
landings should the Japanese occupy the island. He suggested that
Dillon should try and buy one of these and also offered him the two
cars he'd received in exchange for the *Hin Lee*. While Dillon was stuf-
fing his pockets with the guilders to buy the junk Alexander commented that he didn't think there would be any trouble in finding a
crew from the hundreds milling around the town.

Leaving the others to go about the various duties, Warren left the
hotel and walked along the palm-fringed waterfront with its high rollers crashing down on the beaches to the British Consul's office with
its large Union Jack hanging limply over the street. The pavement
was crowded with survivors; some he knew, others knew him and he
acknowledged their greetings with a friendly salute. Children stopped their play and watched him stride up into the office. There he
found Mr Levison, the British Consul, trying to deal with a long
queue of destitute British civilians. Many were almost penniless
when they left Singapore and what few possessions they managed to
carry with them had been lost in the shipwrecks or bartered away on
the journey across Sumatra.

He wanted Levison to send a coded message to the Royal Navy in
Ceylon to find out what was happening to the ship being sent to
evacuate them, as well as by-pass the Dutch and get permission to
take a stay-behind party into the jungle. But he was too late – acting
on instructions Levison had destroyed the codes.

Every evening since he arrived Warren had held a meeting for all
officers to bring them up-to-date with any news he had gleaned.
Tonight was no exception but he did think it politic to defer the bad
news for twenty-four hours – he still hoped the Royal Navy wouldn't
let him down and, despite the odds, would suddenly appear off the
harbour mouth and take everyone off. The Dutch were afraid that
when the 'other ranks' realised the hopeless position they were in
they would take matters into their own hands and, maybe, take over

the town and seize the shipping. They were simply anxious that he kept the men together to avoid bloodshed or massacre of his men by the natives or Japanese.

10th March

Not all those who arrived on the daily train wanted to be absorbed into the restricting military organisation. One of these was a tall, suntanned good-looking Australian captain. He'd just arrived that evening and stood in the dark, tree-lined street opposite the hotel taking in the hustle and bustle, as officers flowed in and out of the high fronted doors. It was three weeks since he had contact with any regular military unit. With a Chinaman as crew he was rowed in a little boat to Sumatra. He had moved from village to village and camp to camp – until now. In the darkness he stood, unshaven, his clothes in rags, cradling his Bren gun – his power – his key to transport problems and his ticket home.

The hotel foyer was crammed with smartly dressed Dutch civilians and British servicemen as he pushed his way through to the crowded lounge. He slumped, exhausted, into a high-backed velvet covered settee, between two other officers. One was a colonel in the Royal Marines and the other a rat-faced featured Australian in the Medical Corps. Colonel Warren and Colonel Coates exchanged looks and stared for a moment at the newcomer before continuing their conversation with Dillon and Alexander.

The captain's body smell began to fill the crowded room as he looked around for companionship. 'I've just come from Singapore,' he said in a loud voice. His statement earned a few glances but he was ignored. In a louder voice he went on, 'I found this bloody Chinese in bed with his wife, so I rammed my gun in his belly and told him to find me a boat. When he did I made the bastard row me to Sumatra. Every time he stopped I waved the gun in his face.'

The room was silent, so quiet that it was deafening.

13th March

'It was evident,' wrote Warren, 'that the Japanese troops were closing in on the town and the Dutch declared it an open city. In a talk with the Governor I offered (again) to form a unit to co-operate with the Dutch troops and carry on guerrilla warfare.

'He turned down this offer as we had few arms and little ammunition' but made no offer to supply Warren with Dutch arms. The Commander also pointed out that he had 'little knowledge of jungle fighting could speak no Dutch and would be more of a nuisance than a help.' He warned me not to allow any men to go on the run. 'Their end,' he said, 'will not be honourable; the jungle will kill them or wild beasts or the natives.'

Commenting on this attitude Warren said that

the Dutch were fearful of the reaction of the natives who were restless and impatient for independence and had already given signs of Japanese sympathies and influence. Along the route across Sumatra, troops had flogged their arms for food, money or clothing and as a result the Dutch had disarmed the troops still retaining their weapons when they arrived at Padang. Although these were said to be in the armoury rumour had it that they were dumped into the harbour. Exactly what the Dutch policy was in Sumatra now that Java had surrendered I never discovered but it was clear that it could only be a matter of days before the Japanese gained control of Sumatra.

That evening in the room full of officers attending his briefing meeting, Warren, with the Dutch Military Commander at his side, broke the news that the British India ship they expected had been sunk.

Standing behind a small table, covered with green baize, Warren studied the restive audience waiting for the murmuring to die down. 'The Dutch are going to surrender,' he said in measured tones but he proposed to stay and work with the Dutch until the end and not attempt to escape. This last comment was intended to reassure 'his' men that he wouldn't desert them like many officers in the past had done. But it had the opposite effect and one officer remembers being incensed to hear him say that he would give his word of honour not to escape. This news produced a quiet and gloomy effect on everyone present and convinced others that the time had come to take individual action to escape.

One of the men selected by Dillon for his escape party was a Lieutenant MRNVR* – he was also the local paymaster for the troops. He approached a Captain Jennings, who was also planning his escape, and asked him to pay out the troops at the Malay School the next day – a job he usually did himself. Apart from thinking it odd Jennings agreed but felt a bit aggrieved later when he realised the chap had left with Dillon† leaving him literally holding the money.

* Malaya Royal Navy Volunteer Reserve.
† Dillon left next day with Ernest Gordon, Lieutenant Hooper commander of the *Jarak* and most of his crew.

Rumour was rife amongst the NCO's and troops and it had been suggested that the officers, quartered in private billets, hotels or the Enderaach Club were out of touch with the men living in the schools.

A self-imposed discipline had emerged amongst the men and there were no reported cases of fighting or drunkenness. Maybe the trouble-makers had left by now. Although some soldiers and officers managed to hide and retain their weapons there were no reported cases of boats being stolen. Realising the end was near groups of soldiers set out each day to search the beaches to the north and south to try and buy boats. They'd clubbed the daily pay together and formed escape parties. The further they travelled from the town the more they came up against hostile receptions from the local inhabitants. They found themselves being mocked or spat at and if they found someone prepared to sell them a boat the seller would be intimidated by neighbours who threatened to report him to the Japanese. With the money they had the soldiers could only consider native dug-out canoes, sometimes with sail. Most of the troops had never been to sea apart from the voyage to Singapore by trooper or the escape to Sumatra and now they faced the daunting prospect of sailing these light craft 1,300 miles to Ceylon or creeping down the coast for 1,000 miles.

14th March

Although Warren was effectively cut off from any Allied command the Dutch kept him up to date with the news. The air-raid on Darwin by 189 Japanese bombers flying at the limit of their petrol consumption, sank an American destroyer, four US troop transports, one British tanker and four Australian freighters. Twenty-three Allied planes were also destroyed. On the ground civil defence workers and hospitals were coping with 538 dead and wounded.

Following the disbandment of ABDA Command and the evacuation of Java, Japanese surface craft, submarines and aircraft, sank most of the escaping ships. This time there were no islands for the survivors and many perished.

The news of the enemy's approach had already reached the local population and as Warren strode away from the Residence the streets were rapidly emptying and the shopkeepers were hurriedly putting up their shutters. He sent one of the soldiers with a message to Colonel Coates at the hospital, informing him of the latest possibility. At the hospital, run by a Canadian Salvation Army Commander Major Meopham and his wife, the doctors and nurses stood by the sick and wounded and waited. They all knew that the Japanese had no respect for hospitals or the wounded and remembered that as the Japanese advanced into the suburbs of Singapore they burst into the hospital wards and bayoneted the wounded, including one actually having surgery on the operating table. In Hong Kong they killed the doctors and lined up to rape the nurses – held down and spread-eagled.

As Warren walked down the now empty streets, the town seemed mean and grubby. He noticed for the first time how narrow the streets were and that piles of manure lay uncollected where they had fallen. Shutters would briefly open and be noisily closed and bolted; leaving a white sheet dangling down and little Japanese flags were appearing on doors and closed shutters. A small crowd of Chinese had gathered around the convent's gateway. The high, wooden, double doors were open and the nurses – including many of the Asian ones – were calmly doing their chores. The men at the gate believed the Japanese might sell off the nurses and were doing a bit of window shopping in anticipation. Colonel Warren sent a message to the nurses to close the doors and make certain that they all wore Red Cross armbands.

He also issued orders, through Sergeant Major Road-night, that all soldiers were confined to their school billets from 6.00 p.m. By that time more than a hundred had decided to chance their luck and slipped away, either into the neighbouring countryside or towards the beach in search of a boat. Levison instructed all the British civilians to concentrate at the Salvation Army Hostel or the Town Hall.

By late afternoon the streets were empty apart from Warren's lonely figure doing the rounds.

Hong Kong had been captured; Malaya had been overrun; Singapore had surrendered; The Dutch had packed in!!

That same day when Warren did his lonely vigil, the Japanese walked into Rangoon. The only ones left were his abandoned ragbag army in Padang.

16th March

Dillon's party left the previous day for Sasak with Warren's money to buy the boats and Warren's cars he'd swapped for the *Hin Lee*. Although they didn't know at the time, they narrowly missed early capture when they turned off the main road only minutes ahead of a Japanese column, spearheaded by armoured cars, racing to capture Padang. Warren funded eight more escape parties and let it be known that money was available for anyone with a reasonable plan.

Shortly after Dillon's party left town Warren was called to see the Dutch Governor and fully expected to be carpeted for encouraging his 'men' to escape. Instead he was told that the Japanese were only 60 miles away at Fort de Kock and would be expected in Padang the next evening. 'In a resigned and tired voice the Governor told me he would surrender the whole of Sumatra,' said Warren.

At 7.00 p.m. Colonel Ferguson Warren left his headquarters with his interpreter, Waite. The following is taken from his recollections with his permission before he died:

'As I left to join the Dutch authorities for the last act of this debâcle I passed a half-crazed European civilian clutching a spaniel, trying to retrace his steps across Sumatra to find his wife.

'There was a strange hush over the town.

'I thought of all those anxious men and women who were awaiting the result of the night's work; of the two *prahaus* at sea, making for Colombo; of the men hiding up in some nearby jungle; of the defeat and ruin of Singapore and the mainland beyond. What was the why of it all?

'We are about to see the end of three hundred years of history.

'It was 1.00 a.m. on the morning of 17th March. There was a spattering of gravel outside the main entrance of the Governor's office and a certain tenseness was felt around the large table at which we were sitting. The Governor and his staff were sitting opposite to me, immaculate in full-dress whites with gold embroidered collars and cuffs, stiff, dignified and obviously concealing considerable emotion; the Dutch army captain and warrant officer in jungle green, seemingly conscious of their inferior rank and work-a-day clothing, sat awkwardly on my left; the British Consul, a small, worried-looking man in a white tropical suit, sat at the end of the table on my right. He had insisted on attending this ceremony in his official capacity and had assumed responsibility for our civilians. His Dutch wife was, I knew, very ill. My own khaki shirt and shorts were dirty and smelt, for the few other belongings I had possessed had gone with the *prahau* a week before.

'The main door of the outer hall was rudely burst open and we turned to watch a young Jap officer stride through the room, his new yellow riding boots squeaking and thumping on the polished wooden floor. He was followed by a Dutch police officer and a bearded bespectacled Jap soldier, armed with rifle and bayonet. A bearded Jap? Not a good beard but nevertheless a beard!

'The Jap strode up to the table, arrogant and truculent, and stood with his legs apart turning his head to glare suspiciously at each of us. Slowly we all came to our feet and returned his stare. Whatever effect it had been intended to produce was interrupted by the bearded sentry dropping the butt of his rifle heavily on the floor, which he followed immediately by emitting a loud belch. Instinctively we turned our heads towards him, a ridiculous and owlishly self-conscious figure.

'The officer slumped quickly into a chair between myself and my interpreter, with a characteristic hissing intake of breath through his teeth. He seemed suddenly tired of acting his charade and removed his cap to mop his shaven head with a dirty neck cloth he was wearing. He ostentatiously selected a cigarette from a shining new silver cigarette case, lit it and started to talk. He had the appearance of being either slightly drunk or doped but was nevertheless in full possession of his senses. The interpreter told us that he was asking for a drink and when a glass of water was brought he turned up his nose. Laboriously he started to scribble on a sheet of paper and giggled childlishly to himself; he thought the girls in Singapore were lovely and this seemed to be his only topic, so the interpreter informed us; he was trying to draw one of the lovely girls.

'This was opera bouffe. Our tension relaxed and we talked more easily among ourselves. The Dutch police officer said that he had met the Jap by arrangement at Fort de Kock and had been driven into Padang with a gun in his ribs, for the Japs suspected some treachery. A general was to be expected in an hour or so to receive our formal surrender. He told me that General Overaakers* had been compelled to surrender and his troops considered it was useless for them to carry on the struggle after Singapore and Java had fallen.

'While the Dutch exchanged news and talked among themselves and the interpreter kept the Jap officer in conversation, the purpose of the gathering around me struck me with some force. Were we really so impotent that we had to surrender ourselves and our men to trash like the fool on my right or the belching sentry behind me? The war had not so far killed my morale even though my experience had to date been all scuttle and run. Norway and France in 1940? We had come out of that with out tails high even though we knew our country had its back to the wall and was hanging on by a shoe-string. But this

* General Overaakers was beheaded by the Japs some years later, it is believed for his part in carrying out the scorched-earth policy in Sumatra.

Malaya business had been different somehow, even after allowing for the same lack of aircraft, tanks and other necessities of modern war. The country, the jungle, had been so unknown to our men; they couldn't tell most of them a Jap from a Chinese, a Malay from an Indian. The *Prince of Wales* and the *Repulse* had somehow started the rot, though God forbid that I should blame the Royal Navy for our position.

'I had been in the War Room at the Naval Base in Singapore when Admiral Phillips had made his decision to put to sea and I remember thinking as I watched him that here, indeed, was history in the making. A historic moment! But that effort had also gone wrong somehow. We still had so many fine fighting types; if I had seen demoralisation and lack of manhood in some, I had also seen the other side of the penny – men taking their bombing and machine-gunning and coming up with the ago-old grins of defiance and contempt. What had been wrong then? Was it our leader? Was it me, even now sitting here waiting to cash in my cheques while my men lay in the darkened billets awaiting the results of my night's work? What did they think about it all?

'An hour passed and there were sounds of movement outside. The Jap officer dropped his childish behaviour and shouted something to us as he jumped to his feet and made for the door. 'They're here, sir' – from my interpreter.

'This was it!

'They entered noisily and we stood up as the sentry banged his butt. This too, was a play, but a grim one. The Jap commander entered followed by about twenty others. They strode purposefully in with the air of conquerors, kicking their legs in front of them, their muddy boots striking heavily on the floor, their curved swords jangling as they walked. The general went to the table opposite me with a few of them, the remainder ranging themselves behind me. A few words were snapped out. 'Chairs,' said my interpreter, and the Dutch moved out to get them. Treating us all as if we did not exist the general sat and talked with two of his staff while the others were being seated, to the accompaniment of noisy throat clearing and hissing intakes of breath as though the coming proceedings were going to be something of great relish.

'I glanced about me. It was as if the pages of history had been rolled back. Vague memories stirred in my mind. Here were Genghis Khan and Tamerlaine and the Mongol hordes of centuries past. These were good fighting men, crude, fierce, proud and confident.

There was little of the undersized myopic Jap in this bunch with the broad, flat, yellow faces with cruel eyes and long wispy moustaches under beehive-shaped sun helmets, bleached and dirty and long past their best; the clothing was stained and made of some cheap cotton material: the sleeves half covering their short gorilla-like arms. A jangle and scraping of chairs as swords were placed between their bow legs and they settled down, filling the room with the sour smell of sweat.

'The jabbering and hubbub gradually died down and we turned our eyes towards the general. He was wearing a British soldier's tropical helmet and shirt with no trimmings or badges of rank that I could see. Helmets were removed and an officer on the right of the general opened the play by suddenly pointing a pencil at me and asking something in Japanese.

' "Do you command the British troops?"

'My interpreter took up his role without further invitation.

' "Yes," this was interpreted back.

' "How many troops are here? Where are they? Where did they come from? Where have you come from?"

'So it went on, the interpreter putting the questions to me and passing the answers back. The questions were simple and there was no point in concealing what the Japs would learn in a few hours' time. We handed over our written surrender and a statement of the disposition of all British nationals in the town. These were read with interest and carefully filed away. They appeared to understand what was set down. The story I told was that I had been sent over from Java just before it fell to look after the British in Padang. I was silent as to the real purpose the port had served or the thousands who had passed through.

'Now the Dutch captain had his turn. He was vague and confused in his answers and the irritation of the Jap was plain. A map was demanded. A thing the size of a postcard was brought in which showed nothing even to the Dutchman. The Jap became suspicious and he started to shout. A map on a large wooden frame was brought, so enormous that some difficulty was found in getting it through the door. The situation was getting slightly ridiculous and I had time to study the officers grouped behind the general. One had a fine head and an aesthetic face and carried himself with aloofness and dignity. The proceedings had little interest for him and he seemed to take pains to show his contempt for them. I put him down as the artillery commander and tried to sort out the remainder of the staff. I was somewhat distracted by the snorting, honking and hissing of a fat, uncouth ruffian immediately behind my chair whose path I was later to cross when he filled the role of Town Major.

'So the affair dragged on. The Governor was questioned closely. Coffee was demanded but none was forthcoming from the back premises; glasses of water were produced instead.

'It was about seven o'clock when the party broke up and the bulk of the Japs departed leaving half a dozen or so behind. I was instructed to keep all my men in their billets and was given a pass to return to my headquarters. This was fastidiously written out in Japanese, with my name in both Japanese and English, by the staff officer who had questioned us. He spoke good English and could not resist telling me he had been to a military academy in France. He was certainly no fool and I felt some satisfaction that here at least was someone with, apparently some civilisation in him.

'I left the building with a sense of unreality strong upon me and walked down the middle of the road with my interpreter. The latter – Waite by name – had done well, though there was little in the miserable proceedings which could be regarded as cause for satisfaction. I felt, however, that our request for decent treatment for the sick and civilians had been fairly received, though I could not understand the farewell remark of the Governor's assistant "Your people will have a bad time," spoken kindly with tears in his eyes.

'The native population stared curiously at us as we passed. All roads were jammed with Jap lorries but the drivers took little notice of us. They were busy on their engines or crawled like monkeys over their vehicles doing odd jobs.

'I decided that it would be safe to make a detour and call at one of the school where several hundred troops were housed. On the way we passed several natives with baskets of live hens. We told them to follow us for we were doubtful of the food situation. They did so with some caution.

'We gave the commanding officer our news, the chickens and some money and then went on our way to my headquarters.

'Three members of the Kempetai – the Jap secret police – were waiting to interview me. They were undersized little rats in shoddy civilian clothes; the questions were a repetition of what I had answered previously, and I told them the same sort of story. They wanted to search the building for arms but I assured them that all arms had been collected into the Dutch armoury. In actual fact we had hidden, around the building, about six revolvers, a few compasses and other escape items.'

At the school Japanese guards took over. One of the men who escaped from Singapore, Sergeant Road-night, decided it was now or never and slipped away under the cover of darkness.* He had been given command of some hundred soldiers who had "lost" their units in the final battle for Singapore and sent back into the fight. He retained control of the survivors and following Percival's surrender, organised their escape to Rengat. Most of his men had been evacuated but he stayed behind with Warren to help run the school when he learnt that officers, appointed by Warren to look after the men, had left to make their own private escape arrangements.

> *8.30 a.m. March 17th 1942. Padang, Sumatra.*
> A Japanese motorised column arrived last night from Fort de Kock at 1.30 a.m. Awaited the arrival of the Jap Commander in Government House in company with the Dutch Governor, his staff and the Dutch Military Commander. Made my formal surrender. St Patrick's Day and my first day as a prisoner. And now what?

An extract from Colonel Alan Warren's diary hastily scribbled when he arrived back from Government House. The Orient Mission had ceased to exist and he was about to create a legend on the River Kwai.

---

* After hiding in the jungle he eventually acquired a native boat and set sail for Ceylon. Ten days later he was found by the Royal Navy and taken to Australia. No one believed his story and he was arrested as a deserter.

CHAPTER SIXTEEN

The Burma Party

Following the surrender of the Dutch East Indies in March 1942 only two Orient Mission's sections still remained active although, technically, no longer part of that Mission. One was Jack Knott's Signals Unit and the other Steve Cummins' Burma Section. Like Malaya, military units in Burma had been starved of both men and equipment and had a lower priority rating, if that was possible, than pre-war units in Malaya.

Until December 1941 the Japanese were over a thousand miles away in Indo-China and Whitehall assumed that the small, under-equipped British army in Burma was safe behind the thick forests and a mountain barrier along the border with Siam. However, in one swift step the Japanese in Indo-China crossed the border into Siam and advanced on Bangkok. Further south landings at Singorra and Khota Bahru sent columns into Malaya. Japanese troops pouring across north Siam moved slowly through the jungle and up rivers before coming to a halt along the border facing the Shan Hills in Burma, a point some 150 miles from Moulmein, a Burmese seaport on the River Salween.

The new Commander in Chief in Burma, Lieutenant-General T.J. Hutton, appointed only a few weeks earlier, considered that the Japanese may attack through Tennasserim to seize Moulmein or thrust through the Shan States. Although he had been Chief of the General Staff in India and no stranger to the lack of men and equipment in Burma, he must have seen disaster staring him in the face when his staff officers brought him up-to-date with his army's deficiencies. All he had was four ill-equipped, half-trained brigades, whose best men had been milked for the Malayan Campaign.

It was about now that Colonel Stephenson, commander of the Burma Levies, came into the picture. About eight weeks earlier he had been asked by the Governor of Burma to raise, train and lead a force of irregulars from amongst the fierce but pro-British hill tribesmen, mainly Shans, Karens, Chins and Kachins. Stephenson had earlier attended Jim Gavin's second course at 101 STS in August.

Realising his potential Jim Gavin had kept in touch and sent him weapons and supplies when he learnt that Stephenson was raising his own private army of hill tribesmen in the Shan Hills. The Governor also learnt of this development and Stephenson was told to present himself to the Residency. Expecting a reprimand he came away with the Governor's commission to raise the Burma Levies.

When Jim Gavin learnt about this new development he sent a small party of specialists under the command of Lieutenant Heath, to Burma to work with Steve Cummins, giving support to the Burma Levies. Their arrival in Burma coincided with the Japanese landing in Siam. Stephenson had been prepared for this and already had his men camping on the border. Within a few days he led a raiding party over the border to attack the strategic north to south railway line. Later, in January, his plans to raid the airfield in Siam, which the Japanese were using as an assembly area, was turned down by the recently arrived 17th Division which had taken over the Moulmein front.

Intelligence reports continually referred to the increasing build up of enemy supplies and men along the border. The expected invasion could only be weeks away and there was every likelihood that it could come through the Shan States. With this in mind Cummins and Stephenson planned to set up well-equipped bases, hidden away in the forests, in areas likely to be overrun by the advancing Japanese. Because of the time needed to train the local recruits manning the bases created a problem. One morning shortly after Lieutenant Heath and Major Seagrim – a new recruit for the Burma Levies – had left to look for a suitable base in the Shan Hills, two lorries packed with heavily armed Burmese soldiers stopped outside the office. In minutes the place seemed full of soldiers. An English-speaking NCO, who appeared to be in charge, explained that they had been volunteered for behind-the-lines work. They were all members of the Burmese Military Police. A pre-war paramilitary organisation, it was used to carry out anti-bandit sweeps in the forest covered hills. It was made up mainly of Gurkhas and local hill people. Having the Governor's commission obviously had its benefits.

Events outside Burma now cast their shadow over the Burma Section's work. First came the news that Burma had been transferred from ABDA Command back to GHQ India. This, in effect, brought Burma Section into SOE (India). Cummins' contact with the Orient Mission had already ceased because of two factors; the upheaval of

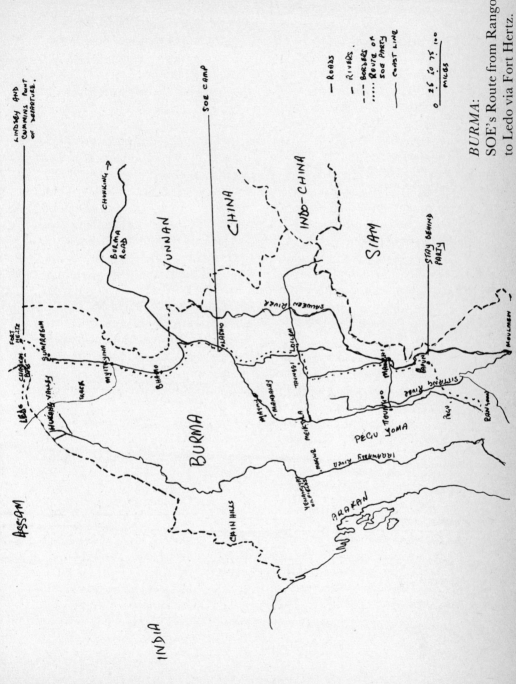

BURMA:
SOE's Route from Rangoon
to Ledo via Fort Hertz.

SOE transferring to Java and Jim Gavin's transfer to China. For about two weeks Cummins worked on his own until one day a Major Lindsey walked into the office: sent by Colin MacKenzie, Chief of SOE (India), to find out what was going on. He arrived in the middle of a high-level flap at HQ Burma. The Japanese had launched their expected attack on Burma.

The enemy's intentions were to seize Moulmein, cut the Burma Road supply route to China and destroy the British army around Rangoon. Only three rivers, the Salween, Bilin and Sittang, provided any natural defence position for the under-equipped, inexperienced 17 Division. In 31 days all three rivers were in Japanese hands and the 17 Division destroyed as a fighting unit.

The destruction of 17 Division was still two weeks away when Steve Cummins led his convoy of jeeps packed with BMPs along the dirt road to Moulmein. News from the front was unreliable but all rumours pointed to fierce fighting. At least five times in the last hour the jeeps pulled off the road and hid from low-flying Japanese Zeros, strafing the lorries packed with wounded, and oxen carts piled high with supplies, trapped on the narrow dirt roads. There was hardly room for two vehicles side by side, and tired, red-eyed infantry, covered in dust, cursed the drivers for forcing them to take an unnecessary step off the road. Fresh from the Malayan debâcle Lieutenant Heath recognised the signs of an army in retreat. Tired, ashen faces, torn, sweat-stained uniforms – lorries nose to tail with mules and oxen carts. All the signs pointed to the army backloading its supplies.

Steve Cummins stopped close to an infantry officer. 'Has Moulmein fallen?'

The officer, who was hardly more than twenty, took in Cummins freshly shaved features, clean uniform and jeeps. 'Four days ago,' he replied.

'Where's the front line?' asked Cummins.

'Fuck knows,' said the officer, wiping a blood stained sleeve across his sweaty, dust-covered face. 'We've been marching for the last twenty-four hours – if these men stop I'll never get them to their feet again! Have you got anything to drink?'

Six water bottles were thrust towards him.

'Thanks,' was all he said as he moved off to catch up with his platoon, taking the water bottles with him.

The effect on Cummins' party was both depressing and one of alarm. Every mile forward they expected to run into Japanese ambushes. Eventually Cummins turned left, off the road, and up a dry weather road through the forest.

In contrast to the road, crowded with exhausted infantry and vehicles, the track they now followed through the forest was empty and only the noise of the jeeps' engines broke the silence. Even the cries of the wild life were muted. For the Europeans the stillness was unnerving and they sat in the vehicles, firmly gripping their weapons and staring into the thick foliage along the track. The Burmese Military Police just sat impassively in the back.

Stephenson had chosen the small town of Papun, on the banks of the Yunsalin River, as a base for his first stay-behind party. Although the town was the administrative centre for the area and the capital of Salween District, it was in fact only about the size of a small English village, consisting of simple, sparsely furnished, native huts with *attap* roofs and unpainted, wooden colonial-type bungalows, built on stone pillars some three feet above ground. Below these houses the village pigs and chickens scratched away for scraps and roots. As the town lay only some thirty miles from Moulmein and less than twenty miles from the Siam border it would be an obvious target if the enemy sent a column over the hills to outflank the retreating British army – in which case Seagrim's guerrillas could harass the enemy and give early warning of the move.

The jeeps, in four-wheel drive, climbed the uphill tracks until finally the forest thinned out to cultivated fields. They drove along the track into the town and stopped outside the District Commissioner's bungalow and were soon surrounded by happy, gesticulating villagers. The party was expected as Lieutenant Heath and Major Seagrim had already visited the area and left Tommy guns and grenades with the locally-born District Commissioner. Now their arrival took on an almost carnival atmosphere as everyone crowded around the jeeps climbing over the packing cases and sacks of food and examining their weapons. After Major Seagrim introduced his party to the District Commissioner, who had by now pushed his way through the crowds around the vehicles, he organised the unloading of weapons ammunition and supplies which were carried to a nearby empty bungalow set aside for him.

Equipping the party with weapons before they left Rangoon had presented Cummins with a problem. This was about the time when contact was broken with Singapore and nothing had been heard from India. This splinter of Orient Mission was isolated and working on its own. All SOE's supplies had been destroyed in the Christmas

Day air raid and 17 Division had made it quite plain that it didn't have anything to spare for 'Stephenson's Home Guard'. Apart from a military presence, the docks were virtually abandoned and Cummins guessed that the *godowns* must be packed with all sorts of items useful to his unit. So, taking a party with him, he drove into the docks and began a search. At the end of the day they rode out with the lorries packed with tinned food, sacks of cereals, ammunition, boxes of grenades and crates of Italian rifles captured in Africa. He also discovered that the American Military Mission was anxious to give away jeeps to anyone who could promise to deliver them to China and he reasoned that there was a possibility that they could finally finish up there so he volunteered to help them out. Six jeeps were added to his motor pool. It was these weapons, supplies and jeeps which now stood in the square at Papun.

In the late afternoon, when all the vehicles had been unloaded and the supplies stacked in the bungalow, Seagrim waved off Lieutenant Heath and his drivers. In a swirl of dust the jeeps turned a half circle in the square and drove off, back down the track into the forest. Standing in the dusty square, watching them recede until they were finally hidden by the dark canopy of the trees, Seagrim probably allowed himself a brief glow of satisfaction. He was to be allowed to be what he enjoyed being – independent. He wasn't concerned about being cut off as he knew the hills like the back of his hand from pre-war hill-climbing holidays in the area. He knew he could walk out at any time. Steve Cummins thought he was ideal for the job and Lieutenant Heath remarked that he seemed an ascetic type who might have made a monk.

His orders were brief. He had been given command of the stay-behind party, made up of the Burmese Military Police section, and he was to raise and train a company of Karen tribesmen. His guerrillas would seek and carry out raids against Japanese lines of communication in the Moulmein area. He explained this to his friend the District Commissioner and villagers that evening as they all sat around the lawn of his bungalow. When he awoke the following morning he now found the lawn crowded with tribesmen who just sat patiently waiting for him to appear. These men had come in from villages miles away and during the next few days he had as many as 200 queueing up outside the bungalow to join his private army.

The next few weeks were spent changing the bow and arrow tribesmen into weapons trained guerrillas. His daily training schedule consisted of the morning on the range, which the Karens built themselves, and creeping around the forest in the afternoon, ambushing each other with unbounded enthusiasm and vigour. Considering the Karens' lack of weapon knowledge, they soon became good marksmen but what worried Seagrim was the high number of misfires from the Italian ammunition during range practice. What, he wondered, would happen when his men went on the offensive?

The last contact the Orient Mission party had with Seagrim was some weeks later. Rangoon had fallen and the British army was in full retreat towards India while the Chinese Divisions, sent to aid them, were themselves being pushed back towards Lashio. The Orient Mission party was attached to the Chinese and while it was in Mawchi, some 50 miles north of Papun, a messenger arrived from Seagrim for more weapons and ammunition for his increasing number of volunteers.

II

About this time Major Knott in Rangoon, was preparing to leave for Chungking while Major Peter Lindsey, in Toungoo, watched the American equipped 5th and 6th Chinese armies move into the town, a hundred miles behind the British lines. They were supposed to be relieving the British 1 Division, holding the Japanese around Pegu at the crossroads of the Rangoon-Mandalay road.

Despite being the best equipped army Chiang Kai-Shek could offer, when the 5th reached Toungoo its officers decided that was as far as it was going. The British Commander had already been ordered by General Slim to hand over to the Chinese and pull his forces out of the area to join the main British force over the hills at Prome. This refusal to go forward left units of the British 1 Division, at Pegu, no option but to fall back for a hundred miles with the Japanese in hot pursuit.

After leaving Seagrim in Papun, Lindsey, Heath and Cummins were caught in the chaos of 17 Division's retreat from Rangoon to Prome. Lindsey split his party, leaving Cummins to go on to Rangoon, where he met Jack Knott, while the rest of the Burma Section went on to Pegu to join 1 Division. There he recruited more hill tribesmen and trained them in guerrilla techniques to protect the division's left flank. When the order to carry out a fighting withdrawal to Toungoo was given, he and Heath carried out a scorched earth policy in the town, including blowing the bridges in the wake of the retreating British 1 Division. Acting as rearguard scouts his

native volunteers stalked enemy troops with crossbows, often creeping within 70 yards of enemy sentries to carry out their silent killing.
Behind enemy lines they acted as road watchers, counting the numbers of lorries and men moving up to the front, they then padded
back through the forest with vital intelligence which was passed on to
the Chinese.

The lack of fighting spirit by the Chinese resulted in one of
Burma's largest rice growing areas being given up without a fight.
Behind the Japanese came Nationalist and anti-British Aung San's
Burmese Independence Army, mopping up stragglers and any units
unfortunate enough to be cut off during the withdrawal. Some
British stragglers, guided by tribesmen, found their way to Major
Seagrim's guerrillas who were able to provide them with food and
guides before passing them on to Lindsey at Mawchi.

Following Major Seagrim's success at Papun, Lindsey decided to
form another native Levy Company at Mawchi, fifty miles away.
This was later commanded by a European named Boyt, the local
timber manager for Steele Bros, who turned up at his office one
morning asking for a job. He set up office in a wooden hut on the
main street and by the end of the first week nearly 3,000 tribesmen
had queued up to join SOE's Levies. Weapons were hard to come by
and Burma Division, now passing through Chinese lines, were reluctant to part with anything. Nevertheless Major Lindsey managed to
scrounge another 250 Italian rifles and a large amount of defective
ammunition.

About this time one of Major Seagrim's natives turned up at Captain Boyt's office with a message requesting any spare arms for volunteers still pouring into Seagrim's training camp, now behind the
lines at Papun. All Lindsey could spare were 150 twelve bore shotguns and 1,000 cartridges – together with fifty 4.10's and two boxes
of grenades. One of the local headmen arranged for seventy porters
to carry the load through the forest.

Two more Europeans arrived in the little town looking for the
'army major'. They were H.C. Smith, late of the Burma Forestry
Service, and another timber man called Thompson. Smith was given
a Field Commission and eighty Kachins and told to screen the area
north of the Toungoo to Mawchi road in case the Japanese attempted a hook-like thrust. Thompson, also commissioned with the rank
of captain, was given a company of untrained Kachins and told to
defend the airfield on the outskirts of Toungoo.

After 1 Burma Division passed through Chinese lines at Toungoo, the defence of the town was passed over to the Chinese 200 Division. The expected Japanese assault on the town followed the usual pattern of heavy air raids to soften up the defenders followed by frontal assaults and hooking movements by enemy patrols through the jungle. Despite fierce fighting the town was cut off, trapping the Chinese 200 Division, which continued to hold out expecting to be relieved by the Chinese 22 Division. As Lindsey had already discovered, Chinese officers, from generals to subalterns made their own choice as to what orders they carried out – and this particular one didn't appeal to them. Field Marshal Viscount Slim in his book *Defeat into Victory* states 'that there is little doubt that this refusal cost us Toungoo – a major disaster, second only to our defeat at Sittang Bridge'. The Chinese in the town had no option but to abandon their 3,000 wounded, their American equipment, guns and vehicles in the break-out that followed.

On the airfield Thompson learnt that the Chinese on his flanks had gone, leaving his men who put up a spirited defence until outnumbered and outgunned, he ordered them to fight their way out before they were overwhelmed. The Chinese had fallen back on Mawchi leaving Smith's men to protect the division's rearguard by setting up a road-block. The first to pass through the ambush position were Thompson and survivors from the airfield carrying out a fighting withdrawal towards the town. When Boyt in Mawchi heard about the coming fight he rushed his men forward in wood-burning estate lorries and arrived just in time to take part in the battle. Referring to the SOE road-block Field Marshal Slim, who was not a supporter of special forces, states that the Levies were swept aside. A rather unfair understatement. The untrained Levies stalked the enemy with shotguns, crossbows and knives killing at least eighty and held up an enemy brigade long enough for the Chinese to reform around the town of Mawchi.

In the town the Orient Mission's staff, including Lieutenant Heath, Corporal Sawyer and Major Lindsey, carried out a well prepared scorched earth policy destroyed valuable equipment at the largest wolfram mine in the world. After running out of supplies and explosives, the SOE unit pulled back to the Hopong crossroads, taking with them Boyt, Smith and Thompson, but leaving the Levies to go back to the villages with their weapons and wait to be contacted later from India.

The Chinese front line had begun to collapse. The enemy had captured Mawchi and after outflanking the Chinese at Bawlake, overran and scattered its survivors. There was nothing else left for SOE to do but fall back in their jeeps along roads crowded with stragglers and leaderless groups of Chinese to Lashio.

From the verandah outside the SOE office in Lashio, Cummins watched four battered and mudstained jeeps drive into the compound. Joined by Sergeant Benson he walked across the muddy carpark and saluting welcomed a very tired and hungry Major Lindsey to Lashio. Commenting on the absence of staff, Cummins broke the news that the China Mission had been cancelled and all its personnel ordered to make their own way to India. Some had been stuck in Maymo – not reaching Lashio – and pulled out with the rearguard of 17 Division retreating over the Ava Bridge on the Mandalay road.

Tired and hungry, sitting in the jeep, slumped over the driving wheel, Major Lindsey listened to Captain Cummins' report, only lifting his eyes to nod to Sergeant Benson when he heard about the wireless link with Calcutta via Chungking. The rest of the party began to unload the vehicles and someone organised the Chinese cook to produce a large meal. After a bath and a change of clothes Lindsey led the team into Lashio to see what they could do in the way of destroying the large supply and fuel dumps in the town. They found the narrow streets choked with Chinese soldiers and refugees.

Every day Japanese bombers flew leisurely overhead, unloading their bombs without opposition. Most of the population joined the soldiers and refugees fleeing to China. Close on the heels of the retreating Chinese army came thirty Japanese tanks, armoured cars and six hundred lorry-borne troops.

After sending a few supply dumps sky-high and mining bridges the SOE section packed all their belongings on to the jeeps. Finally booby-trapping the compound Cummins' jeep led the way out through the gates and drove off along the mountain track. The following day, the 29th, the Chinese abandoned the town.

The track, running parallel with the Chinese border, led to the small mountain village of Bhamo. Like every road from Lashio this too was packed with refugees and defended by men belonging to the Burma Frontier Force. By the second day the convoy was well clear of the congestion and had the road almost to themselves. All around them the tree-covered hills rose thousands of feet. In the distance they could see ridge after ridge of mountains bordering China. Occasionally the road ran alongside deep gorges and hundreds of feet below they had glimpses of the Irrawaddy gorges and boulders as large as houses.

One morning they almost crashed into a tree lying across the road blocking a bridge over a gorge. Sensing an ambush, the convoy drew slowly to a halt and the men climbed out and spread themselves out to cover the bridge and the fallen tree. Almost immediately a dark skinned Oriental with a rifle as long as himself appeared from amongst the trees above the road. He turned out to be a native officer with the North Karen Levies: one of Lindsey's recent volunteers questioned him in his own language, Chingpaw. From him they learnt that the Karen Levies' commanding officer was none other than Colonel Stephenson, whose HQ was in a town three days' walk away.

Leaving the Karens to their road block, Lindsey's party drove on to Myitkyina, which seemed to be the most likely town for Stephenson's HQ. Some hours later they unexpectedly met him in charge of a convoy, packed with native troops, rushing up the track intent on blowing the bridge before the Japanese arrived. Lindsey learnt that his men had been only hours ahead of the Japanese ever since leaving Lashio.

The only things between the Japanese and Myitkyina were Stephenson's Levies, the SOE party and the bridge. Very little is known of what next took place but Jack Barnard, the young officer from Mike Calvert's Bush Warfare Centre, recalls meeting Stephenson in town some two days later. He told him that the Levies and the SOE party arrived too late and the enemy had already captured the bridge but the SOE party managed to avoid trouble and returned to Myitkyina with Stephenson's Levies.

Steve Cummins found the town crowded with thousands of Indians, Anglo-Burmese, Eurasians, all junior civil servants and their families and relatives. They had followed the Governor who arrived earlier, guarded by a small unit of Gloucesters. They hoped he would look after them and arrange their evacuation to India. The Governor steadfastly refused to leave Burma and the refugees but eventually his wife, Lady Dorman-Smith, who had insisted on staying with her husband, was persuaded to fly out from the little dirt airstrip, just outside the town. About two American DC3's were flying in each day picking up some two hundred refugees for India. They left so overloaded that some of them could hardly lift off at the end of the runway. When Churchill learnt of the situation in the town he personally intervened and ordered the Governor to leave.

The town was now within air-strike distance of Japanese bombers and on 6th May, as a Dakota was taxiing down the runway, four

Japanese fighters came in low over the tree tops, line astern and almost at ground level over the airstrip. Each one pumped high explosives into the plane until she exploded. Her smoke mushrooming above the trees could be seen from the town and marked the grave of her barbecued passengers and crew. By now the Japanese were only a few miles away and all further evacuation flights were cancelled. The refugees had been expecting a round-the-clock evacuation programme, it was rumoured, planned for 15th May – still nine days away. With all flights cancelled and the enemy troops expected in town at any hour some 45,000 former civil servants of the Raj, together with their elderly parents, wives and children, fled. Almost all had already trekked hundreds of miles, through tropical terrain, dumping warm clothing and blankets to lighten their loads – particularly as they expected to be flown out. Now faced with crossing the mountains to India on foot, together with an early monsoon, they discovered that food, clothing and essential items needed for the trek had long since disappeared from the bazaars.

Looking around the town on 6th May, Major Lindsey realised there was nothing to be achieved by stopping and moved his men out. After helping themselves to food and petrol from a military supply dump, before blowing it up, the SOE jeep convoy drove along the rocky track to Sumprabum, a large village deep in the heart of the Triangle, in the mountains of Upper Burma.

It was at this point, although no one realised it, that the Mission's work came to an end. It is worth reflecting that in four months it had partially armed some 1,500 loyal Karen tribesmen who covered the British army's left flank during the initial retreat: on the way out of Burma they managed to organise guerrilla units amongst the Shans (Major Seagrim) in the east and from the Kachins (Toungoo) in the north-east.

Beyond Sumprabum was Fort Hertz – literally the most far-flung outpost of the British Empire, high in the mountains bordering China. The Burma Government officials still remaining moved on to Fort Hertz. Lindsey understood that the area was going to be used as a base for guerrilla attacks against the Japanese and Colonel Stephenson certainly intended to use it as the next base for his Burma Levies. The journey from Myitkyina to Fort Hertz would cover some 200 miles so Major Lindsey decided to go as far as possible by jeep then hire porters for the remainder of the journey.

The dirt track the jeeps had been following from Myitkyina stopped in the village square of Sumprabum. The mountain village was

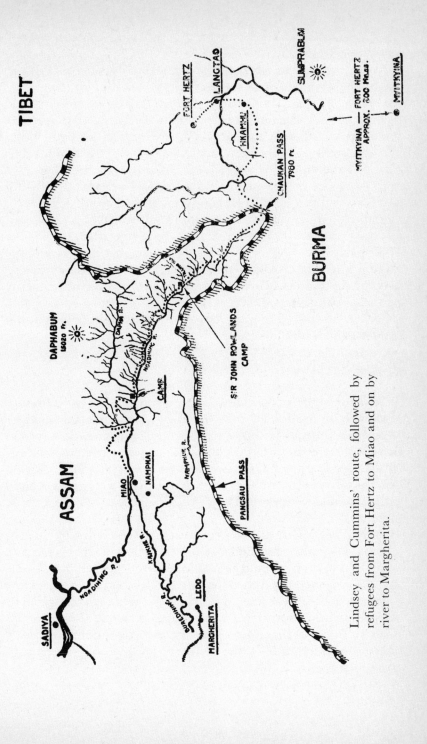

Lindsey and Cummins' route, followed by refugees from Fort Hertz to Miao and on by river to Margherita.

made up of rough wooden native huts surrounding a bazaar. The few shops, owned by Chinese, also supplied the local platoon of Sepoys quartered in the Burma Frontier Force barracks on the edge of the village. Almost immediately an Irish priest, Father Stuart, appeared from some building. He had some thirty refugees sheltering at his mission and was anxious to know if they had any spare medical supplies and whether he could expect help from any outside source. Steve Cummins told him they could do nothing to help and warned him that large groups of refugees were heading for the village. He later discovered that most had taken an earlier fork towards the mountains and the dreaded Hukong Pass.*

From the native NCO at the barracks Cummins learnt that only mule tracks went on to Fort Hertz. The route was so bad the porters were refusing to accompany European parties unless they were properly equipped and provisioned for the eighty mile journey through mountainous forests. A Government official who looked after the village had already rescued three parties and was turning others back. The NCO thought there were some 500 Sahibs (Europeans) in the town trying to reach Fort Hertz.

<h1 style="text-align:center">III</h1>

In the shade of the Sepoy Barracks, Sergeant Benson sat in front of his set with his headphones on, listening to Major Knott's hand on the morse key, transmitting a reply from Chungking. Benson had signalled the previous day that the SOE party had arrived in the village and that Myitkyina had fallen to the Japanese. He also reported that Major Lindsey, with Cummins and himself, were moving on to Fort Hertz as soon as porters could be arranged, for the eighty mile journey.

In the village square the Government official put up a notice warning every new arrival that the terrain beyond the village was hazardous and no attempt should be made to reach the fort but Major Lindsey was determined to go on. He split his party, leaving Corporal Sawyer, Boyt, Gardner and Thompson behind at Sumprabum as a forward unit to work with Brigadier Upton, the Commanding Officer from Myitkyina. He was trying to form a unit made up of stragglers arriving in the village. Apart from Upton, the unit con-

---

* Twelve months later the British and American army engineers drove a road from Ledo in India through this pass in the drive to Mandalay.

sisted of Colonel Stubbs, the Commanding Officer, Burma Frontier Force in Myitkyina, who had arrived with some Sepoys and Colonel Stephenson, who also turned up with a group of Burma Levies. They had acted as rearguard when Upton's brigade left for India. The brigadier refused to go and stayed behind to form a redoubt at Fort Hertz. Stragglers from the Lashio Battalion, together with Gurkhas, Chins and some lost Gloucesters, eventually formed a ragtail army sheltering in the village.

The journey across Burma for the SOE party had been hazardous but it in no way prepared the three men for the long climb through the jungle and mountains to Fort Hertz. Nevertheless they managed the eighty mile journey in five days, assisted by some twenty porters. On the fifth day the forest began to thin out and the party found themselves on a flat, featureless plain. Beyond they could see a Beau Geste-type bastioned Fort Hertz.

The fort seemed surrounded by small buildings which, as they approached, they discovered were old colonial-type bungalows with attractive lawns. Their occupants had fled. A large, single-storey building they found to be an empty hospital. The nearby little post office, with its closed sign on the door, had been abandoned. As the party filed past the empty buildings the side door of the Court House banged in the wind. Neither was there any sign of life from the Fort which stood silhouetted against the snow-capped mountains, which rose in layers as far as the eye could see.

As the party approached the high double doors leading into the Fort they were met by a European who turned out to be the Assistant District Commissioner for Sumprabum. He had arrived a few hours earlier with the Government party led by Sir John Rowlands. Inside the compound was cluttered with dumped baggage and porters milling around a group of some hundred Europeans including a woman and her baby.

When Major Lindsey discussed the position with Sir John, he discovered that there seemed to be no plans of setting up a military base at the Fort and the Government party intended to walk to India, some 250 miles, via the almost impassable Chaunkan Pass.

While Cummins was exploring the fort and the nearby airstrip and Lindsey was discussing their situation with Sir John Rowlands, Sergeant Benson unpacked the wireless equipment again and strung out his aerials in front of the Fort watched by an inquisitive crowd of porters. With Station 'H' (Mobile) on the air and in contact with Chungking once more, Benson sent Lindsey's message giving news of the Government party's intended trek and seeking orders from Calcutta. Later that day, 14th May, the reply came back – they were to close down, bury their equipment and join the Government party.

The route Sir John proposed to take had only been walked by five previous European explorers – none in the last fifty years. The only map had large unsurveyed areas indicating that for some 200 miles the journey would be through uninhabited mountains and unexplored forests. The only good point was that it wouldn't be full of refugees like the passes further south. Some ninety porters agreed to go with the party as far as the Chaungken Pass but then would return, leaving the hundred or so Europeans to make their way to Burma the best way they could. Most of the party were under the mistaken impression that a rescue party was striking out from Burma and would meet up with them on 27th May. This rumour, on misinformation, almost caused disaster.

The party set out on the 14th in a long straggling Indian file. Steve Cummins, Lindsey and Sergeant Benson carried small packs and their weapons. The wireless set was buried and its location marked on Lindsey's map.

Sir John sent a small party ahead to mark out the trail across this forgotten world. Behind, the slow moving party, after covering only twelve miles in two days, camped for three days to allow the porters to go back and bring out more supplies left behind at the fort. The party had trekked through tangled forests and across fast flowing streams, spanned by swaying bamboo bridges. Both Steve Cummins and Lindsey soon realised the mistake of joining this slow-moving party. By the end of the week the van of the party was again on the move, following the markers.

Recounting the story to Jim Gavin some months later, Steve Cummins recollects the first part of the journey to the pass was through thick jungle, over innumerable hills, anything from 1,500 feet to 6,000 feet high. On a good day they would march some five miles in ten hours. The monsoon had broken early and the ground had become a quagmire. Some members of the party sank up to their thighs in red mud as they pulled themselves, step by step, up the mountains or scrambled down rock faces. It rained continuously and every night they cut bamboo and small trees to build a shelter. They often went days without a fire and went to bed wet and hungry. In the morning, at first light, Cummins and Lindsey went around cursing, cajoling and pleading for everyone to get on their feet and march. The rains and melting snows turned passable streams into rushing rivers. Some rivers were waded chest deep, others were safely crossed by hacking down large trees on the river banks; when they were felled they spanned the raging torrents. On other occasions the tree trunks were lashed together with ropes and bamboo enabling the party to be rafted across.

Apart from the markers there was no path other than animal tracks. Often the terrain was so impossible that the party spent days wading along the river bed to make progress. Eventually, after climbing some 8,000 feet, the party reached the Changken Pass. By now they were covering less than three miles a day and everyone was exhausted.

On the 23rd Cummins was surprised to see Corporal Sawyer and the Burma Levy officers. They had walked across the mountains from Sumprabum. The village was evacuated when a large force of Japanese appeared up the track with a fighter plane scouting ahead for them. Brigadier Upton, Colonel Stephenson and Colonel Stubbs together with Dr McRobert, a surgeon from Rangoon hospital, who had been treating the refugees, left with the Sepoys for Fort Hertz. When news of the Japanese column reached the village everyone had split up and made their own plans. When Cummins' porters arrived back at the village with the news that the Sahibs had left Fort Hertz for India, Sawyer with Captain Boyt and Gardner decided there was nothing left but to follow Cummins and walk out to India.

Almost everyone in the Government party expected to be rescued any day and were so convinced that the planes flying overhead were looking for them that two large bonfires were lit to attract attention. The planes in fact were on a regular run to China and no notice was taken of the beacons.

The rain continued to pour down without a break and everyone huddled in makeshift, leaky, bamboo shelters. About 26th May Major Lindsey agreed that Corporal Sawyer, Boyt and Gardner should make a dash to India, travelling light with little food. Boyt and Gardner set off with a civilian, aptly named Moses, along the valley in the pouring rain and were soon lost from view in the mist. Two days later Corporal Sawyer also left with a small party made up of a civilian named Jardine, two escaped prisoners of war, Captain Fraser and Sergeant Pratt from the Hussars and two other officers McCrindle and Howe.

A large party of Gurkhas had stumbled on their camp and sheltered for a few days with them. They now volunteered to help carry the food and baggage. On 2nd June the party moved off into country worse than that already covered. In one day alone they criss-crossed rivers some fifteen times, they hacked their way through bamboo and climbed hill after tortuous hill. The column had by now broken up into small groups. The stronger members were in the lead and depending on the state of exhaustion the survivors attached themselves to others in similar condition. The sick were carried on improvised stretchers made from bamboo, army webbing and blankets and the less sick took turns as stretcher bearers. The Gurkhas, concerned at the slow pace the party was making, were becoming impatient and asked permission to strike out on their own.

It was three weeks since the first party had left to fetch help and since then at least three other parties went ahead searching for rescue parties. Nothing had been heard of any of these apart from abandoned weapons and discarded baggage, binoculars and in one instance a map case. It was assumed that some if not all had perished. In view of the deteriorating conditions of the travellers Cummins and Lindsey decided to leave the main party in yet another bid to fetch help. The following morning the main party arrived at a river in full flood. There was no path along the bank and the groups waded through the water when the forest became too thick. Late in the afternoon they discovered a dilapidated lean-to which they first assumed to be a refugee shelter but inside they discovered Corporal Sawyer's party, exhausted and starving, waiting for the river (Tilung Hka) to drop in order to ford it. As the rest of the main party gradually stumbled in, Cummins and Lindsey bullied everyone to build shelters for themselves.

The party was trapped by this river for about twelve days all the time gradually eating into the food stocks. About the 12th the SOE party decided to try and ford the river. The main party now had only two weeks' food left and unless help reached them soon everyone would perish. There had been some talk of building rafts but eventually the party waded out into the river chest deep in ice cold water from the snow topped mountains. Wading diagonally across the surging river, they were joined by the Gurkhas and three civilians, Jardine, Kendal and Moses. The Gurkhas, clinging to one another, formed a human chain. The force of the river on everyone's back pushed them downstream towards the opposite bank. The roar of the river drowned any instruction shouted by the party lining the east bank.

Eventually reaching the bank, Cummins clung to its steep sides and looked around in time to see Corporal Sawyer being swept away. Another casualty was Captain Fraser, who had decided to join them and was now swept down-stream and trapped by his webbing against a tree. The force of the water forced his body under and at great risk to themselves others waded back into the river and hacked away at the harness. Eventually, more dead than alive, they freed him and dragged him ashore but there was no sign of Corporal Sawyer. After some hours resting Cummings, Kendal and Lindsey moved on. It had been previously agreed that when the party reached the west bank it would split into smaller groups thus offering more opportunities of getting through.

Describing the rest of the journey to Major Gavin, Cummins remembers forests being infested with sand flies and leeches. Their bites and sores wouldn't heal and the slightest knock on any part of the body caused large bruises and sores. Lindsey had badly bruised himself crossing the river and this was giving him trouble. Despite a lot of perseverance, the hoped for disciplined, eight miles a day march, became less each day. Jardine was also very ill and needed treatment. Finally on Saturday, 19th June, after carrying them across the flooded Dalpha River, Cummins left both exhausted men on a sandy beach alongside the river.

His own condition was also desperate. He was both mentally and physically exhausted, his uniform was in rags held together by bits of rattan. His boots had disintegrated and his revolver oiled and holstered, hung from his leather belt feeling as if it weighed a ton. Searching his pockets all he had was two ounces of rice.

He had only the vaguest idea where he was but assumed it to be some fifty miles from the nearest habitation – in India – a prospect of some ten days' march. Stumbling through the trees along game tracks he no longer heard the roar of the river. It was still raining hard but this no longer worried him nor the leeches which dropped on him as he brushed past the trees. All he saw was the ground under his feet. He still retained the discipline of the march – thirty minutes' walking then stopping for five minutes but after each stop it was difficult to set off again.

Occasionally wild animals dashed off into the undergrowth, usually wild pig or deer. Later in the day, however, a line of elephants appeared on the path. Too exhausted to move away he slumped against a tree. The elephants seemed to be shouting at him and he knew he must be on the verge of going out of his mind. Suddenly brown skinned soldiers crowded around him and in their midst appeared a European leading a search party.

Cummins was sufficiently coherent to give him general directions where to find his two companions. A search party was sent off to find them while the rescue team bivouacked for the night. Steve Cummins' mumbled directions were sufficient and Jardine and Lindsey were brought in that day.

The following day after explaining that more groups were close behind and giving instructions where to find the Government party, Major Lindsey and Captain Cummins rode off on two elephants and eventually reached the local military headquarters. Here Lindsey insisted on telephoning the RAF and persuaded them to make supply drops to the main party. Only when this had commenced did he and Cummins make their way to Delhi and report to Colin MacKenzie.

CHAPTER SEVENTEEN

The China Party

Major Knott and his Signals Unit arrived at Rangoon in February 1942; taking up the story, Jack Knott recollects standing on the deck of the little tramp steamer. SS *Rajputna*, one evening some miles downstream from Rangoon. The night sky, above the silhouette of the trees on the horizon, was filled with a red glow. No one spoke. They all knew. Rangoon was on fire.

His thoughts were interrupted by the ship's engines throbbing noisily. Its propeller churned up the dirty brown river water which seemed white and luminous in its wake. The steamer had been anchored all day waiting for permission to enter Rangoon harbour – like Singapore all shipping was banned from entering or leaving harbour during daylight. As the little steamer began to move up river, passengers could see the dark shapes of blacked out warships and freighters at anchor waiting their turn to join the convoy.

One of Knott's men, Corporal Bond, had been sent on in advance to make all the necessary arrangements for landing stores and securing accommodation. All the remaining Signals personnel at 101 STS, Sergeant Shufflebottom and seven other ranks, accompanied Knott to Rangoon.

As the ship approached the harbour, recalls Knott, the entire city seemed to be deserted and in flames. Fires raged, unchecked, around the waterfront and swirling black clouds swept along the dockside and over the roof tops. Soldiers appeared from the shadows and helped the ship's crew to tie up alongside. As for Corporal Bond, he was nowhere to be found.

Anxious to avoid losing all the equipment in the next daylight air raid, Major Knott sent Sergeant Shufflebottom to look for Burma Defence HQ and hopefully, Corporal Bond. All around the city fires were raging and bodies lay unattended. Apart from the occasional lorry racing across intersections, the cratered streets seemed empty. Phantoms lurked amongst the shadows, moving beyond the light of the flames. Most of the population had fled but what Shufflebottom didn't know was that the city, at night, was taken over by lunatics released from the asylums before the staff fled and escaped convicts from bombed prisons. The only authority remaining in the city was the British army and it had its hands full trying to control looters and arsonists. General Hutton had asked the War Office for a division just to maintain internal security in Rangoon. Shufflebottom searched the city for three hours before someone directed him to the Burma Defence Bureau Buildings. There the luckless Corporal Bond, sleeping comfortably in bed, was unceremoniously turned out.

The following morning Knott took three Signalmen and a wireless set to the Bureau and made contact with Killery. On board the *Rajputna*, Sergeant Shufflebottom had the unenviable task of getting the stores unloaded. Before long the silver-winged enemy bombers were over the crowded harbour. Around the docks Gunners, who had arrived some weeks earlier on the SS *Darvil* from Singapore, together with university professors, manned obsolete Italian artillery pieces captured in Africa. From the nearby airfield American P 40s, flown by American mercenary pilots, 'The Flying Tigers', slow-moving British Brewster Buffaloes and worn out Mark 1 Hurricanes, took off again and again, heavily outnumbered, to inflict heavy casualties amongst the bombers. When the enemy planes broke through to the harbour every ship, most of them packed with American supplies for China, blazed away with little six inch guns, Bren guns, Lewis guns, flares, even revolvers. About the time Knott arrived in Rangoon, Field Marshal Viscount Slim recollects* that the city was defended by 35 Allied aircraft while the Japanese could put 150 into the air. Appeals for reinforcements were refused because they were needed for Singapore.

Every time a plane appeared over the docks, friend or foe, the native dockers fled, scattering the loads. The dock area, close to the ship, was badly cratered and nearby warehouses were burning. Along the dockside flames from a burning building leapt across a gap sending a second building alight and the flames threatened to engulf a car park packed with civilian lorries. A lorry full of Gloucesters suddenly appeared around the corner, and the soldiers, scrambling out of the back before it stopped, raced around the car park driving the lorries to safety. The Gloucesters were short of every weapon, piece of equipment and transport and 'A' Company, whose soldiers had rescued the lorries, took every opportunity of making up their

---

* *Defeat into Victory.*

deficiencies by stripping the lorries they rescued.

At the Bureau Jack Knott had just finished his first transmission to Killery when Steve Cummins walked into the wireless room. 'Hello,' said Cummins, 'what are you doing here?' It seemed to Cummins that almost overnight the bureau was full of Orient Mission bods. Apart from Jack Knott and his Signals Unit the building were full of Frenchmen pretending to be British officers and clerks and instructors from 101 STS. Amongst these was Pierre Boulle, who, unknown to Knott, had one of his precious Mark 1 wireless sets. This was just as well as all the Orient Mission's stores which Jim Gavin had stockpiled in Rangoon for China had been destroyed in the Christmas Day air raid. It fell upon Steve Cummins to get the Anglo-French China party away. A Free French Major had arrived from London and he and Baron de Langlade were flown to Chungking. The American Military Mission had large stocks of lorries, jeeps and cars, part of the US supply programme for China. With help from contacts in the Mission, lorries and jeeps were scrounged for the Anglo-French party.

By mid-February 17 Division, having stood and fought at two rivers, the Salween and Bilin, retreated across the Sittang. In a last ditch attempt to stop the Japanese advance, the rear-guard was overwhelmed. Someone pressed the panic button and blew the centre span of the only bridge across the river, trapping two Brigades on the wrong side. Having lost a major part of its transport, supplies and men, all that remained of 3,500 officers and men of 17 Division were 1,420 survivors. The Japanese deployed 70,000 men, mainly veterans of campaigns in China or fresh from successful battles in Malaya.

The loss of Rangoon could only be weeks away. On 20th February all units were warned to prepare to evacuate the burning city, leaving it in the hands of looters. Refugees poured out into the villages or took the road to Mandalay as the army began to backload 1,000 tons of stores a day. Remembering the situation Jack Knott recollects he and Steve Cummins, with Sergeant Shufflebottom, loading kit bags and stores at the railway yards. Later they stood guard over the loaded wagons to stop marauding Regimental Quartermasters looking for extra rolling stock.

The railway yards were full of army lorries and troops and enemy aircraft were continually overhead. Ack-ack guns alongside the railway blasted off shell after shell, filling the sky with puffs of smoke and the yards with shrapnel. Sitting in a slit trench with a steel helmet firmly on his head, Knott was thankful to see the train finally disappear down the track with Sergeant Shufflebottom riding shot-gun in the wagon. The journey was to take some four days – through some of the wildest country in the whole of Burma. Refugees clung to every window and ledge and camped out on the carriage roofs. Eventually the train rattled over a viaduct 850 feet above the Salween, in north Burma, into Lashio.

Knott expected the railway and the road to Pegu to be cut at any time. The Japanese were locked in battle with the Burma Division near there and fresh enemy reinforcements were arriving all the time. Enemy troops had also infiltrated through the British lines, some dressed in British uniforms, to create road blocks and carry out ambushes. To add to the problem the local population were largely anti-British, and at the best, hostile, and gave the Japanese a great deal of co-operation. The pre-war enemy agents had obviously done their job well. No one really knew how far enemy patrols had infiltrated and from hour to hour whether the railway line through Pegu was still open. Trains would leave Rangoon for Mandalay and some hours later Railway Administration staff in Rangoon would telephone their counterparts in Pegu to see if the train had arrived. If it had the line was still open and they would send off another.

The last days of Rangoon were at hand and the Army ordered the general evacuation of all civilians, so with the expectation of having to fight their way through enemy road blocks, Knott's unit packed all the remaining equipment and themselves into a 15 cwt truck and joined the long line of refugees and crowded army lorries moving slowly along the road to Mandalay. What little air cover the retreat had was supplied by American P 40s flown by The Flying Tigers, 'which were good and capable', Knott remembers, 'even superior to the Japanese Zeros.' Despite this they regularly abandoned their truck in the face of low level strafing by enemy fighters.

A few days later the party drove along the winding road, past the white pagodas leading into Maymo. Along the side of the road slumped groups of refugees unable to walk another step. They found the streets of the town packed with servicemen of every nationality Gurkha, British, Australian, American airmen, Indian Sepoys and Burmese. Every train disgorged hordes of civil servants, affluent businessmen and their families as well as service families evacuated at the last moment from Rangoon. The whole town seemed to be in utter confusion. In the midst of this lorries belonging to Army Headquarters, Burma, pushed their way through the crowds looking for the new Headquarters.

The Burma Levies' Commanding Officer, Colonel Stephenson, was also passing through the town. The capture of Pegu had separated him from his Levies, who were now under the command of SOE's Major Lindsey and with Burma Division, north of Pegu. Trapped in Rangoon, the Governor ordered Stephenson to leave and form new companies amongst the Kachin and Naga hill tribes. Shortly afterwards the Governor himself was ordered to leave Rangoon and he also took up residence in Maymo. When he heard Major Knott had arrived in the town he invited him to tea. Remembering the occasion Knott recalls 'being most hospitably received' by Sir Reginald Dorman-Smith. News had just come in about the loss of the Dutch East Indies and Singapore and 'the Governor was interested to hear my account of the Malayan Campaign and the conditions on the road between Rangoon and Maymo'. Reflecting on their meeting Jack Knott later remarked that he 'admired his Excellency's astonishing calm and collectiveness.'

The following morning Knott left the crowded summer capital and drove up the Burma road, full of American army lorries taking supplies to China. They found the SOE compound in Lashio just off the Hse Paw road, about a half mile outside the town on the edge of an airstrip. The little wooden town with its narrow dirty streets was full of hawkers. An enormous number of Chinese, Shans and Burmans were continually pouring in from the surrounding hills to set up roadside stalls – all hell bent on getting rich quick while the good times lasted.

The local police had given up any attempt to control the situation and corruption, smuggling and graft with rife. The local bazaar was full of sophisticated equipment – all hijacked by dacoits or Japanese-led bandits along the Burma road. More than once Major Knott bought wireless spares from there. 'It was the nearest thing to a Hollywood version of a wild west town I've ever experienced,' commented Jack Knott thirty years later. On the hill overlooking the compound the Signals Unit built itself – what Knott termed – a pathetic bamboo hut. Into it went the wireless transmitters and outside they erected the aerials. They made contact with Station 'Y' in Rangoon almost straightaway. His men had been keeping in continuous listening watch for him. They told him that they had left Rangoon with the rear-guard of the re-equipped 17th Division and were held up at a Japanese road block near Prome. Despite their difficulties and many adventures, they kept in touch with Lashio throughout the retreat to India, where they were taken over by SOE (India).

Knott next tried to make contact with Spencer Chapman who he believed to be transmitting from north Malaya. He kept a continuous watch for Chapman's call sign DJJ but he never came on the air. But, unknown to Knott, a second transmitter in south Johore, manned by Sergeant Cross, was daily calling Station 'Y'. Unaware of his existence neither Lashio nor Station 'Y' listened in on his frequency. Even if they were Sergeant Cross reflected after the war that he doubted whether his transmitter was powerful enough to reach Rangoon or Lashio.

No one in SOE (India) in Delhi really knew what was left of the Orient Mission's Burma Section. MacKenzie had sent Lindsey to find out but he had disappeared around Mawchi. Not a man to suffer this type of situation, Colin MacKenzie flew off in an American DC3 for Lashio to find out for himself.

Lashio was the railhead for the Burma road – the last town of any size before reaching China. Surrounded by high, desolate mountains, the area seemed to trap the monsoon rain clouds. For the SOE staff the clouds seemed to remain stationary over the compound. Torrential rains sent rivers of water through Knott's flimsy bamboo Signals hut to form large muddy lakes, inches deep around the hut.

The camp was built next to the airstrip and, taking up the story, Jack Knott remembers standing in the shelter of his hut watching Steve Cummins escorting a very senior officer with a limp around the compound. There were usually big, tough-looking American flyers in leather flying jackets drifting around looking for the English women working in SOE's office. Often disappointed they would offer to settle for a bottle of Scotch. That day the camp was full with French members of the Anglo-French party held up on their way to Kunming in China, and Mike Calvert's bush-hatted Australians who had been there for weeks, waiting to join up with Chinese guerrillas in China.

The Chinese border guards wouldn't let the British cross into China. No one seemed to know what the problem was. It was assumed that the guards wanted a fat bribe which they always levied on all vehicles, even those carrying American aid to China. If it wasn't a bribe it must be some Chinese cock-up at a very senior level, mused SOE staff.

What had happened was that a devious political situation had developed in Chungking. It had been agreed at a meeting between Churchill and President Roosevelt that Chiang Kai Shek would command all United Nations forces in China but one unforeseen side effect was a request – more a demand – that a Chinese General should command Keswick's China Mission. Keswick refused to allow this and was ordered to leave. The British Ambassador tried to smooth things out but Chiang Kai Shek made himself unavailable. Some weeks later Chiang Kai Shek left on a tour of India and the Ambassador was transferred to Moscow. It was against this background that MacKenzie arrived in Lashio.

He found the town packed with American vehicles rushing supplies to China before the Burma road was closed by the advancing Japanese. Moving in the other direction, into Burma were the Chinese 5th and 6th Armies Chiang Kai Shek had sent to help the British troops locked in battle around Pegu, trying to keep open China's only supply link from the west. He had also sent two squadrons of Flying Tigers to protect Rangoon – its harbour full of ships carrying American aid for China.

The Chinese troops moving through Lashio lived off the land and local villagers soon learnt to lock up their food and their daughters. In the opinion of the recently arrived American General Stillwall the Chinese Generals not only kept back their soldiers' pay but also sold the rations and weapons. Cowardice and bribery were paramount, smuggling above duty.

Since his arrival in Lashio a few weeks earlier, Major Knott had become a familiar figure racing around the town in his two-seater, racy, sports car on scrounging missions to make up his station's equipment deficiencies. One of his acquisitions was a brand new, high powered, American transmitter which 'fell off the back of a lorry'.

Shortly after MacKenzie's visit things began to happen recalls Jack Knott and the compound was soon astir with activity. The Free French and the Australians began to move out for Kunming in China where the French hoped to recruit volunteers from amongst the French community for special operations in Indo-China. The Australians expected to link up with bands of Chinese guerrillas* in Japanese-occupied areas and then move across country to operate close to Shanghai – which was in Japanese hands. Knott's Signals Unit was also ordered to Kunming but the remainder of 101 STS's China Mission† was disbanded and its personnel ordered to make their own way to India.

* Of battalion strength and arranged with Warren when he visited Chungking in November.
† Its role was taken over by an American OSS unit also known as 101.

Before they finally moved out. Steve Cummins told Knott that he would remain behind and wait for Major Lindsey, SOE (India), who was somewhere near Toungoo. In view of the deteriorating military situation which may have put Cummins and Lindsey behind the lines, Jack Knott decided to leave Sergeant Benson and his wireless with Cummins. This would be known as Station 'H' but once it was on the move it would become Station 'H' Mobile. Sergent Shufflebottom was told to collect all the equipment not needed, leaving it with Benson. 'The following day,' said Jack Knott, 'I moved out with Sergeant Shufflebottom, a corporal and a couple of Orient Mission bods whom Cummins was smuggling into China, to join Keswick in Chungking. These rode shot-gun for us over the roof of the world to Kunming.'

When the Signals unit reached Kunming they were housed in the grounds of the British Consulate and almost immediately Knott opened up the set and made contact with Benson in Lashio and Station 'Y' retreating with 17th Division along the road to Mandalay. Despite this, Station 'Y' kept a listening watch for Spencer Chapman in Malaya but possibly still didn't know about Sergeant Cross's station in Johore.

In spite of all the promises made by the Chinese, special operations based at Kunming didn't really get started. There was no apparent Chinese military action and Pierre Boulle with the Free French was convinced that the Chinese General with whom he was staying, sent one of his men through the front line to his Japanese counterpart for iced beer. Curiously enough, despite the Japanese invasion of the Chinese mainland, Chiang Kai Shek didn't consider China to be at war with Japan but just involved in 'an incident'. China had contacts with the Japanese at various levels and Hong Kong the link was through a secret agent belonging to the Chinese Central Investigation and Statistics Bureau, part of the Chinese Secret Service.

When Knott arrived in Chungking, after opening up his station in Kunming – he found a new British Mission had been formed, known as 204 Mission. Its role would be to provide training and technical help to the Chinese guerrillas. Its commander may have been unaware of the Chinese duplicity but this seems unlikely. Although the Chinese had agreed with Warren to raise six guerrillas battalions very little had been accomplished as the Australians found out to their cost. The Mission's diplomatic skirmish with Chinese officials was still in the future so when Knott joined them it was based at the British Embassy. It was here, in his office, that Keswick briefed

Knott on what he hoped would be SOE's future work. The prime intention, remembers Knott, 'was to infiltrate into north Burma and Thailand'.* Although Warren's proposals to form and equip SOE-led Chinese guerrillas battalions had been abandoned one of his projects still remained – the SOE Training School – and this was being actively discussed with the Chinese.

During the weeks that followed Knott remembers endless meetings with Chinese generals and senior government officials and vast quantities of ceremonial tea being drunk. The Chinese were evasive, tepid to the idea of a training school and often unco-operative. In fact they were just playing for time until the American 101 Mission arrived. Major Knott had brought with him his last remaining wireless set and, spreading his aerials across the roof of the Embassy, he opened up the first wireless link between Chungking and the SOE base in Calcutta.† It seemed to have some face-saving significance, recalls Knott. The Chinese seemed impressed and Keswick was delighted.

In spite of the apparent image-making coup SOE's days in China were numbered. Various American special service units were arriving and competing for Chinese favours, to be bought with weapons, equipment and cash. Although French, British, Russians and Americans had military personnel in China there was no overall Allied Command except that exercised by Chiang Kai Shek. The Generalissimo was supreme, and he didn't like the British. He was suspicious of their country's motives, which wasn't surprising considering its actions in China in the previous sixty years; and his staff complained about British duplicity.

In about March 1942 the Chinese finally ordered SOE to leave China. Their departure was summed up in a note from the British Embassy to GHQ India. 'The SOE', it commented, 'got into such bad odour with the Chinese because its personnel were almost exclusively representatives of British interests and their tactless and misguided activities, that Chiang Kai Shek himself ordered them out of China and refused them permission to operate.'** By the time this occurred Knott had already left for India to take charge of the embryo SOE Signals network.

* The OSS also took over this role with Merrill's Marauders.
† From Chungking Knott made contact with Station 'H' Mobile operated by Sergeant Benson.
** File – WO 208 129 HN 00745 at PRO Kew.

CHAPTER EIGHTEEN

Orient Mission Survivors Reach India

Following their arrival in India, Major Lindsey and Captain Cummins made their way to SOE's secret offices in Delhi. After reporting to Colin MacKenzie they went on to Meerut – a military hill station holiday centre and coincidentally also a SOE base camp. It was here that Cummins again met up with his old friend and Commanding Officer, Major Jim Gavin, and his wife. Jim Gavin remembers that despite the hardship, and being very much underweight, Cummins seemed fairly fit. He was one of the few who reached India, after trekking across Burma, still carrying his weapon. One member of his party who had also trekked across north Burma and India, discovered that many of the small post offices in the hills still had large stocks of Queen Victoria stamps* – obviously issued during the first flush of youth of the Indian postal system. He arrived in Meerut with his pack full of sheets of Victorian stamps but no weapon.

John Davis and Richard Broome were also in town having arrived in Calcutta after sailing across the Indian Ocean in a native junk. The native crew, who initially helped them familiarise themselves with the unwieldy craft, were put ashore as previously arranged on one of the small islands outside Padang.

The navigation was taken over by Ivor Lyon while Jock Campbell carefully rationed the supplies. About halfway across they almost ran out of water but were saved by rain showers, collecting the water in pans and large canvas sheets. To help out the rations fishing lines were hopefully put overboard but apart from one small fish their efforts went unrewarded. Campbell then cut the rations.

During lulls in the monsoon enemy aircraft flew sorties searching for escape vessels. Twice they were discovered – each time they tried to disguise themselves as innocent traders by planting Broome's and Davis's 'boys' on deck while the Europeans packed below. This didn't fool the enemy pilots who, after making a pass across the bows, banked around for a second run and sprayed the boat liberally with bullets.

* Which was hardly surprising since many tribesmen were illiterate.

They had with them Warren's wireless (ex Goodfellow and Rosher). He couldn't get it to work and neither could they, apart from the time signals from Ceylon. This at least helped with the navigation until the batteries ran out. The spare was found to be unserviceable so Lyon continued the navigation by dead reckoning.

In the middle of the ocean, during a lull in the wind, Passmore fell overboard. Before they managed to reach him the wind came up and it was some time before they hove to. By this time he was almost out of sight. Eventually they reached him but only a few yards ahead of triangular fins cutting their way through the water at high speed.

After 34 days at sea they sighted land but it wasn't until 16th April that they actually sailed within swimming distance of the shore. By that time everyone was too exhausted to attempt it so Lind took the boat in to beach it. At the last moment a freighter was seen heading towards them on a converging course. With everyone on deck frantically waving and shouting, Lind steered towards her but the ship, the SS *Anglo Canadian*, didn't seem to see them and changed course away. Lind quickly changed tack and again approached her. Again she changed course and it became obvious that the skipper was trying to avoid them. Eventually, after a game of sea tag, the ship stopped and allowed them to come alongside. A Jacob's ladder was dropped over the side and the crew's grim faces looked down on them over the ship's rails.

Remembering the occasion thirty years later, John Davis recalls that in spite of everyone being in poor shape, Jock Campbell was first up the ladder. By the time he and Passmore arrived on deck Campbell was on the ship's bridge talking to the Captain who assumed Campbell was in charge. For the rest of the voyage the skipper worked through him. Davis remembers he and Passmore looking at each other incredulously, then shrugging their shoulders, too weak to argue, accepted the situation.

Later the skipper explained his mysterious changes of course after he had seen them in the water. When he first sighted the junk he thought it might be a Japanese decoy and tried to get away. Bringing them up to date with the news he told them about Darwin being bombarded, Colombo being heavily attacked and some 100,000 tons of shipping being sunk around the coast during the last four days. The enemy Navy was expected off Trincomalee on Ceylon's west coast, any day and the authorities had cleared the harbour. Local people were rioting to get on board the ships leaving the quayside. He wasn't going back, not even to land them, so they could either travel with him to Calcutta or go back to their junk. They opted for India and the ship's crew used the junk for gun practice.

They discovered later they they had missed Jim Gavin by only a few days. The SS *Krain* eventually reached Trincomalee after almost running out of fuel in the middle of the ocean. Unable to bunker extra fuel at Batavia, nor rations, the ship had sailed at half speed and the passengers and crew were reduced to a cup of water and a ship's biscuit a day.

Shortly after the ship escaped through the Sunda Straits only a few hours before it was closed by the Japanese invasion fleet, Jim Gavin began to stagger about. His voice sounded almost as if he had a cleft palate and his wife made him go to bed. As more symptoms, including a high temperature, began to appear the skipper diagnosed diphtheria and Barbara spent the next three weeks nursing him as he steadily got weaker.

Unknown to them a large enemy naval force comprising five aircraft carriers three battleships, two heavy cruisers and nine destroyers closed-in on Ceylon. In their first raid on Colombo, enemy carrier-borne bombers wrecked the naval dockyards inflicting heavy damage as well as sinking an armed merchant cruiser and a destroyer. All the air cover the RAF could provide (32 planes) was sent up to intercept but only eight returned to base.

When news of the approaching task force reached RN HQ in Ceylon all its ships were cleared from harbour. Two heavy cruisers, the *Cornwall* and the *Dorsetshire*, discovered the enemy force but were sunk. A few days later HMS *Hermes*, an aircraft carrier with all its planes still on board, was also sunk.

Blissfully unaware of the sea battles, the *Krain* limped into Trincomalee only to find it was also being cleared of shipping. The Shipping Control Officer said that the enemy force was expected at any moment and to prove their point 94 enemy planes swooped in and pounded the harbour and its installations. The RAF lost nine of its eleven Hurricanes. It looked very much as if this was going to be Gavin's fourth evacuation in four months.

When the ship docked it became the centre of a full scale riot as thousands of civilians, crowding the dockside, tried to storm the ship. Dragging himself from the bunk, Gavin took command and his men beat off and subdued the mob with rifle butts and shots in the air. By now he was in a state of complete collapse and was rushed to hospital as a terminal case.

Before being carried off on a stretcher Jim Gavin ordered Lieutenant L. Seeleur, RE, to take command and try to reach India where he should hand over the men and equipment to Colin MacKenzie, SOE's India Mission. After some time in hospital, Gavin grew stronger and was allowed to continue his journey with Barbara to SOE at Delhi. From there he went to the SOE camp at Meerut. Here the army doctors decided that the stress and strain on his heart had been too great and his general physical condition was poor, so he found himself on a troopship to England with every likelihood of being discharged. Despite these odds he convinced Baker Street that he was fit and well and joined SOE Middle East operations before finally retiring as a Major-General.

Those left behind in Java after the *Krain* sailed, also escaped. Killery of course had already left and reached Australia: Egerton Mott found a sailing boat and after various adventures finally reached Australia. Boris Hembry and Lowe convinced a skipper of a small tramp steamer that they were first class stokers and fired the ship's boilers all the way to Australia.

Both Basil Goodfellow and Major Rosher reached India. The latter disappeared into the grey world of Secret Service activities while Goodfellow joined SOE (India) and set up Section B, responsible for clandestine work in Malaya and Sumatra. Here he met again Boris Hembry who made his way to India, rejoined the Force and spent his time on secret missions in and out of enemy-occupied Sumatra and Malaya. Two other sections were formed: 'A' dealt with Burma, Siam and Indo-China and later 'C' was established for SOE activities in China.

Section B also attracted the old team of Richard Broome and John Davis – both soon to be promoted Colonels – who volunteered to go back into Malaya to search for Spencer Chapman. Both, on separate occasions, were landed on Malayan beaches and they too disappeared for some twelve months. The fault again was poor wireless equipment. It was assumed that all three (including Chapman) had been captured so when they managed to repair the equipment sufficiently to get a weak signal transmitted, Section B, HQ in Colombo believed they were 'sending' under duress. Davis and Broome had been found by the Communist guerrillas and Chapman was also with them. Eventually all three and others were brought out.

Richard Broome's boy, who escaped with him, volunteered for active duty and after parachute training and a course at a Special

Training School, was dropped by parachute into Malaya.

Colonel Knott arrived in India, from China, to set up the wireless communications and was joined by Major McMillan, who escaped from Java and made his way to India.

Moving in the other direction, Jock Campbell and Ivor Lyon, together with Sergeant Morris, rescued from a life of bedpans and blankets at the British Military Hospital, left for Australia. From there they mounted commando raids against shipping in Singapore Harbour. Lyon was captured during the second raid and executed in Singapore by the Japanese in July 1945.

In Singapore in April 1942 the Japanese searched for Warren – the leader of the British sabotage groups operating behind their lines. He had been named on a safe conduct pass signed by him and found on a captured member of one of the stay-behind parties. During the search of the POW camps the Japanese Kempetai discovered and he believed, beheaded Scott whom they considered to be the Propaganda Chief in Singapore. Warren didn't totally escape their clutches. He was interrogated but managed to convince them that he was only a RN officer and not the Army colonel they were searching for. After this narrow escape he shaved off his moustache and his head of hair, then volunteered to take charge of the first group of prisoners to be sent up-country to work on what was to be the Railway of Death. He was probably the first British colonel on the River Kwai.

Another prisoner was Sergeant Wright who had been captured by counter-intelligence in Siam before the war broke out and was probably the first prisoner of war in the battle for Malaya. He managed to convince them that he was only a deputy manager of a tin mine and was interned. Later he joined the prisoners working on the Death Railway. He survived the war and now lives in Swansea.

Was the casualty rate high? Not amongst the regular SOE staff. The first casualty before the war broke out was Sergeant Wright's fellow wireless operator who was caught and shot, using his transmitter, by Siamese counter-intelligence agents. A fatal accident at 101 STS took the life of an experienced weapons NCO and the same accident seriously wounded Captain Lowe. A third fatality occured when Corporal Sawyer was drowned trekking out of Burma.

It was a different story, of course, amongst the volunteers. The miners and engineers risked their lives in Siam, especially those massacred at Pinyok. Vanrennan, Harvey and Graham were executed in Kuala Lumpur; others like Captain Smyllie, Major Barry in Johore

and Bryan Tyson died a lonely death in the jungle waiting for someone – anyone – to contact them. There seems to be no record of what
eventually happened to Sergeant Regan whose death remains a mys-
tery. It is possible that he was killed in a running gun fight when the
Japanese burst in on a secret meeting of guerrilla chiefs at Batu
Caves. Most were wiped out but some did manage to escape into the
surrounding jungle.

Three stay-behind parties survived the war. Chapman's adventures have become a legend.* In Burma SOE (India) re-established
contact with Major Seagrim, but he was later captured by the
Japanese and executed before they fled from Rangoon at the end of
the war. Following Major Barry's death, Sergeant Cross took charge
of the party and spent the remainder of the war trying to break into
Allied transmissions without success. Eventually he trekked through
the jungle to make contact with a British party parachuted into
Malaya. They really didn't want to know him in case the landing was
compromised and told him to go away. Eventually they were passed
on to another SOE party who got them out.

* *The Jungle is Neutral.*

Conclusion

Official Indifference

The problem experienced by the Orient Mission in 1941/42 resulted largely from the reluctance to allow it to set up any kind of structure, especially in the Malayan Peninsula. In its short life of barely ten months it accomplished more than could be expected of it.

Against all odds and official indifference it opened up a Special Training School, trained and equipped European stay-behind parties as well as more than 200 Communist guerrillas. It also trained and armed the part-time Hong Kong Recce Regiment and the native Burma Levies. Both organisations stayed behind and fought on long after the regular army had retreated or surrendered. In Siam the SOE volunteers seized their objectives at the outbreak of the war but were forced to abort them due to lack of military support or change of plans. The China party, finding itself in the cockpit of international politics was less successful.

In Paragraph 51 of Percival's Despatch* the General refers to the Orient Mission's part in the war. He complains that it suffered from an excess of secrecy and lack of knowledge on the part of the gentlemen responsible.

Like Killery, Warren also came up against what seemed to be a mental barrier by the military towards the Orient Mission. As one GHQ officer put it to him 'send those SOE bods back to Blighty and not First Class either'. However Jim Gavin believes that this feeling was actually expressed towards the non-military members of the Mission. All his uniformed staff always received full co-operation from their counterparts in the regular military units.

Lack of Wireless Equipment

In the months leading up to the outbreak of war with Japan British forces in Malaya and Burma lacked almost everything from trained soldiers to essential equipment and weapons. Colonel Knott's

---

* Page 194 – 'Singapore 1941/42'.

experience was typical – if lucky, one made do with pieces of old equipment. Very little, if any, consideration had been given to providing lightweight powerful radio transmitters for use in difficult or tropical terrain. As Knott points out, the equipment was primarily designed for European conditions with easy access to electricity.

Again time was the limiting factor. The Signals Unit arrived in late July, barely four months before the Japanese assault. However if the Orient Mission had been allowed to create jungle bases, each one could have been supplied with a transmitter and been in regular contact with GHQ during every step of the enemy advance down the peninsula, not only providing valuable intelligence concerning the flow rate of reinforcements to the front line but also co-ordinating guerrilla activity. But wireless sets were in short supply and some battalions lacked even one.

Scorched earth policy

When Brigadier Lyons and the Resident Counsellor Forbes*, in Penang, decided to evacuate all Europeans from the island they became embroiled in both a political and peace-time attitude towards a scorched earth philosophy. Briefly summed up this meant that the military could destroy its own stores and, with permission, European civilian installations, but not that owned by the native population. In addition the Governor was responsible for the destruction of all stocks of rubber and tin as well as Radio Penang. Enmeshed in the unexpected evacuation of Penang and anticipating the Governor's authority, Warren arranged for Gavin and his men to carry out wide-scale demolitions – assisting the Fortress Engineer – but the destruction of Radio Penang, being clearly the Governor's decision, was left to the Station's staff. In view of the sudden evacuation of the civilians it is probable that the staff left before the Governor's instructions (if any) to destroy the Radio Station arrived. Consequently the transmitter fell intact into enemy hands – and was quickly used to good effect by the Japanese.

Because no scorched earth plans existed valuable time was lost searching the *godowns* for stocks of rubber and tin. As a result vast quantities fell into enemy hands. For many fishermen their boats were the sole means of livelihood and wealth, so, when the demolition teams began to move amongst the boats, the owners quickly hid them in the surrounding creeks.

---

* Senior Civil Servant in Penang.

In Malaya the rapid evacuation by the RAF from its airfields, especially in north Malaya, left much to be desired. Hastily abandoned, undamaged airfields at Alor Star, Taiping and Sungei Patani enabled enemy planes to refuel and stock with 'Churchill supplies' – captured fuel and bombs. This was why Warren took the opportunity of sending Gavin and his party to the abandoned RAF airfield outside Kuala Lumpur. Their work, putting the airfield out of commission, if only for a few days, possibly saved 11 Division, choked nose to tail in lorries, retreating down the Kuala Lumpur to Seremban road.

Stay-behind parties and the guerrillas
When war came to Malaya and the Orient Mission's plans were finally agreed European volunteers were recruited, trained and armed in less than three days. Freddy Chapman masterminded the first wave of stay-behind parties in north Malaya. He then joined them in the jungle. This, as it turned out, was unfortunate because he knew nothing about the later parties in Johore.

Within weeks the guerrillas, their numbers now swollen to some three thousand, were in action attacking the Japanese lines of communication. Spencer Chapman and his men were doing the same but acting independently. Because of the rapid withdrawal of British troops in Malaya and the subsequent loss of Singapore the Orient Mission lost touch with both organisations.

If Spencer Chapman had gone into the jungle with the last European party in January he would have had time to establish a relationship with MCP HQ officers and, together, could have co-ordinated their plans for action against the enemy lines of communication. In a letter to Spencer Chapman* after the war Percival suggests that the whole subject of stay-behind parties should have been organised earlier. Was this defensive criticism on his part?

In July 1941 Shenton Thomas asked Percival to give Killery as much help as possible. Percival admits that it took him longer to study the SOE proposals, submitted to him in October, than it should have done. Warren didn't get the authority to put in the stay-behind parties until almost New Year's Day. By that time half of Malaya had already been lost. In October 1941 Percival's Chief Engineer Brigadier Simpson proposed that guerrilla forces be trained for operations behind enemy lines, supported by previously

* 'Singapore 1941/42'.

created dumps of arms, ammunition and explosives, but nothing came of the idea.

In the same letter to Chapman, Percival pondered whether GHQ should have done more to help. If Percival had given the Orient Mission the support the Governor requested in July 1941, a well established line of communications could have been built using secret jungle bases well stocked with supplies and wireless transmitters.

Hindsight is a wonderful bed companion and it is interesting to speculate on the possible outcome of the war in Malaya had Killery and Warren been given the men and resources needed to carry out guerrilla warfare behind Japanese lines.

In those last days before Percival surrendered, the stay-behind parties and the Communists' guerrillas were playing mayhem against the enemy lines of communication. Vital supplies and reinforcements were not getting through and enemy troops destined for the front were needed to guard bridges, trains and installations. If Java had held out for one more week McMillan might have made contact with Berry's transmitter and through him MCP HQ. Acting as control and in touch with Warren on the Sumatran east coast, men and supplies could have been passed into Malaya. Extensive guerrilla activity behind enemy lines, relieving pressure on Singapore, might have prolonged its siege and drawn off enemy troops destined for Burma, giving Alexander time to re-establish a strong defence position at Pegu instead of fighting a rear-guard action against battle-experienced enemy troops fresh from victories in Malaya.

A prolonged siege of Singapore would have also affected Japanese plans for north Sumatra which required troops from Malaya to carry out the invasion schedule.

However this can be only speculation which historians need finally to analyse. From the beginning the Orient Mission found the odds stacked against it and what was eventually done was often as a result of personal initiative which seemed a good idea at the time.

Appendix

A Copy of Colonel Warren's letter to ABDA Command

Tuesday 24 Feb

Hotel D'Oranji
Padang
Sumatra

Addressed to Colonel Field

Dear Colonel

If Killery is still near you will you please pass this to him. I am writing to you as being someone who I am certain is in Java.

I have received two messages from Java – one from Procurator-General (?) dated 15th or so telling me to continue with my plans and send a rep. to Java; the last from you telling me to make for Padang or Sibolga. I arrived at Padang today on a recce of the possibilities of the situation. Gordon-Bennett's staff will tell you the situation here.

You will find Capt Broome's report attached. I have two officers still in Malaya and have had no news from them. They left Bagan on 12 Feb. Communications with my Base at Labuan Bilik are such that I cannot get in touch with my rep. there until tomorrow. I had intended sending Broome to Batavia as opportunity offered but as Gordon-Bennett's ADC can take his I don't think it is now necessary.

The report may interest you. It raises this point. Can we help the Chinese further i.e. by passing in arms or a W/T set. If so I and some of my party will stay and look after affairs. If we have no arms etc. then I and my party had better leave Sumatra for wherever Killery says.

Padang seems to be organised – as a distributing centre for British personnel. We can look after ourselves and either muck-in with all other military personnel or find our own – perhaps to Java. If Killery has any wish for us to go to Java or Colombo with you – please say which, as I understand things here British military personnel are being sent to Colombo.

In determining our future disposal I hope K will note what Broome says about the movement of aircraft at sea off the Malayan coast. The report of my remaining two officers may put a different complexion on this. To make the link with Malaya reasonably secure I think a high speed naval vessel is necessary. She could be hidden during the day in the mangrove swamps near Bagan or Labuan Bilik and operate at night. The Dutch must of course be right in the picture. I have told Colonel Overaakers (Comdy Centre, Sumatra) most of my activities – he is most helpful. Japanese patrol craft may in future raise difficulties.

Summing up my position I think the following are main points:

1 I have still to get into the picture at Padang.
2 I stay in Sumatra until you or Killery says we can do more good.
3 I want to know where I and party am to go if I have to leave Sumatra i.e. to Java or Colombo.
4 If I am to stay on the north coast and try to keep communications going with Malaya may consideration be given to the provision of a high speed craft – reliable with fuel reserves at Base: also to the provision of W/T set; also to getting Dutch fully into picture in Java.
5 Lieuts. Vanrennan and Graham are still in Malaya (S. Bulah) north of Port Swettenham. I will forward their report earliest opportunity if of value. I must remain until they return or get news of them.
6 I am at present investigating the possibility of joining up with the general evacuation plan from here or of getting a boat and making our getaway if necessary.
7 All is well with us.
8 Please send communications for me to Col. Overaakers – HQ at PRAPAT or TOBAMER.

Yrs sincerely

A.G. Warren

Bibliography

Background research and papers used in compiling the story of the Orient Mission.

1 General background

Death of a Navy 1941-1945	A. D'Albas	Robert Hale Ltd.
Sunk	M. Hashimoto	Cassell & Co.
North of Singapore	C. Wells	Jarrolds
Malay Waters	H.M. Tomlinson	Hodder & Stoughton
The Royal Australian Navy	G. Herman Gill	Canberra Australian War Memorial
Singapore to Freedom	Oswald Gilmour	E.J.Burrow
Inside SOE	E.H. Cookridge	Arthur Barker
Baker Street Irregulars	Bickham Sweet-Escott	Methuen
Chronology of the War at Sea Volume 1.	Rohwer and Hummelchen	Ian Allan
The Navy at War 1939-1945	Capt. S.W. Roskill R.N.	Collins
Grand Father Long Legs	Ian Morrison	Faber & Faber Ltd.
Chronology and Index of the Second World War	Royal Institute of International Affairs	Newspaper Archive Development Ltd.
War in the Shadows	Robert Asprey	MacDonald & Janes
Operations Most Secret	Ian Trenowden	William Kimber
South East Asia in Turmoil	Brian Crozier	Penguin Books
Japan's Imperial Conspiracy	David Bergamini	Heinemann
Pacific Onslaught	Paul Kennedy	Pan/Ballantine

Malaya

Pai Naa	Dorothy Thatcher and Robert Cross	Constable
Red Jungle (in paperback *The Three They Couldn't Kill*)	John Cross DCM	Robert Hale
The Jungle is Neutral	F. Spencer Chapman	Chatto & Windus
One Man's Jungle	Ralph Barker	Chatto & Windus
Sinister Twilight	Noel Barber	William Collins

Index